Best Hikes along the Continental Divide

From Northern Alberta, Canada to Mexico

Edited by Russ Schneider

Contributions by Will Harmon, Bill Schneider, Bill Hunger, Caryn and Peter Boddie, Laurence Parent, and others

FALCON®

HELENA, MONTANA

A FALCON GUIDE ®

Falcon® Publishing is continually expanding its list of recreation guidebooks. All books include detailed descriptions, accurate maps, and all the information necessary for enjoyable trips. You can order extra copies of this book and get information and prices for other Falcon® guidebooks by writing Falcon, P.O. Box 1718, Helena, MT 59624 or calling toll free 1-800-582-2665. Also, please ask for a free copy of our current catalog. Visit our web site at http://www.falconguide.com

CAUTION

Outdoor recreational activities are by their very nature potentially hazardous. All participants in such activities must assume the responsibility for their own actions and safety. The information contained in this guidebook cannot replace sound judgment and good decision-making skills, which help reduce risk exposure, nor does the scope of this book allow for disclosure of all the potential hazards and risks involved in such activities.

Learn as much as possible about the outdoor recreational activities in which you participate, prepare for the unexpected, and be cautious. The reward will be a safer and more enjoyable experience.

♻ Text pages printed on recycled paper.

*Dedicated to the preservation of public land
along the Continental Divide*

Contents

Acknowledgments

This project would not have happened without the significant support and contributions of the following FalconGuide authors: Caryn Boddie, Peter Boddie, Will Harmon, Bill Hunger, Laurence Parent, and Bill Schneider. Hikers who helped with individual hikes in one way or another include Ed Madej, Fred Swanson, Rosemary Rowe, Paul Donharl, Mike Murphy, Crystal Boddie, Doug Crocker, Brian Dempsey, Robin Boddie, Jim Haynes, Don Wagner, Tyler Garbonza, Ruth Mooneyham, Sandy Mooneyham, Chris Frye, Pieter Dahmen, and the folks at Mountain Miser Ltd. In addition, we would like to thank the U.S. Forest Service, National Park Service, Bureau of Land Management, and Parks Canada for preserving land for recreation and wildlife. In addition, Falcon employees and freelancers deserve thanks for producing a user-friendly and accurate guidebook.

Preface

This book is the brainchild of Bill Schneider, conceived in response to growing interest in the Continental Divide and the Continental Divide National Scenic Trail (CDT). Instead of approaching this project from the traditional through-hiker point of view, we chose to provide selected hikes to a more general audience. Most people only get a couple of days or weeks at a time to go hiking and do not have time to cross a major portion of the continent. This book is the key to their experience of hiking along the divide for just a few days at a time.

We began by compiling hikes from Falcon's vast library of hiking books, and dug around for all of the best hikes along the Continental Divide. We did not want to limit your exploration to just the divide in the United States: we included eleven hikes in Alberta that enable you to explore some of the most spectacular glaciated regions of the northern divide. All hikes in this book come from guidebooks published by Falcon, including *Hiking Alberta*, *Hiking Glacier and Waterton Lakes National Park*, *The Trail Guide to Bob Marshall Country*, *Hiking Montana*, *Hiking Yellowstone*, *Hiking Wyoming*, *Hiking Colorado*, and *Hiking New Mexico*. As Falcon increases its library of hiking books, we will continue to provide new information on areas to visit along the divide in future additions.

Once you explore these regions you will realize the importance of preserving them for others to enjoy. We produced this book to support conservation and responsible recreation along the divide, and we urge you to support the designation, maintenance, and work toward the completion of the CDT. The CDT faces many obstacles and needs your support, especially in Wyoming and New Mexico; let's make the difference between a dream and reality. See page 209 for information on supporting the CDT.

Map Legend

Interstate	00	Campground	⛺
US Highway	00	Cabins/Buildings	▪
State or Other Principal Road	00 000	Peak	9,782 ft.
National Park Route	00	Hill	
Forest Road	0000	Elevation	9,782 ft. X
Interstate Highway	⟹	Pass/Saddle	)(
Paved Road	⟹	Glaciers	
Gravel Road	⟹	Lava Flow	
Unimproved Road	===⟹	Falls	
Trailhead	○	Gate	•—•
Main Trail(s)/Route(s)		Mine Site	✗
Alternate/Secondary Trail(s)/Route(s)		Overlook/Point of Interest	▣
Cross Country Trail		National Forest/Park/ Wilderness Boundary	
Parking Area	Ⓟ		
River/Creek		Map Orientation	N
Spring	○⌐		
Intermittent Stream		Scale	0 0.5 1 Miles
Continental Divide		Continental Divide Trail = CDT	
		Continental Divide Route = Divide Route	

Map Overview:
Continental Divide

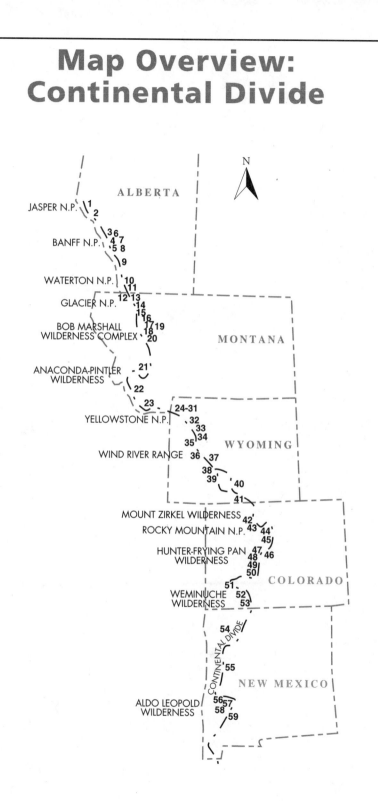

N

ALBERTA

JASPER N.P.   1
              2

              3 6
BANFF N.P.   4 7
              5 8

              9

WATERTON N.P.   10
                11
              12 13
GLACIER N.P.   14
              15
              16
BOB MARSHALL 17 19
WILDERNESS COMPLEX 18
              20

MONTANA

ANACONDA-PINTLER   21
WILDERNESS
              22

              23
                  24-31
YELLOWSTONE N.P.   32
              33
              34
              35

WYOMING

WIND RIVER RANGE   36   37
              38
              39   40

              41

MOUNT ZIRKEL WILDERNESS   42
ROCKY MOUNTAIN N.P.   43 44
                      45
HUNTER-FRYING PAN   47   46
WILDERNESS   48
              49
              50

COLORADO

              51
WEMINUCHE   52
WILDERNESS   53

              54

CONTINENTAL DIVIDE

              55

NEW MEXICO

              56
ALDO LEOPOLD   57
WILDERNESS   58
              59

Introduction

The Continental Divide traverses the Rocky Mountain spine of North America for more than 3,200 miles from Northern Alberta, Canada into Mexico. *Best Hikes along the Continental Divide* details many of the most spectacular sections. It draws from the work of many experienced FalconGuide authors to present a sampling of the best backpacking and dayhiking trips.

The Continental Divide channels waters flowing from melting snow into either the Arctic, Atlantic, or the Pacific Oceans. North of Triple Divide Peak in Glacier National Park, Montana, waters east of the divide flow into the Arctic Ocean and waters west of the divide flow into the Pacific Ocean. South of Triple Divide Peak, waters east of the divide flow into the Atlantic Ocean and waters west of the divide continue to make it to the Pacific until the Panama Canal.

The height of the divide ranges from around 5,000 feet at several low spots in Montana, Wyoming, and New Mexico to 14,000 feet in Colorado. The different elevations and resultant differences in snow pack and rainfall create many diverse environments including alpine tundra, desert scrub, and evergreen forest. Most areas of the divide stay snow covered until May or June, especially north of New Mexico.

The divide passes through famous national parks like Banff, Jasper, Waterton Lakes, Glacier, Yellowstone, and Rocky Mountain. The divide catches snow for clear waters of many famous wilderness areas like the Bob Marshall Complex and Anaconda-Pintler in Montana; Teton, Bridger and Huston Park in Wyoming; Never Summer, Collegiate Peaks, Indian Peaks, and Weminuche in Colorado; and San Pedro Parks, Aldo Leopold, and Gila in New Mexico. Hikes in all these parks and wilderness areas have been incorporated into this book.

We included hikes like Triple Divide Pass (Hike 13) that take you to the places where the waters divide, hikes like Wolf Creek Pass–Divide Trail (Hike 52) or Lost Man Pass and Deadman Lake (Hike 49) that take you across 12,000 foot sections along the divide, and we even included a trip underneath the divide with the Colorado Midland Railroad Trail (Hike 48).

To hike in all these areas is to hike the Rocky Mountains and to tour the best alpine splendor North America has to offer. Whether you start in Banff, end in the Gila, or simply wander somewhere in between, these hikes are sure to leave you speechless, tired, and dreaming of sunny days on the mountaintop.

MAKE IT A SAFE TRIP

The Scouts have been guided for decades by what is perhaps the best single piece of safety advice—Be Prepared! For starters, this means carrying survival and first-aid materials, proper clothing, a compass, and topographic maps—and knowing how to use them.

Perhaps the second best piece of safety advice is to always tell somebody where you are going and when you plan to return. Pilots must file flight plans before every trip, and anybody venturing into a blank spot on the map should do the same. File your "flight" plan with a friend or relative before taking off.

Close behind your flight plan and being prepared with proper equipment is physical conditioning. Wilderness travel is more fun and safe when you are fit. To whet your appetite for more knowledge of wilderness safety and preparedness, here are a few more tips:

- Check the weather forecast. Be careful not to get caught at high altitude by a bad storm or along a stream in a flash flood. Watch cloud formations closely, so you are not stranded on a ridgeline during a lightning storm. Avoid traveling during prolonged periods of cold weather.
- Avoid traveling alone in the wilderness.
- Keep your party together.
- Be extremely careful around thermal areas. In some cases, a thin crust can break and cause a severe burn.
- Study basic survival and first aid before leaving home.
- Never eat wild plants unless you have positively identified them.
- Before you leave for the trailhead, find out as much as you can about the route, especially the potential hazards.
- Avoid exhausting yourself or other members of your party by traveling too far or too fast. Let the slowest person set the pace.
- Consult your maps before you become confused on a trail. Follow them as you go along, from the moment you start moving up the trail, so you have a continual fix on your location.
- If you do get lost, sit down and relax for a few minutes. Carefully check your topographic map and take a reading with your compass. Then, confidently plan your next move. It can be smart to retrace your steps until you find familiar ground, even if you think it might lengthen your trip. Many people get temporarily lost in the wilderness and survive— usually by dealing with the situation calmly and rationally.
- Stay clear of all wild animals.
- Take a first-aid kit that includes, at a minimum, the following items: sewing needle, snake-bite kit, aspirin, antibacterial ointment, two antiseptic swabs, two butterfly bandages, adhesive tape, four adhesive strips, four gauze pads, two triangular bandages, codeine tablets, two inflatable splints, moleskin, one roll 3-inch gauze, CPR shield, rubber gloves, and lightweight first-aid instructions.

- Take a survival kit that includes, at a minimum, the following items: compass, whistle, matches in a waterproof container, cigarette lighter, candle, signal mirror, fire starter, aluminum foil, water purification tablets, space blanket, and flare.

The best defense against unexpected hazards is knowledge. Read up on wilderness safety in *Wild Country Companion* by Will Harmon (Falcon 1994).

LIGHTNING

The high altitude topography of the Continental Divide is prone to sudden thunderstorms, especially in July and August. If you get caught by a lightning storm, take special precautions. Remember,

- Lightning can travel far ahead of the storm, so be sure to take cover before the storm hits.
- Do not try to go back to your vehicle. Instead, seek shelter. Even if the trailhead is only a short way back, it is not worth the risk. Lightning storms are usually brief and from a safe vantagepoint you might enjoy the sights and sounds.
- Be especially careful not to get caught on a mountaintop or exposed ridge, under large, solitary trees, in the open, or near standing water.
- Seek shelter in a low-lying area, ideally in a dense stand of small, uniformly sized trees.
- Stay away from anything that might attract lightning, such as metal tent poles, graphite fishing rods, or pack frames.
- Get in a crouch position and place both feet firmly on the ground.
- If you have a pack (without a metal frame) or a sleeping pad with you, put your feet on it for extra insulation against shock.
- Do not walk or huddle together. Instead, stay 50 feet apart, so if lightening strikes anyone, others in your party can give first aid.
- If you're in a tent, stay there in your sleeping bag with your feet on your sleeping pad.

HYPOTHERMIA

Be aware of the danger of hypothermia—a condition in which the internal temperature of the body drops below normal. It can lead to mental and physical collapse and death.

Exposure to cold, wetness, winds, and exhaustion causes hypothermia. The moment you begin to lose heat faster than your body produces it, your body starts involuntary exercise such as shivering to stay warm. It makes involuntary adjustments to preserve normal temperature in vital organs, restricting blood-flow in the extremities. Both responses drain your energy reserves. The only way to stop the drain is to reduce the degree of exposure.

As energy reserves are exhausted, with full-blown hypothermia, cold reaches the brain, depriving you of good judgment and reasoning power. You will not be aware that this is happening. You will lose control of your hands. Your internal temperature will slide downward. Without treatment, this slide leads to stupor, collapse, and death.

To defend yourself against hypothermia, stay dry. When clothes get wet, they lose about 90 percent of their insulating value. Wool loses relatively less heat, but cotton, down, and some synthetics lose more. Choose rain clothes that cover the head, neck, body, and legs, and provide good protection against wind-driven rain. Most hypothermia cases develop in air temperatures between 30 and 50 degrees Fahrenheit, but hypothermia can develop in warmer temperatures.

If your party is exposed to wind, cold, and wet, think hypothermia. Watch yourself and others for these symptoms: uncontrollable fits of shivering; vague, slow, slurred speech; memory lapses; incoherence; immobile, fumbling hands; frequent stumbling or a lurching gait; drowsiness (to sleep is to die); apparent exhaustion; and inability to get up after a rest. When a member of your party has hypothermia, he or she may deny any problem. Believe the symptoms, not the victim. Even mild symptoms demand treatment, as follows:

- Get the victim out of the wind and rain.
- Strip off all wet clothes.
- If the victim is only mildly impaired, give him or her warm drinks. Then get the victim in warm clothes and a warm sleeping bag. Place well-wrapped water bottles filled with heated water close to the victim.
- If the victim is badly impaired, attempt to keep him or her awake. Put the victim in a sleeping bag with another person—both naked. If you have a double bag, put two warm people in with the victim. For more information on Hypothermia, see *Wilderness First Aid* by Gilbert Preston, M.D. (Falcon 1997).

LEAVE NO TRACE

Hiking along the Continental Divide is like visiting a museum. You obviously do not want to leave your mark on an art treasure in the museum. If everybody going through the museum left one little mark, the piece of art would be quickly destroyed—and of what value is a big building full of trashed art? The same goes for wilderness along the Continental Divide, which is as magnificent as any masterpiece by any artist. If we all left just one little mark on the landscape, the wilderness would soon be despoiled.

A wilderness can accommodate human use as long as everybody behaves. Because a few thoughtless or uninformed visitors can ruin it for everybody who follows, all wilderness users have a responsibility to know and follow the rules of no trace camping.

Nowadays most wilderness users want to walk softly. But some may not be aware that they have poor manners. Often their actions are dictated by the outdated habits of a past generation of campers who cut green boughs for evening shelters, built campfires with fire rings, and dug trenches around tents. In the 1950s, these "camping rules" may have been acceptable. But they leave long-lasting scars, and today such behavior is absolutely unacceptable. The wilderness is shrinking, and the number of users is mushrooming. More and more camping areas show unsightly signs of heavy use.

Consequently, a new code of ethics is growing out of the necessity of coping with the unending waves of people who want a perfect wilderness experience. Today, we all must leave no clues that we have gone before. Canoeists can look behind the canoe and see no trace of their passing. Hikers, mountain bikers, and four-wheelers should have the same goal. Enjoy the wildness, but leave no trace of your visit.

THREE FALCON PRINCIPLES OF LEAVE NO TRACE

- Leave with everything you brought in.
- Leave no sign of your visit.
- Leave the landscape where you found it.

Most of us know better than to litter—in or out of the wilderness. Be sure you leave nothing, regardless of how small it is, along the trail or at the campsite. This means you should pack out everything, including orange peels, flip tops, cigarette butts, and gum wrappers. Also, pick up any trash that others leave behind.

Follow the main trail. Avoid cutting switchbacks and walking on vegetation beside the trail.

Leave "souvenirs," such as rocks, antlers or wildflowers where you find them. The next person wants to see them, too, and collecting such souvenirs violates park regulations.

Avoid making loud noises that may disturb others. Remember, sound travels easily to the other side of the lake. Be courteous.

Carry a lightweight trowel to bury human waste 6–8 inches deep and pack out used toilet paper. Keep human waste at least 200 feet from any water source.

Finally, and perhaps most importantly, strictly follow the pack-in/pack-out rule. If you carry something into the backcountry, consume it or carry it out.

Leave no trace—and put your ear to the ground in the wilderness and listen carefully. Thousands of people coming behind you are thanking you for your courtesy and good sense. For more information on minimum impact recreation see the book *Leave No Trace* by Will Harmon (Falcon 1997).

Using this Guidebook

DIFFICULTY RATINGS

To help you plan your trip, trails are rated by difficulty. However, difficulty ratings for trails serve as general guides only, not the final word. What is difficult to one hiker may be easy to the next. In this guidebook, difficulty ratings consider both how long and how strenuous the route is. Here are general definitions of the ratings.

Easy—Suitable for any hiker, including children or elderly persons, without serious elevation gain, hazardous sections, or places where the trail is faint.

Moderate—Suitable for hikers who have some experience and at least an average fitness level. Probably not suitable for children or the elderly unless they have an above-average level of fitness. The hike may have some short sections where the trail is difficult to follow, and often includes some hills.

Difficult—Suitable for experienced hikers with above-average fitness level, sections of the trail are often difficult to follow. They may even include some off-trail sections that could require knowledge of route-finding with a topographic map and compass, sometimes with serious elevation gain, and possibly some hazardous conditions.

DISTANCES

In this guidebook, most distances came from National Park Service or Forest Service signs and brochures, but some trail mileage was estimated. Since it is difficult and time-consuming to precisely measure trails, most distances listed in any guidebook, on trail signs, or in park brochures are usually somebody's estimate. Keep in mind that distance is often less important than difficulty. A rocky, 2-mile uphill trail can take longer and require more effort than 4 miles on a well-contoured trail on flat terrain. The moral of this story is if the distance is slightly off, there is no need to get too excited.

TRAFFIC

Traffic ratings give you an idea of the amount of people you will see along the trail and the signs of heavy use that may be characteristic of this trail.

Heavy—describes trails that are well known, receive heavy traffic at peak season, and where you are likely to see other hikers.

Moderate—describes areas where you might see people during peak season, but during odd times you may see nobody and the signs of impact are slight.

Light—describes areas where it is unusual to see large groups and the trail shows almost no negative signs of use.

ELEVATION GAIN

Elevation gain gives you and idea of how much climbing you will have to do on each trip. If you dislike hills, pick a hike with little or no elevation gain (less than 200 feet). Consider, however, that hikes near the divide, which often involve climbing ridges and mountains, are usually rewarded with views.

MAPS

There are a variety of maps for areas along the Continental Divide, but in preparing this book, we produced maps for each area. I suggest you also use a Trails Illustrated Maps or the U.S. Geological Survey Quadrangle map for the area you plan to visit. You can usually special order any USGS Quad from your local sport store, or you can order them directly from the USGS at the following address:

U.S. Geological Survey
Box 25286, Federal Center
Denver, CO 80225
1-800-USA-MAPS
www.mapping.usgs.gov

For Alberta you will need topographic maps in the National Park Service 1:50,000 series and other 1:50,000 series maps for Alberta. To get these contact:

Canada Map Office
130 Bentley Road
Ottawa, Ontario, Canada KIA OE9
1-800-465-6277

FOR MORE INFORMATION

This is usually the agency address of the local Forest Service or District Ranger. You should contact these offices before you get to the trailhead to learn of any changes in access, regulations, or natural conditions that may affect your trip.

FINDING THE TRAILHEAD

This is detailed information about finding the trailhead. If you speak to a ranger directly, have him or her circle your trailhead on the map. Always make sure you are at the trailhead you think you are before setting out. It is easy to find your way back to a known spot, but very difficult to find your way back to a place you thought was somewhere else.

SHARING

Everybody hopes to have a wilderness all to themselves, but that rarely happens. Instead, we have to share the trails with other hikers, mountain bikers, and backcountry horsemen.

If you meet a stock party on the trail, move off the trail on the uphill side and quietly let the stock animals pass. It is too difficult (and sometimes dangerous) for the stock animals to yield. Hikers should yield to horses. Mountain bikers should yield to both hikers and horses.

BACKCOUNTRY USE REGULATIONS

Backcountry use regulations are not intended to complicate your life. They help preserve the natural landscape and protect visitors. Each area you hike in has specific regulations for that area. Check with the local Forest Service or Park Service office for complete and up-to-date regulations. Hikes in national parks will include a section with specific regulations.

The following backcountry use guidelines are typical of many wilderness areas and national parks:

- A permit is often requiring for overnight use of the backcountry.
- Build campfires in established fire rings and only at campsites where campfires are allowed.
- In areas with bears, suspend food at least 10 feet above the ground and 4 feet horizontally from a post or tree.
- Carry out all trash. If you can pack it in, you can pack it out.
- Dispose of human waste at least 200 feet from any water source, or campsite, or sight of a trail.
- Have a valid fishing permit if you intend to fish.

Do not:
- Feed, touch, tease, frighten, or intentionally disturb wildlife.
- Toss, throw, or roll rocks or other items inside caves, into valleys, canyons, or caverns, down hillsides, or into thermal features.
- Possess, destroy, injure deface, remove, dig or disturb from its natural state any plant, rock, animal, mineral, cultural, or archaeological resource.
- Violate a closure, designation, use or activity restriction or condition, schedule or visiting hours, or public use limit.

The Continental Divide in Alberta, Canada

The Continental Divide in Alberta cuts through endless ranges of ice-clad mountains. The divide forms the southwestern border of the province and the backdrop for such famous Canadian National Parks as Jasper and Banff. This book includes six hikes in Banff National Park and several in Jasper National Park. We also included several less-visited areas outside of the national parks for exploring the Continental Divide. The hikes cover territory from alpine passes to teal blue glacial tarns.

Alberta's backbone of mountain ranges catches more precipitation than any other part of the province, most of which is from snow during the winter months. The hiking season runs from July through September, and many snowfields linger on through July on alpine trails. Alberta is also bear country so take all necessary precautions.

THE CONTINENTAL DIVIDE IN JASPER NATIONAL PARK

Canada's largest national park—Jasper, just north of Banff—has 1,000 kilometers of trails with several high alpine trips near the Continental Divide. Trails are less heavily used here than in Banff, although a few popular routes remain crowded during peak season. Jasper operates a quota system on its backcountry trails in an effort to preserve the quality of the wilderness experience for visitors. If you plan to spend a night or more in the backcountry, you must first obtain a use permit. Quotas for busier trails fill rapidly, particularly in July and August. Plan and select several backup trips. The park staff will also take reservations to fill up to thirty percent of each trail's quota. You may book a slot on a specific trail up to three weeks before your actual trip by writing to the Park Superintendent, Jasper National Park, P.O. Box 10, Jasper, Alberta, TOE 1EO. In your request include the number of people in your party, your destination, the proposed route, and the dates you plan to be in the backcountry.

1 Geraldine Lakes

General description:	A moderate day or strenuous overnight hike over rugged terrain to a remote lake basin.
Distance:	8.5 miles (14.2 km).
Difficulty:	Moderate.
Traffic:	Moderate.
Elevation loss:	1,340 feet (406 meters).
Maps:	Jasper National Park.
For more information:	Park Superintendent, Jasper National Park, P.O. Box 10, Jasper, Alberta TOE 1EO, 403-852-6176.

Finding the trailhead: From the Icefields Parkway (Highway 93), turn west onto Highway 93-A at the Athabasca Falls junction. Drive north for about half a mile and turn left onto the Geraldine Access Road, a rough dirt road that climbs rapidly into the forest. Follow this road 3.7 miles (6 km) to a small parking area at the top of a series of switchbacks. The trail leaves directly from the road and is marked with a sign.

The hike: A hiking companion once described the route into the Geraldine Lakes as a miserable, root-infested, ankle-busting slog. These epithets probably tell more about the hiker than the trail, but there is some truth in them. Hikers who venture beyond the first lake will encounter trackless boulder fields, steep scrambles up rocky headwalls, and a confusion of cairns. Bad weather intensifies the risk of a slip or losing the rail. But these same obstacles preserve the wild, remote character of the upper basin, and the alpine ridges above the upper two lakes offer some of the best terrain in the park for wandering and exploring along the Continental Divide.

Day hikers can easily reach the second lake, but the upper basin is best explored from a basecamp set up at the designated site on the south end of the second lake. The first mile or so of the trail to the lowermost lake is wet and spongy, tangled with tree roots and decaying logs. This section of the trail climbs gradually through a dense forest before dropping over the last 200 yards to the outlet stream and the first lake. The trail hugs the northern shore, skirting a small boulder field before stair-stepping up the first headwall beside a noisy cascade.

From the top of this headwall, the trail vanishes in a maze of boulders. Watch for cairns and stay within earshot of the stream to pick up the track again as it skirts a copse of stunted trees. The trail then crosses to the left of the rock-strewn valley bottom and passes a shallow pond. After breaking through a stand of taller trees, hikers are rewarded with unobstructed views of the 330-foot waterfall streaming from the second headwall. The trail threads through more extensive boulder fields, then climbs up the loose scree of an avalanche gully to gain the level of the second basin.

The second Geraldine Lake, looking west.

Ten miles (6 km) from the trailhead, a low ridge atop the headwall provides good views of Mount Fryatt to the southeast and Whirlpool Peak to the north. From here the track is better defined as it drops to the second lake and contours another 0.5 mile (1 km) around the east shore to the backcountry campsite.

Geraldine Lakes

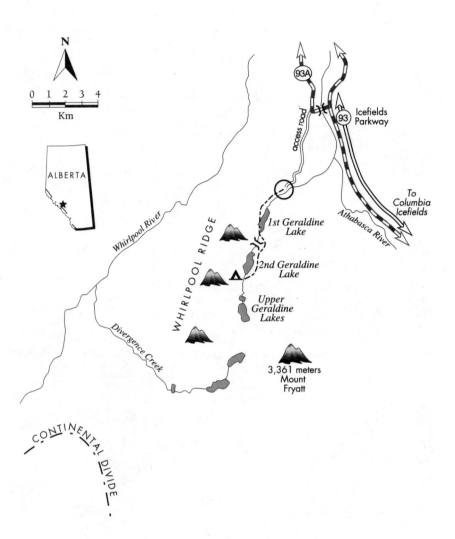

Overnighters will want to pack lightly because of the boulder hopping and punishing climbs up the two headwalls. Wear sturdy shoes and bring a compass and topographic map for reconnoitering the basin above. A third large lake lies beyond the campsite, best reached by paralleling the stream bed south. It is also possible to traverse to the top of the open pass at the head of the Geraldine Basin for a look into the headwater lakes of Divergence Creek directly south.

2 Wilcox Pass

General description:	An easy day hike to a broad alpine pass with stunning views of the Columbia Icefield. The hike is located above the Columbia Icefield Visitor Center near the border between Banff and Jasper National Parks. The trail is not on the Continental Divide, but features excellent views of the divide and the Columbia Icefield.
Distance:	6.8 miles (11.3 km) one way.
Difficulty:	Easy.
Traffic:	Heavy.
Elevation gain:	1,000 feet (303 meters).
Maps:	Jasper National Park; Columbia Icefield 83 C/3, Sunwapta Peak 83 C/6.
For more information:	Park Superintendent, Jasper National Park, P.O. Box 10, Jasper, Alberta TOE 1EO, 403-852-6176.

Finding the trailhead: The trailhead is easy to find, just off the Icefields Parkway on the access road to the Wilcox Creek Campground, 0.6 mile (1 km) north of Sunwapta Pass or 1.2 miles (2 km) south of the Columbia Icefield Visitor Center.

Athabasca Glacier from Wilcox Pass.

Wilcox Pass

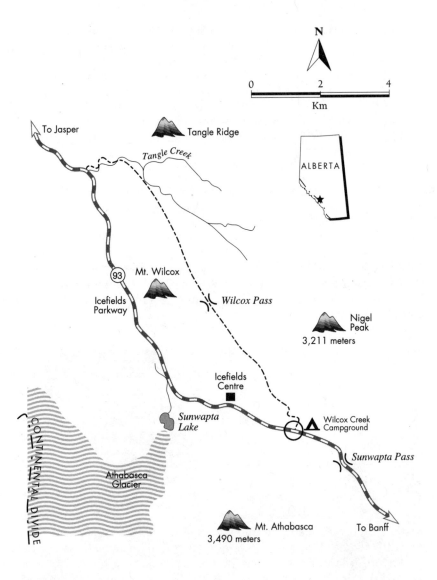

The hike: This 6.8-mile (11.6 km) day hike offers more than its share of alpine scenery, yet the hike itself is not too demanding, particularly if you stop for lunch at the top. Take along a warm hat and a jacket; even in mid-summer, days can be cool and wind or rain raises the risk of hypothermia.

Until the turn of the century, glaciers filled the valley where the Icefields Parkway now runs and Wilcox Pass was the route trappers and outfitters took over Sunwapta Divide. The pass can be hiked from either direction, but the southern trailhead is the more scenic approach to the pass.

The trail switchbacks steeply for roughly 1.2 miles (2 km) through an old growth forest of subalpine firs before leveling off on a high bench overlooking the Columbia Icefield to the west. From here to the pass itself, the trail meanders through alpine tundra and around melt water ponds.

The plants and soil of this harsh climate are extremely fragile, so stay on the path and limit your cross-country travel to numerous bighorn sheep trails. At the top of the broad pass, numerous sheep trails lead west of the main trail, providing access to 8,856-foot (2,700-meter) Mount Wilcox. The slopes of Mount Wilcox offer shelter from the winds and a panoramic view of Mount Athabasca and the Athabasca Glacier sloping away from the massive Columbia Icefield. In good weather, look for the tracks of climbers on the snowy faces of Mount Athabasca. Mount Wilcox also provides views of Wilcox Pass itself, where bighorn sheep, deer, grizzlies, eagles, and moose are sometimes sighted.

Many hikers simply return to the Wilcox Creek trailhead, making a 4.8-mile (8 km) round trip. For those continuing north, the trail is lightly used and grows faint, following the headwaters of Tangle Creek. A marker points out the flank of Tangle Ridge to the north, and the trail again looses definition as it descends into the trees. From here the trail is better defined as it drops sharply down to the Tangle Creek Trailhead and parking lot 6 miles (10 km) north of the Wilcox Creek Campground by way of the Columbia Icefields Parkway.

THE CONTINENTAL DIVIDE IN BANFF NATIONAL PARK

In 1887, just fifteen years after Yellowstone became the world's first national park, Banff was designated Canada's first national park. Today, Banff is the premier tourist attraction in Canada, host to more than three million visitors each year. The Continental Divide forms the west edge of the park and offers some of the best scenery found anywhere in the Canadian Rockies.

Anyone planning to camp in the backcountry must first obtain a backcountry use permit from a visitor information center in the park. Permits can be requested by mail from the Park Superintendent, Banff National Park, P.O. Box 900, Banff, Alberta TOL OCO. Include the number of people in your party, your destination, the proposed route, and the dates you plan to be in the backcountry.

3 Peyto Glacier

General description:	A strenuous day hike to the toe of Peyto Glacier spilling from Waputik Icefield.
Distance:	8 miles (13.3 km).
Difficulty:	Strenuous.
Traffic:	Light.
Elevation loss:	1,500 feet (455 meters).
Maps:	Banff National Park; Hector Lake 82 N/9.
For more information:	Park Superintendent, Banff National Park, P.O. Box 900, Banff, Alberta TOL OCO, 403-762-1500.

Finding the trailhead: Turn west onto the access road at the summit of Bow Pass and turn right into the large parking lot. An asphalt path leads 400 yards to the wooden deck of the viewpoint. Continue uphill about 10 yards past the deck; the trail drops from here through a thick forest in a frenzy of switchbacks.

The hike: Each year, thousands of tourists stop at the viewpoint overlooking the turquoise waters of Peyto Lake, but few people venture beyond the interpretive trail for a close-up view of the lake and the glacier that gives it its color.

Peyto Lake and the Mistaya Valley.

Peyto Glacier

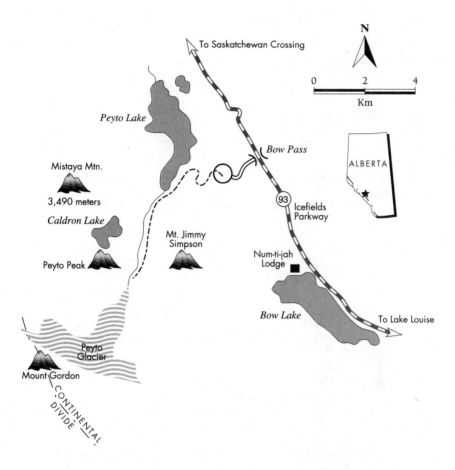

A set of switchbacks rapidly drops the trail from the viewpoint to the head of Peyto Lake in 1.5 miles (2.5 km) of hiking.

At the bottom, a gravelly glacial plain flanks the inlet stream. Walk south across these flats, following the stream to where it cuts through a ridge of trees, actually an old moraine. About 100 yards to the left of the stream, the trail enters the trees and climbs the ridge, then continues south over the cobbles and glacial debris for another 2.4 miles (4 km) to the toe of the glacier. Stone cairns mark most of this route as it follows the headwaters of the Mistaya River to their source between Peyto Peak and Mount Jimmy Simpson.

The names of this region are a mixture of Indian and pioneer history. *Mistaya* is the Stoney Indian name for the "great" or grizzly bear; Peyto Lake is named after Banff Park Superintendent Bill Peyto, early explorer of the park.

The final approach to the glacier is steep, with unstable footing. Do not attempt to climb on the glacier without proper equipment and know-how. Also, remember to save some time and energy for the demanding climb back up from Peyto Lake to the viewpoint. Carry plenty of water. The streams and Peyto Lake carry too much glacial sediment to treat for drinking.

4 Hector Lake

General description:	A short day hike—with a major river ford—to the shores of a large, glacier-fed lake in the Bow Valley, just west of the Icefields Parkway, about 11 miles (18 km) north of the junction with the Trans-Canada Highway in Banff National Park. Highlights include fishing, fording the Bow River, views of the Waputik Range and Balfour Pass. This hike is down in the valley below the Continental Divide, but is one of the more interesting rambles in the area, offering views of the divide and surrounding peaks.
Distance:	3 miles (1.8 km).
Difficulty:	Easy, but with potentially dangerous ford of the Bow River.
Traffic:	Light.
Elevation loss:	200 feet (60.6 meters).
Maps:	Banff National Park; Hector Lake 82 N/9.
For more information:	Park Superintendent, Banff National Park, P.O. Box 900, Banff, Alberta TOL OCO, 403-762-1500.

Finding the trailhead: The trailhead is marked with a sign on the west side of the Icefields Parkway 0.6 mile (1 km) north of the Hector Lake viewpoint. Park on the west side of the road along the widened shoulder. The trail begins at the north end of the pull out.

The hike: Although Hector Lake lies within 1.2 miles (2 km) of the Icefields Parkway, few hikers visit its shores. The Bow River threads between the road and lake, presenting a dangerous ford when the water is high. **Fording the Bow should be attempted only by strong hikers with previous experience in crossing swift rivers, and then only during low water.** It is best to try this hike in late August, September, or October, but beware of daily fluctuations in the river's flow. Glacier-fed rivers are usually at their lowest in the morning and tend to increase through the day as warmer

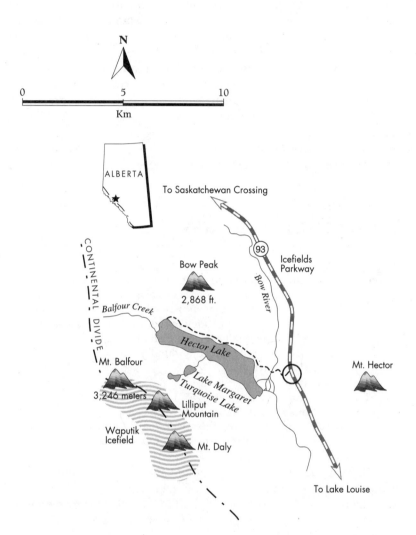

temperatures add meltwater to the current. To the hiker, this means that a knee-deep stream may become a waist-high torrent by mid-afternoon. Exercise caution.

For the first half mile, the trail drops down onto the densely timbered Bow River floodplain. The route is muddy and potholed much of the distance to the river, partly a symptom of the heavy use from people going to fish the Bow River. Don't stray off the trail just to keep your boots dry—such detours only lead to more widespread damage.

At low water, the river can be forded where the trail leads to the water's edge. If this looks risky, another ford can be found about fifty yards downstream where the channel splits around a small island. The current can be strong at either ford—if the water reaches your waist, turn back and be content to stroll the banks of the Bow.

If you manage to cross the river, proceed upstream along the bank to pick up the trail. From here, the trail enters the forest again for an easy one mile walk to the cabins of an old outfitting camp on the eastern shore of Hector Lake. Pulpit Peak, Lilliput Mountain, and other peaks of the Waputik Range rise beyond the lake. Look for osprey and eagles in the crowns of trees ringing the shore. Also, keep an eye—and ear—out for bear and moose, particularly in the brushy thickets along the Bow River.

5 Wenkchemna Pass

General description:	A moderate day hike into a remote glacial valley, located southwest of Lake Louise in Banff National Park. Special attractions include Moraine and Eiffel Lakes and Valley of the Ten Peaks, an array of impressive, glacier-clad mountains.
Distance:	12 miles (20 km) round trip.
Difficulty:	Strenuous.
Traffic:	Heavy.
Elevation gain:	12,400 feet (3757.6 meters).
Maps:	Banff National Park; 82 N/8.
For more information:	Park Superintendent, Banff National Park, Box 900, Banff, Alberta TOL OCO, 403-762-1500.

Finding the trailhead: To reach Moraine Lake and the trailhead, take the Lake Louise access road from the Trans-Canada Highway. Within 2.1 miles (3.5 km), the road to Moraine Lake forks off to the left. This road ends in 6.6 miles (11 km) at a large parking lot at the foot of the lake. Walk down to the lakeshore and past the lodge to the trailhead.

The hike: Wenkchemna Pass rises to just over 8,580 feet (2,600 meters) at the head of the Valley of Ten Peaks, so named because of the row of saw-toothed mountains forming the valley's southern wall. At the mouth of this valley, the peaks are mirrored in the turquoise waters of Moraine Lake, a popular tourist destination.

The trail to Wenkchemna Pass leaves the lakeshore path and steadily switchbacks for 1.5 miles (2.5 km) to the junction with the Larch Valley Trail. Take it slow on the initial climb and follow all the switchbacks—this is

Wenkchemna Pass

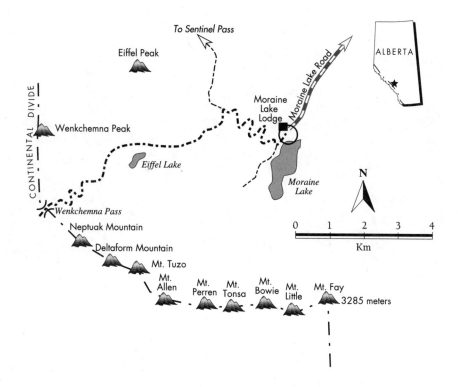

the steepest section of the trail and there is no point in burning the thighs at the outset by shortcutting. The dense spruce and fir forest here shades the trail, easing the work of gaining elevation.

At the Larch Valley junction, stay to the left on the level grade heading west. From here, the trail wends gradually out of the trees and across open slopes, always facing the jagged peaks across the valley. The rock-strewn Wenkchemna Glacier fills the valley floor, with Moraine Lake shining at the mouth. Listen for rockfalls and avalanches across the valley. Also, keep an eye out for deer and bighorn sheep, and for bears browsing on the slopes along the trail.

Roughly 3.6 miles (6 km) into the hike, the trail crosses a scree slope above Eiffel Lake and then traverses an old rockslide and fields of glacial cobble, at one point following the crest of an esker or small ridge of debris in the middle of the glacier's footprint. From here, several routes to the pass are possible, some marked by cairns of piled stones. Snow may linger on this final slope into July, longer in the gullies and on sections of the proper trail. The snow may offer good footing early in the day, providing a more direct approach to the pass.

Moraine Lake from the trail to Wenkchemna Pass.

Western winds often snarl over the saddle that marks the pass, but a scattering of boulders at the base of Wenkchemna Peak to the north offers a choice of sheltered lunch spots with views into remote regions of Yoho and Kootenay National Parks. Mountain goats are common here—hikers may smell their musky scent before actually sighting one.

6 Plain-of-Six-Glaciers

General description:	An easy day hike with a moderate climb just before the turn around point. Hike location starts from the Chateau at Lake Louise in Banff National Park. Six active glaciers are observable from a safe distance.
Distance:	8 miles (13.3 km) round trip.
Difficulty:	Easy.
Traffic:	Heavy.
Elevation gain:	1,200 feet (363.6 meters).
Maps:	Banff National Park; Lake Louise 82 N/8.
For more information:	Park Superintendent, Banff National Park, P.O. Box 900, Banff, Alberta TOL OCO, 403-762-1500.

Plain-of-Six-Glaciers

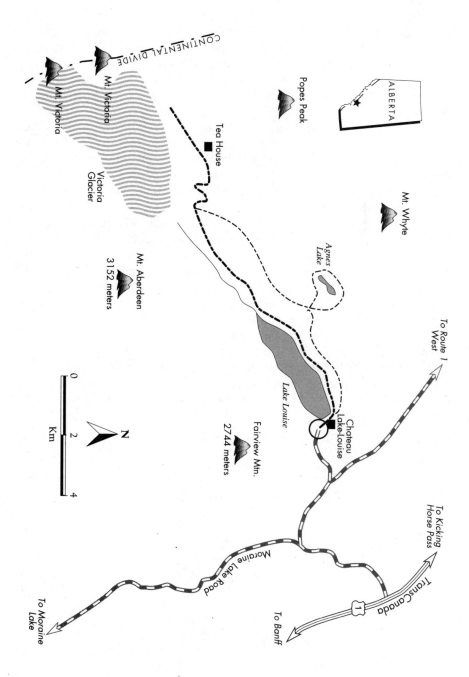

Finding the trailhead: To get to the trailhead, take the Lake Louise exit on the Trans-Canada Highway and follow the signs on the spur road for Lake Louise. Park in the visitor lot for the chateau and follow the asphalt path to the lake's eastern shore.

The hike: The trail to the Plain-of-Six-Glaciers is one of the more heavily used routes within Banff National Park. However, trails become popular with good reason, and this particular hike offers several rewards.

The trail wraps around the northern shore of Lake Louise and is paved until it leaves the water's edge for the gradual ascent toward the Plain-of-Six-Glaciers.

Within 1.2 miles (2 km) from the chateau the trail begins to climb, but the grade steepens notably only after the junction with the Mirror Lake highline trail roughly 1.8 miles (3 km) into the hike. Over the next 1.5 miles (2.5 km) the trail twists up the side of this glacier-scoured valley in a series of switchbacks, rewarding the hiker with views of Mount Victoria and Mount Lefroy with each turn in the trail.

At 3.5 miles (5.5 km) the trail levels off just below a two-story teahouse where fresh squeezed lemonade and home baked muffins tempt hikers to while away the afternoon. But the trail continues, skittering along the crest of a lateral moraine for another 0.6 mile (1 km) to a precarious rock pile below Abbot's Pass. Mountain goats sometimes lounge on the grassy ledges above the trail. This is also a good vantage point for scanning the surrounding glaciers for avalanches or for watching the progress of climbing parties approaching the stone hut atop the pass.

The return trip to Chateau Lake Louise takes about two hours unless you opt to follow the Mirror Lake highline trail. The highline trail is often less crowded, but requires additional climbing before dropping back down toward Lake Louise. This route also adds about 2.4 miles (4 km) to the round-trip distance.

7 Consolation Lakes

General description:	An easy, half-day stroll through a subalpine forest to a pair of sparkling lakes below the walls of Bident Mountain. Hike is located south of Lake Louise in Banff National Park, with views of Bident Mountain, Mount Quadra, and Mount Temple; Babel Creek, Lower and Upper Consolation Lakes.
Distance:	3.7 miles (6.2 km).
Difficulty:	Easy.
Traffic:	Moderate to Heavy.
Elevation gain:	200 feet (60.6 meters).
Maps:	Banff National Park; Lake Louise 82 N/8.
For more information:	Park Superintendent, Banff National Park, P.O. Box 900, Banff, Alberta TOL OCO, 403-762-1500.

Finding the trailhead: From the Lake Louise access road, follow the Moraine Lake Road 6.6 miles (11 km) to the parking lot at the end of the road. The trail begins on the boardwalk next to the picnic area below Moraine Lake. Look for the sign mentioning the Moraine Lake Overlook and Consolation Lakes.

Bident Mountain towers above Lower Consolation Lake.

Consolation Lakes

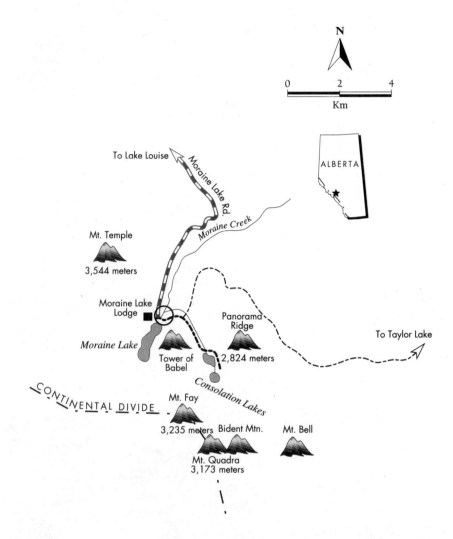

N

0   2   4
Km

To Lake Louise

Moraine Lake Rd.

Moraine Creek

ALBERTA

Mt. Temple
3,544 meters

Moraine Lake
Lodge

Panorama
Ridge

To Taylor Lake

Moraine Lake

Tower of
Babel

2,824 meters

Consolation Lakes

CONTINENTAL DIVIDE

Mt. Fay

3,235 meters   Bident Mtn.   Mt. Bell

Mt. Quadra
3,173 meters

The hike: The Consolation Valley was named in counterpoint to Desolation Valley, the original label pinned to the raw, boulder strewn canyon above Moraine Lake now known as Wenkchemna Valley. And the short, shady, gently graded trail into Consolation Lakes should well console weary hikers. No other trail in the park requires as little effort to reach such a gem of an alpine lake basin.

The trail begins as a boardwalk leaving the Moraine Lake picnic area. Bear left through the boulder field below Moraine Lake—a short side trail to the right climbs the rock pile for a view of the lake. After winding through the boulders, the main trail settles into a steady but easy ascent along Babel Creek through a spruce and fir forest.

As the trail rounds the foot of the Tower of Babel (a ridge running north from 10,171-foot (3,101-meter) Mount Babel), the grade eases and the noise of Babel Creek draws nearer. Just over a half mile (1 km) from the trailhead, the trail to Taylor Lake forks off to the left, immediately crossing Babel Creek. Continue straight on the main trail for another 0.6 mile (1 km) to a small meadow along Babel Creek. Watch for moose and elk here, especially in the early morning. Just 550 yards (500 meters) more brings you to the mouth of a large amphitheater with Lower Consolation Lake shimmering at the head of Babel Creek.

Pick your way across the boulder field on the west bank of the creek to reach the lower lake. To continue on to the upper lake, cross the stream by hopping boulders (in higher water a retreat downstream to a narrower section may be necessary) and follow the grassy path around the east shore of the lower lake. Cross the scree slope and climb the mounds of glacial debris separating the two lakes. The second lake affords a better vantage of Consolation Pass and Mount Bell to the south.

Although this trail attracts a good number of visitors, hikers seeking a sense of remoteness and solitude can still enjoy this trail at sunrise or sunset, particularly later in the season when the crowds have thinned.

8 Twin Lakes

General description:	A moderate one- or two-night backpacking trip to a pair of high lakes nestled in nearly identical settings against the eastern face of Storm Mountain, located just southwest of Castle Junction on the western border of Banff National Park.
Distance:	10 miles (16.7 km).
Difficulty:	Moderate.
Traffic:	Light to moderate.
Elevation gain:	1,900 feet (575.8 meters).
Maps:	Banff National Park; Banff 82 O/4; Mount Goodsir 82 N/1.
For more information:	Park Superintendent, Banff National Park, P.O. Box 900, Banff, Alberta TOL OCO, 403-762-1500.

Finding the trailhead: From Castle Junction, drive west on Highway 93 for 4.8 miles (8 km) to the Vista Lake viewpoint. The viewpoint is a large parking area on the south side of the road overlooking the 1968 Vermillion Pass burn. The trail is marked with a sign and drops quickly from the southeast corner of the parking lot.

Vista Lake with the route to Twin Lakes in the background.

The hike: Most veteran backpackers own stout hearts and sore knees, giving credence to the old rule that you go uphill with your heart and come down with your knees. With this in mind, you will find the ascent to Twin Lakes a genuine workout, while the retreat back down to civilization is more gradual and forgiving. Moreover, you will find the destination—Twin Lakes—more than rewarding for your efforts.

From the Vista Lake viewpoint, look south over the lake and the low ridge beyond to scan the first several miles of the route. The trail descends

Twin Lakes

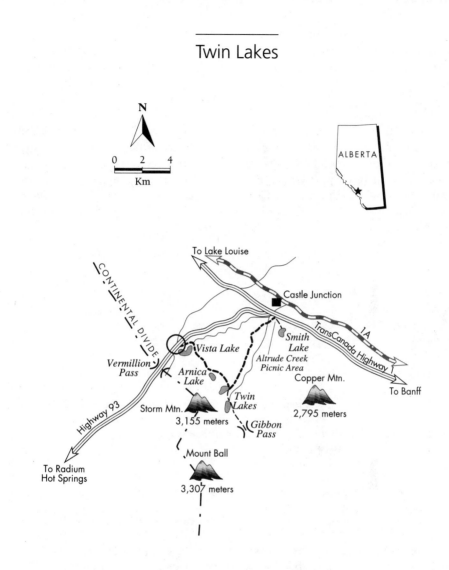

quickly over the first 0.9 mile (1.5 km) to the shore of Vista Lake, crosses a bridge over the outlet stream on the lake's eastern end, and then begins climbing at a moderate pitch. Another 0.5 mile (1 km) further, a side trail from the Storm Mountain Lodge joins the main track. Bear right and continue the uphill grunt as it steepens. This is the hottest, most tedious part of the climb, as it is open to the sun until the trail leaves the burn and enters the shady forest.

The trail soon levels off before dipping slightly to Arnica Lake, 3 miles (5 km) from the trailhead. The talus slopes and cliffs of Storm Mountain provide a dramatic backdrop to Arnica Lake, which is also a popular day hike destination for anglers hoping to land one of the lake's cutthroat trout.

Leaving Arnica, the trail scales an outlying ridge from Storm Mountain, reaching 7,495-foot (2,285-meter) Arnica Summit in a strenuous 2,600-foot (800 meter) push. From here, it is about two thirds of a mile down to Upper Twin Lake and the designated campsites. Both of the Twin Lakes are set against the cliffs and snowfields of the Continental Divide, ringed by subalpine forest laced with alpine larch. Total distance from Vista Lake viewpoint is 4.8 miles (8 km).

If you have arranged a shuttle or are willing to hitch hike back to your car, leave the Twin Lakes Basin by dropping to the trail junction below the lower lake and turn left. Follow this gradually descending trail through meadows and larch parklands, over a marshy section plagued with roots and rocks, down to the Altrude Creek picnic area, a distance of 4.8 miles (8 km). Near the trailhead, the trail crosses Altrude Creek and joins an old quarry road for the final 600 yards (500 meters).

Note: End of Banff area hikes

---

9 Three Isle Lake

General description:	An easy overnight or moderate day hike to a large subalpine lake tucked below the Continental Divide. Highlights include Upper Kananaskis Lake, Three Isle Lake, outstanding mountain scenery, wildlife.
Distance:	7.2 miles (12 km) one way.
Difficulty:	Moderate.
Traffic:	Moderate.
Elevation gain:	1,600 feet (484.8 meters).
General location:	West of Kananaskis Lakes in Peter Lougheed Provincial Park.
Maps:	Peter Lougheed Provincial Park Summer Trails brochure; 82 J/11.
For more information:	Park Superintendent, Peter Lougheed Provincial Park, Box 130, Kananaskis Village, Alberta TOL 2HO, 403-591-7222.

Finding the trailhead: Turn west onto the Kananaskis Lakes Trail from Kananaskis Trail (Highway 40). Follow this road to its terminus at the North Interlakes parking lot next to the earthen dam. Walk across the dam and spillway and turn left onto the old fire road.

The hike: For scenery and easy access to the backcountry, few trails match the route into Three Isle Lake near the western boundary of Peter Lougheed Provincial Park. Hikers enjoy excellent views of Upper Kananaskis Lake and surrounding mountains in the early going, and the trail runs nearly level for much of the first 4.2 miles (7 km) of this 7.3-mile (12 km) hike. The

Three Isle Lake

final destination, a large subalpine lake cupped below the bulk of Mount Worthington, offers a pleasant backcountry campground and unrivalled opportunities for day hiking above timberline.

The first 3.6 miles (6 km) follow an old fire road that rolls through the forest above the north shore of Upper Kananaskis Lake. About 1.5 miles (2.5 km) from the trailhead, the main track drops from a junction with the upper lakes trail and eventually crosses the Upper Kananaskis River on a stout log bridge. Shortly after the bridge, the main track meets the Lyautey trail and then runs 1.2 miles (2 km) to the Forks, where the Lawson trail branches to the right. A set of campsites straddles the Lawson trail just beyond the junction.

From Forks, the trail climbs beside Three Isle Creek toward a steep headwall guarding the lake basin. After leaving the creek (which drains not from the lake but from the glaciers on Mount North over to the south), the trail switchbacks up the face of the headwall, crossing from right to left before attaining the lip and dropping down to the lake's eastern shore. The Three Isle Campground lies on the northeast end of the lake, providing a good base camp from which to explore the basin.

The most popular day hike from camp consists of following the main trail along the north shore of Three Isle Lake and climbing to South Kananaskis Pass, 1.2 miles (2 km) from the campground. The pass offers views down Beatty Creek into British Columbia and north along the divide. For even better vistas, climb west to a large cairn and continue for another mile over rolling alpine terrain to the unnamed summit north of Mount McHarg. To the north, Palliser Pass and the rugged peaks along the southern border of Banff National Park come into view. To the southwest, the deep valley of the Palliser River falls away.

Most hikers return to Upper Kananaskis Lake by retracing their steps, but if time allows, a more adventurous loop can be completed by descending Beatty Creek and traversing North Kananaskis Pass to Turbine Canyon.

10 Crowsnest Mountain

General description:	A strenuous day hike to the top of Crowsnest Mountain, one of the finest viewpoints in the Canadian Rockies. The hike features high-alpine terrain and excellent views of the Continental Divide to the west.
Distance:	7.5 miles (12.5 km) round trip.
Difficulty:	Strenuous.
Traffic:	Light.
Elevation gain:	3,300 feet (1000 meters).
General location:	North of Crowsnest Pass in southern Alberta where Highway 3 crosses the Continental Divide into British Columbia.
Maps:	82 G/10.
For more information:	Crownest District, P.O. Box 540, Blairmore, Alberta, Canada TOK OEO, 403-562-3210.

Finding the trailhead: From the town of Coleman, drive west 1.8 miles (3 km) on Highway 3 to the Allison Creek Road. Turn north on this paved road and drive 1.5 miles (2.5 km) to a fork in the road. The left fork leads to a

Crowsnest Mountain

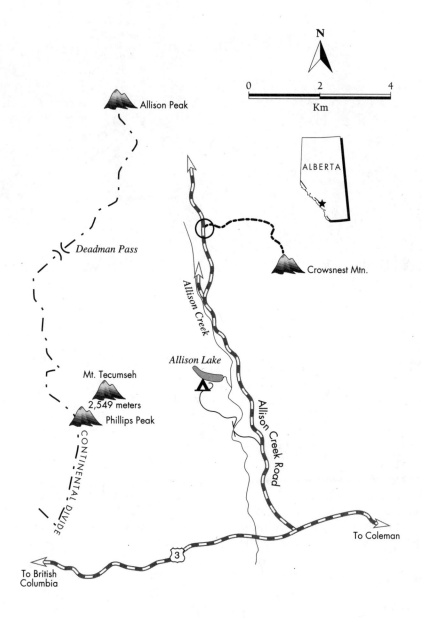

Crowsnest Mountain stands alone, an outlyer from the peaks of the Continental Divide. A 360-degree view awaits hikers on the summit. PETER ALLEN PHOTO

lakeside campground operated by the Alberta Forest Service (sites are in a lodgepole pine forest and the lake offers good fishing for rainbow trout). Take the right fork—a gravel road—to reach the hiking trail, driving 4 miles (under 7 km) to the trailhead sign. Continue past the sign another 300 yards to a narrow road and parking area on the right.

The hike: Crowsnest Mountain is a 9,198-foot (2,804 meter) pyramid of history turned upside down. The mountain was formed by a violent upheaval along the Lewis thrust fault, which folded the older Paleozoic rock on top of the younger Mesozoic formations. Today this geologic anomaly rewards determined hikers with commanding views of Alberta's rugged backbone, the Canadian Rockies.

Plan a full day for the 7.2-mile (12 km) roundtrip to the summit and back, and wait for fair weather. Pack along a sweater and windbreaker or raincoat, and carry plenty of drinking water. The trail begins with a steady climb through a second growth pine forest, an area once thinned by fire and logging. The track is well-defined and offers glimpses of the mountain through the trees until timberline is reached at the 2.4-mile (4 km) mark.

From timberline, the route traverses a steep scree slope to the base of massive limestone cliffs. Follow a series of cairns to a broad cleft or chimney in the cliffs. Here the trail becomes an arduous scramble up the rocky debris within the chimney, finally opening onto the gentle terraces of the upper slopes. The summit route contours directly to the top over loose, shingle-like stones.

Stunning panoramic views greet the successful hiker, with Tornado Mountain dominating the northern horizon. To the west lies Deadman Pass, a low gap on the Continental Divide between 8,672-foot (2,644-meter) Allison Peak to the north and 8,361-foot (2,549-meter) Mount Tecumseh to the south.

Retrace your steps to return to the trailhead.

THE CONTINENTAL DIVIDE IN WATERTON LAKES NATIONAL PARK

In 1932, an international accord with the United States established the Waterton–Glacier International Peace Park, but Waterton had been a Canadian National Park since 1914. Waterton townsite provides most services found in large towns. No registration is required for day trips, but overnight trips require a special permit, which can be purchased at the visitor center outside Waterton townsites. Backpackers must stay in the established campground.

11 Carthew Pass

General description:	A moderate day hike to a high alpine pass overlooking the remote northern mountains of Glacier National Park in the United States. The hike is just east of Cameron Lake near the southern boundary of Waterton Lakes National Park.
Distance:	10 miles (16.7 km) round trip.
Difficulty:	Moderate.
Traffic:	Moderate.
Elevation gain:	2,100 feet (636.4 meters).
Maps:	Waterton Lakes National Park.
For more information:	Park Superintendent, Waterton Lakes National Park, Waterton Park, Alberta TOK 2MO, 403-859-2224.

Finding the trailhead: From Waterton townsite, drive west 9.6 miles (16 km) on the Akamina Parkway to the Cameron Lake parking lot at the end of the road. Follow the lakeshore trail to the left past the boat rental concession to the bridge over Cameron Creek. The trail to Summit Lake and Carthew Pass begins here.

Carthew Pass

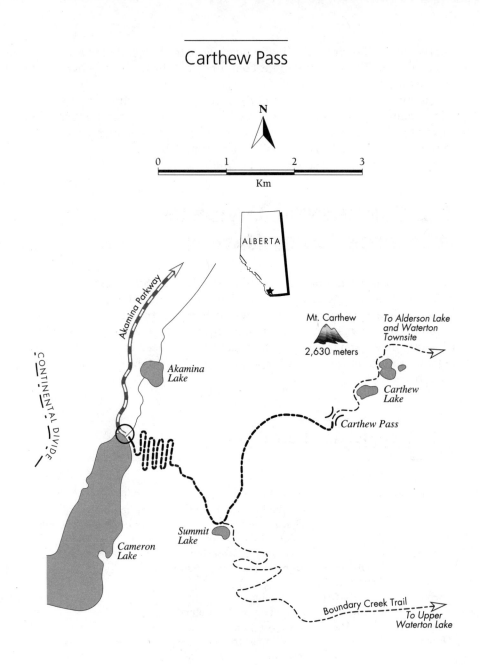

N

0   1   2   3

Km

ALBERTA

Akamina Parkway

CONTINENTAL DIVIDE

Akamina Lake

Mt. Carthew
2,630 meters

To Alderson Lake
and Waterton
Townsite

Carthew Lake

Carthew Pass

Cameron Lake

Summit Lake

Boundary Creek Trail
To Upper
Waterton Lake

The hike: From the forested shore of Cameron Lake to the blustery, barren summit of Mount Carthew, this hike is packed with mountain lakes, wildflowers, panoramic views, berry patches, glimpses of glaciers, and wildlife. Many day hikers on this trail venture no further than Summit Lake, but those who go the extra distance to Carthew Pass will find it well worth the effort. Be sure to carry plenty of drinking water (do not drink from Summit Lake without first boiling or purifying the water), and pack along a raincoat and a warm sweater.

From Cameron Lake, the trail rises gradually through a 300-year-old forest of spruce and fir in a series of long, gentle switchbacks. Watch for the pale turquoise of Cameron Lake peeking through occasional breaks in the forest canopy, and keep an eye to the trail-side foliage for thimbleberries and huckleberries in season.

After climbing for 1.8 miles (3 km), the trail levels and dips slightly to the north shore of Summit Lake some 2.4 miles (4 km) from the trailhead. Most hikers stop here for lunch, but an earlier start allows those more adventurous to continue hiking up to Carthew Pass, 2.4 miles (4 km). Turn left at the trail junction just above Summit Lake and climb over the low spur into a wide subalpine basin. The trail crosses below a broken rock band frequented by bighorn sheep then sweeps across the southern arm of Mount Carthew at timberline.

As you climb above stands of stunted fir, larch, and whitebark pine, the southern horizon opens to reveal glaciers hugging the walls of Mount Custer and Chapman Peak, with Nooney and Wurdeman Lakes cupped in their respective cirques. The trail ends its long contour by zig-zagging steeply up a red scree slope to the pass at 7,544 feet (2,300 meters). The pass, and the summit beyond, should be attempted only during fair weather and with plenty of daylight remaining. The ridge offers no shelter from wind, rain, or lightning, and storms brew quickly in this region.

For even more spectacular views, hikers can climb the spur leading north from the saddle to the summit ridge of Mount Carthew. The peak itself lies 0.6 mile (1 km) north along this barren ridge and offers a 360-degree panorama of mountains, glaciers, and glistening lakes. Total distance from the trailhead to the summit is just less than 6 miles (10 km); allow about 4 hours for the one-way trip.

The Continental Divide in Montana

There are 760 miles of the Continental Divide in Montana. This is more of the divide than all other states and provinces except Colorado. It also passes through the largest contiguous habitat area in the lower 48 states, the Glacier–Bob Marshall Wilderness Complex. The hikes along this section of the divide pass through Glacier and Yellowstone National Parks, seven national forests, the Bob Marshall Wilderness Complex, and the little known but spectacular Anaconda–Pintler Wilderness. Special permits are required for Glacier National Park.

THE CONTINENTAL DIVIDE IN GLACIER NATIONAL PARK

From the western side of Waterton Lakes National Park just north of Glacier National Park, the Continental Divide crosses into some of the most scenic country in the United States. Like the Rocky Mountains of Banff and Jasper, the divide in Glacier passes several glaciers. Weasel Collar Glacier is visible from the Boulder Pass hike and almost all of the deep U-shaped valleys of Glacier show signs of past glacial carving. Tragically, most of the visitors to Glacier National Park only see the divide at the Logan Pass Visitor Center, but those few adventurous souls who do plunge into the wilderness discover a wealth of natural beauty at every turn of the trail.

A special treat for the Continental Divide enthusiast, Triple Divide Pass separates water from three oceans. Creeks flow in each direction to each of the Atlantic, Arctic, and Pacific Oceans.

A backcountry camping permit is required for backpacking in Glacier National Park. Competition for premier sites is fierce, especially for sites in Boulder Pass. In order to get permits for the following hikes, you need to apply for them, using the advance reservation system or by going to visitor centers, 24 hours in advance of your trip. For more information, call or write Glacier National Park, West Glacier, Montana 59936, 406-888-7800.

12 Boulder Pass

General description:	A six-day backpacking trip from Kintla Lake to Upper Kintla campground to Boulder Pass or to Goat Haunt Ranger Station.
Distance:	To Upper Kintla campgroud, 11.6 miles; to Boulder Pass, 17.7 miles; to Goat Haunt Ranger Station, 31.4 miles.
Difficulty:	Moderately strenuous (east to west), strenuous (west to east).
Traffic:	Moderate.
Elevation gain:	3,470 feet.
Maps:	Kintla Lake, Kintla Peak, Mount Carter, Porcupine Ridge USGS quads.
For more information:	Glacier National Park, West Glacier, Montana 59936, 406-888-7800.

Finding the trailhead: Drive north on Glacier Route 7 from Polebridge to its northern terminus at Kintla campground. The trail begins at the northeast corner of the campground, near the lakeshore.

Key points:

0.0	Trail sign. Trail follows shore of Kintla Lake.
3.6	Junction with connecting trail to Kishenehn Ranger Station. Keep right for Boulder Pass trail.
6.3	Kintla Lake campground. Trail leaves Kintla Lake, moderate uphill to Upper Kintla Lake.
9.0	Foot of Upper Kintla Lake. Trail follows shore of Upper Kintla Lake.
11.6	Upper Kintla campground. Trail crosses Kintla Creek and ascends steeply to Boulder Pass campground.
17.2	Boulder Pass campground.
17.7	Boulder Pass. Junction campground is 0.1 mile to the left. Stay to right for Boulder Pass trail, which descends moderately steeply into Hole-in-the-Wall.
21.2	Junction with trail into Hole-in-the-Wall campground (0.5 miles)—Stay left for Brown Pass.
22.8	Brown Pass. Junction with trail to Bowman Lake. Stay left for trail to Goat Haunt Ranger Station, which descends moderately steeply to Olson Creek.
24.9	Hawksbill campground. Trail gradually descends through Olson Creek Valley.
25.1	Junction with spur trail to Lake Francis campground.
27.9	Lake Janet campground.
30.9	Junction with Waterton Lake trail. Stay right for Goat Haunt Ranger Station; turn left to Waterton Township (8.7 miles).
31.1	Suspension bridge over Waterton River.

Thunderbird Mountain from Boulder Pass overlook.

The hike: The Boulder Pass trail provides access to some of the most rugged and beautiful high country areas in Glacier National Park. High elevations between Boulder and Brown Passes lead to high snow accumulations and late snow melt, making this trail impassable early in the season. This trail may be entered and exited via three trailheads: Kintla Lake, Goat Haunt Ranger Station, and Bowman Lake (see separate listing). Any combination of hiking experiences, from day hikes to extended expeditions, are available to hikers on this trail.

The trail begins at Kintla Lake, which is set in a forested valley between tree-clad hills. As the trail winds around the north lakeshore, watch for signs of mule deer and mountain lions that inhabit the dense forest. Approximately 3.5 miles from the campground, a primitive connecting trail from Starvation Creek joins the Boulder Pass trail from the north. The Boulder Pass trail continues to follow the lakeshore for another 3 miles to Kintla Lake.

Shortly after the campground, at the head of the lake, the trail passes the Kintla Lake patrol cabin, where the trail leaves the lakeshore to begin a gentle ascent to Upper Kintla Lake. The trail passes up wooded benches, just out of sight of the cascades of Kintla Creek. Occasional avalanche chutes from Long Knife Peak provide vistas of Park Peak and the Harris Glacier across the valley. The trail reaches the foot of Upper Kintla Lake some 2.5

Boulder Pass

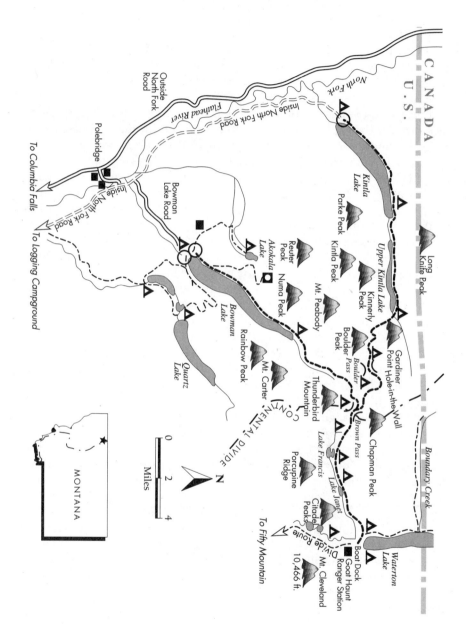

miles beyond the patrol cabin. The cockscomb peak at the head of the lake is Gardner Point. The trail follows the north shore of the lake, providing views of Kinnerly Peak across the valley. After 2.5 miles, the trail reaches a spur trail to the campground at the head of the lake, which is beautifully situated among stands of fir and spruce.

Leaving the lakeshore and campground behind, the trail crosses Kintla Creek and begins a steep ascent along the western slope of Gardner Point. There are many switchbacks through scattered stands of spruce and open jungles of cow parsnip (a favorite springtime food for grizzlies) before the trail emerges into alpine parkland at the head of the small valley. All along this section of the trail there are views of Kintla and Kinnerly Peaks to the southwest, and the Agassiz Glacier at their feet. Looking back toward Upper Kintla Lake, Long Knife Peak can be seen, marking the boundary between Canada and the U.S. The trail then reverses its direction, climbing northward to the Boulder Pass Campground. Just below the pass, the trail passes through stands of young alpine larch, an uncommon tree that exists here near the southern extreme of its range.

From the west end of Boulder Pass, the trail winds for several miles through a high, glacier-carved valley, across moraines left by retreating glaciers. Pyramid-shaped piles of rock called cairns mark the location of the trail so that it can be found in times of deep snow. At the east end of the pass, the trail branches into two parts. The more northerly path is now a goat path, which ascends the terminal moraine of Boulder Glacier and winds upward for a mile to a lookout point, high above the Bowman Valley. This lookout affords the most spectacular views of Thunderbird Mountain and many of the high peaks of the Livingston and Lewis Ranges.

The more southerly path descends onto a rocky shelf occupied by several tarns and continues its decent around the curve of the Hole-in-the-Wall, a perfectly formed hanging cirque which sits some 1,800 feet above the floor of the Bowman Valley. There are deep snowdrifts along this section, usually until August. When the trail reaches the eastern edge of the Hole in the Wall, a spur trail descends to the floor of the cirque, where a beautiful alpine campground is located among meadows of wildflowers and subalpine firs. This campground is frequented by mountain goats and several pestiferous mule deer, which should not be fed for any reason.

After passing Hole in the Wall, the trail continues its gentle descent to Brown Pass, a low saddle at the base of Thunderbird Mountain. Huckleberries grow in great profusion along this section of trail and provide a free food source for hikers and animals alike when they ripen in early August. At the pass is the junction with the Bowman Lake trail. A short jaunt of 0.3 mile down this trail brings the hiker to the Brown Pass campground, a pleasant area set among windblown firs. Looking eastward from Brown Pass, the jagged spur ridge shaped like a wolf's lower jaw is Citadel Peaks, and the massive peak behind it is Mount Cleveland, at 10,466 feet, the highest point in the park. After Brown Pass, the Boulder Pass trail descends steeply beneath the Thunderbird Glacier to a tarn at the head of Olson Creek Valley. A steep snowdrift extends down to the edge of the water in spring, and several early-season hikers have slid down the drift to receive an icy and unplanned bath. The pond itself is set among dense willows and may harbor an occasional moose.

Once the trail reaches the valley floor, it begins a long, slow descent to the Waterton Valley. The trail passes through an open section to Hawksbill Campground, a small area situated below a cliff-like spur ridge scraped sheer on both sides by glaciers. The trail continues eastward through open forest to the junction with a spur trail to Lake Francis campground, which lies on the shore of a beautiful lake beneath rocky cliffs. The lake is noted for its mosquitoes and fine rainbow trout fishing. The trail continues to the Lake Janet campground, which is located on the bank of Olson Creek, some distance from its namesake lake. Grizzly bears are frequently spotted in the avalanche paths on the ridge above this campground.

The trail continues down the Olson Creek Valley past shallow, and sometimes mucky, Lake Janet, and into a forest of Douglas-firs. An occasional opening in the canopy provides a backward look at glacier-clad Porcupine Ridge, as well as views of Citadel Peaks and Mount Cleveland ahead. Finally, the trail makes a brief descent to the floor of the Waterton Valley and meets the Waterton Lake trail. To reach Goat Haunt Ranger Station, the trail turns south and east, crossing the Waterton River via a suspension bridge and then turning north to the ranger station complex.

13 Triple Divide Pass

General description:	A day hike from Cut Bank Campground to Triple Divide Pass.
Distance:	7.2 miles.
Difficulty:	Moderate.
Traffic:	Moderate to light.
Elevation gain:	2,380 ft.
Maps:	Cut Bank Pass, Mount Stimson USGS quads.
For more information:	Glacier National Park, West Glacier, Montana 59936 406-888-7800

Finding the trailhead: Take Montana Highway 49 (North of East Glacier or south of Saint Mary) to the junction with the Cut Bank Creek Road, 17 miles north of East Glacier. Turn west and drive 4 miles over a gravel road to the Cut Bank Campground. The trail starts on the right before you enter the campground loop.

Key points:
0.0   Trail sign. Trail climbs gently, following the North Fork of Cut Bank Creek.

Hiker and marmot below Triple Divide Peak.

Triple Divide Pass

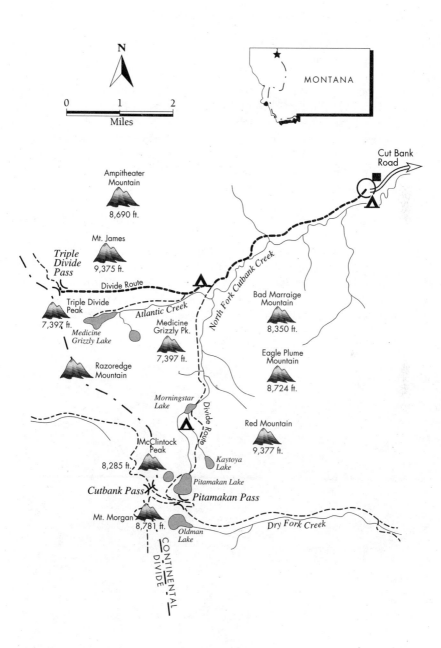

1.0	Junction with old chalet road. Stay right for Medicine Grizzly Lake and Triple Divide Pass.
3.9	Junction with Triple Divide trail. Turn right for the pass and Medicine Grizzly Lake. Trail begins gradual ascent of Atlantic Creek Valley.
4.3	Atlantic Creek campground.
4.6	Junction with Medicine Grizzly trail. Turn left for Medicine Grizzly Lake (1.4 miles). Stay right for Triple Divide Pass. Trail climbs north side of Atlantic Creek Valley.
7.2	Triple Divide Pass.

The hike: The Triple Divide Pass trail begins at the Cut Bank Creek Ranger Station and follows Cut Bank Creek for almost 4 miles before ascending the Atlantic Creek Valley. Both Medicine Grizzly Lake and Triple Divide Pass may be visited on a long day hike, while a campground near the confluence of Atlantic and Cut Bank Creeks provides overnight facilities for backpackers. Triple Divide Pass connects the Cut Bank Creek trail with the Red Eagle Lake trail, allowing access for hikers on extended trips into the St. Mary drainage.

The Cut Bank Creek Valley is less visited than some in the park, but it is a beautiful valley, characterized by fir parklands, rushing streams, and towering red mountains from which graceful cascades descend. The trail begins just beyond the Cut Bank Rangers Station at the reopened Cut Bank Campground. The trail crosses low-elevation meadows before entering an open forest of lodgepole pine and Douglas-fir. The trail climbs imperceptibly as it follows the north bank of the creek, and openings in the trees

Split Mountain from Triple Divide Pass.

reveal a small rocky canyon as the creek passes below the foot of Bad Marriage Mountain. About 4 miles up the trail, there is a junction with the Triple Divide Pass Trail.

From the trail junction, the Triple Divide trail climbs gently to the north, passing through the Atlantic Creek campground. The trail forks about 0.6 mile from the junction, with the left fork following the valley floor for 1.4 mile through beargrass-studded parklands to Medicine Grizzly Lake. The right fork rises steadily along the north wall of the valley, climbing high above Medicine Grizzly Lake. Across the valley, an unnamed lake lies in a hanging cirque embedded in the north face of Medicine Grizzly Peak. The trail continues its pleasant grade upward without a single switchback, passing tiny waterfalls and emerging into a meadowy bowl below the pass.

Triple Divide Pass derives its moniker from the peak of the same name that overlooks the pass to the west. Water flowing from the various sides of this peak will eventually reach the Atlantic, Pacific, and Arctic Oceans. An alpinist's route to the summit crosses the steep talus bowl to the south and climbs the second of two couloirs, which pierces the Atlantic valley headwall to reach a flat saddle. From this point, it is an easy scramble up the south slope of the peak to the summit.

Wildlife is abundant near the pass. Hairy marmots, chipmunks, and both golden-mantled and Columbia ground squirrels make their homes in the talus surrounding the pass. Bighorn sheep are frequently sighted on the surrounding slopes. Herds of bighorn are segregated by sex—rams and ewes are rarely found in the same herd during the summer months. These animals begin rutting in September, and the thunderous cracks of colliding rams may be heard as early as late August. Looking northward from the pass, Norris Mountain dominates the head of the valley, while Split Mountain rises on its northern perimeter. The south faces of the peaks surrounding Little Chief Mountain can be seen in the background.

14 Dawson–Pitamakan Passes

General description:	A day hike or backpacking trip from Two Medicine campground to Dawson Pass, around to Pitamakan Pass and back.
Distance:	18.8 miles.
Difficulty:	Moderately strenuous.
Traffic:	Heavy.
Elevation gain:	2,935 feet.
Maps:	Squaw Mountain, Mount Rockwell, Cut Bank Pass USGS quads.
For more information:	Glacier National Park, West Glacier, Montana 59936, 406-888-7800.

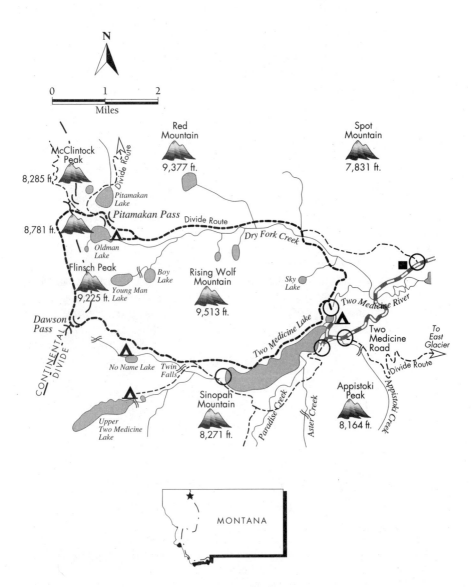

N

0   1   2
Miles

Red Mountain
9,377 ft.

Spot Mountain
7,831 ft.

McClintock Peak
8,285 ft.

Divide Route

Pitamakan Lake

Pitamakan Pass   Divide Route

8,781 ft.

Dry Fork Creek

Oldman Lake

Flinsch Peak

Boy Lake

Rising Wolf Mountain

Sky Lake

9,225 ft.

Young Man Lake

9,513 ft.

Two Medicine River

Dawson Pass

Two Medicine Lake

Two Medicine Road

To East Glacier

CONTINENTAL DIVIDE

No Name Lake

Twin Falls

Divide Route

Sinopah Mountain

Paradise Creek

Aster Creek

Appistoki Peak

Appistoki Creek

8,271 ft.

8,164 ft.

Upper Two Medicine Lake

MONTANA

Finding the trailhead: Two Medicine north shore trailhead, on the north side of Two Medicine campground, at the outlet of Pray Lake. Boat travelers will begin from the upper boat dock, meeting the trail before Twin Falls.

Key Points:

    0.0   Trail sign. Trail follows north shore of Two Medicine Lake.

    3.3   Junction with trail leading to Twin Falls and the south shore trail. Stay right for Dawson Pass.

    4.8   Junction with trail to No Name Lake and campground (0.2 miles). Stay right for Dawson Pass. Trail ascends steeply to Dawson Pass.

    6.7   Dawson Pass. Trail runs north, following the west face of the Continental Divide.

    9.9   Cut Bank Pass. Junction with trail into Nyack Creek. Stay right for Pitamakan Pass.

  10.0   Pitamakan Pass. Junction with the trail down Cut Bank Creek. Stay right for Oldman Lake and Two Medicine campground. Trail descends steeply toward Oldman Lake.

  12.0   Oldman Lake.

  12.9   Oldman campground. Trail descends gently, following the Dry Fork Creek.

  16.4   Junction with Dry Fork trail. Stay right for Two Medicine campground. Trail turns south, traversing the flanks of Rising Wolf Mountain.

  18.8   Two Medicine campground.

Looking into the Upper Nyack Valley.

The hike: The Dawson–Pitamakan trail runs from Two Medicine Lake to the Continental Divide and around into the Dry Fork drainage to form a long loop. It offers spectacular views of the spires of the southern Lewis Range, as well as good wildlife viewing opportunities along its entire length. The trail may be hiked in its entirety in a single day, but it takes several days to fully explore the wonders of this region.

The trail begins at the Two Medicine auto campground and winds around the north shore of the lake, beneath the hulking mass of Rising Wolf Mountain. Openings provided by avalanches from the mountain above allow excellent views of the peaks across the lake. The trail winds through a mixed forest which grades into spruce stands before finally emerging to an opening below Sinopah Mountain at the head of the lake. At this point, a connecting trail from the south shore trail and the upper boat dock joins the Dawson Pass trail. Travelers using the tour boat enter the trail here, having cut off the first 2 miles of the trail. A short side trip of 0.3 mile down this connecting trail brings the hiker using the North Shore trail to Twin Falls.

From this point, the trail ascends gently into the Bighorn Basin, a glacier-carved bowl filled with scattered stands of subalpine fir and lush meadows. At mile 4.8, a spur trail descends to No Name Lake, with its attendant campground. The Dawson Pass trail continues to climb the southern slope of Flinsch Peak, offering views of Mount Helen and the knife-edge wall of the Pumpelly Pillar. After 2 miles and 1,200 feet of steady climbing, the trail reaches the windy saddle of Dawson Pass. From this spot, vistas open to the glacier-carved valley of Nyack Creek to the south and the Lupfer Glacier, nestled high on the east slope of Mount Phillips across the valley. From Dawson Pass, mountaineers will find a fairly easy ascent up the south face of Flinsch Peak to its summit.

From Dawson Pass, the trail turns north, following the Continental Divide along its west face around Flinsch Peak to an unnamed saddle at the head of the Dry Fork Valley. The trail crosses dry barren rockscapes all along the divide and backward glances reveal outstanding views of Lone Walker Mountain, Caper Peak, Battlement Mountain, and the spiny summit of Mount St. Nicholas. This area is also home to bighorn sheep. The trail continues around Mount Morgan, and rocky pedestals on a spur ridge provide an ideal lunch spot among breathtaking views of Mount Stimson and Mount Pinchot across the valley, as well as the peaks to the south and north. The trail winds around to Pitamakan overlook, which affords stunning views to the north and west.

From this point, the trail turns east, following the north slope of Mount Morgan. A connecting trail from the Nyack wilderness rises to meet the Dawson–Pitamakan trail in the course of its gentle descent to Pitamakan (Pit-ah'-muh-kun) Pass, high above the large lake of the same name to the north. The trail to the north descends to Pitamakan Lake in the Cut Bank Creek Valley. Looking southward, the partial horn of Flinsch Peak soars above Oldman Lake, while pyramid-shaped Rising Wolf Mountain rises further to the east. The trail descends steeply, switching back frequently through rocky ledges covered with wildflowers and firs, before reaching a spur trail that leads to the campground at the foot of Oldman Lake. This lake receives a fair amount of angling pressure, but remains good fishing for Yellowstone cutthroat trout in the 1- to 3-pound class. The campground is set in an open stand of old-growth whitebark pines, about 100 yards east of the lakeshore.

After leaving the campground, the trail descends through parklike stands of fir separated by beargrass-studded fields along the Dry Fork. As the trail continues down the valley, it enters drier meadows of tall grasses reminiscent of high plains habitats. Nearing the foot of the valley, the trail enters a sun-dappled forest of lodgepole pine. Some 2.4 miles before reaching the Two Medicine campground, a trail forks to the east, leading 2.6 miles through marshy aspen stands to the entrance station on the Two Medicine Road. The main trail swings southward, around the forested base of Rising Wolf, to terminate at the footbridge below Pray Lake.

15 Firebrand Pass

General description:	A day hike from the Lubec trailhead on U.S. Highway 2 to Firebrand Pass.
Distance:	4.8 miles.
Difficulty:	Moderately strenuous.
Traffic:	Moderate.
Elevation gain:	2,210 feet.
Maps:	Summit, Squaw Mountain, Mount Rockwell USGS quads.
For more information:	Glacier National Park, West Glacier, Montana 59936 406-888-7800

Finding the trailhead: At mile marker 203 on US 2, follow the dirt road across the railroad tracks to a barricaded dirt road that runs for 0.5 mile to the site of the old Lubec Ranger Station (which was burned in 1980). The Firebrand Pass trail begins at this site.

Key Points:

0.0	Trail sign. Trail climbs gently, following Coonsa Creek.
1.4	Junction with Autumn Creek trail. Turn right for Firebrand Pass. Trail follows along the flanks of Calf Robe Mountain.
2.4	Junction with Firebrand Pass trail. Turn left for Firebrand Pass. Trail ascends rather steeply around the northeast face of Firebrand Pass.
4.8	Firebrand Pass. Trail descends steeply to Ole Lake.
7.7	Ole Lake campground.

The hike: The Firebrand Pass trail begins at a false summit near Marias Pass and winds around Calf Robe Mountain to Firebrand Pass before drop-

Firebrand Pass

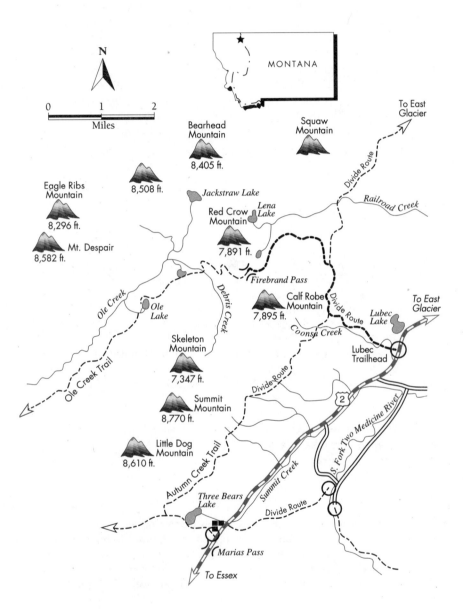

MONTANA

N

0   1   2
Miles

To East
Glacier

Bearhead
Mountain
8,405 ft.

Squaw
Mountain

8,508 ft.

Jackstraw Lake

Eagle Ribs
Mountain
8,296 ft.

Red Crow
Mountain
7,891 ft.

*Lena
Lake*

Railroad Creek

Mt. Despair
8,582 ft.

Divide Route

Ole Creek

Firebrand Pass

Debris Creek

*Ole
Lake*

Calf Robe
Mountain
7,895 ft.

Divide Route

*Lubec
Lake*

To East
Glacier

Coonsa Creek

Lubec
Trailhead

Skeleton
Mountain
7,347 ft.

Ole Creek Trail

Divide Route

Summit
Mountain
8,770 ft.

2

S. Fork Two Medicine River

Little Dog
Mountain
8,610 ft.

Autumn Creek Trail

*Three Bears
Lake*

Summit Creek

Divide Route

Marias Pass

To Essex

ping down into the Ole Creek Valley. Ole Lake can also be reached via a longer, less scenic route up the Ole Creek Valley from the Walton Ranger Station or from the Fielding trailhead. Firebrand Pass makes a reasonable destination for day hikers, while backpackers will find backcountry campsites at Ole Lake.

The trail starts out on the north bank of Coonsa Creek, which it follows for 0.5 mile before turning slightly north and climbing gently to the junction with the Autumn Creek trail. Hikers bound for the pass should turn north at this junction and follow the Autumn Creek trail for a mile as it leaves the forest and enters grassy meadows near the junction with the Firebrand Pass trail, which takes off to the west. Following the Firebrand Pass trail as it winds upward around the open slopes of Calf Robe Mountain, hikers will see Squaw Mountain straight ahead and Red Crow Mountain as the trail reaches the north slope of Calf Robe Mountain. The forest on both sides of the pass burned in the hot fires of the early 1900s.

THE CONTINENTAL DIVIDE THROUGH THE BOB MARSHALL WILDERNESS COMPLEX

The divide in northern Montana passes through the largest continuous expanse of wilderness in the lower 48 states. The complex actually includes three wilderness areas, the Scapegoat, Great Bear, and the Bob Marshall, named after the legendary Robert Marshall, who was at the forefront of the movement to protect wilderness in the United States. The high mountain passes of the "Bob," as locals call it, enable the visitor to experience a world deep in the wilderness, far away from civilization.

16 Gateway Pass Loop

General description:	An extended loop backpacking vacation from Swift Dam Trailhead, passing Haywood Creek along the North Fork of Bird Creek to Badger Pass at 8.1 miles, then turning south on the Strawberry Creek Trail (161) to Gateway Gorge Trail, then passing Gateway Pass, and finally connecting with the South Fork of Birch Creek back to the Swift Dam Trailhead.
Distance:	29.6 miles.
Difficulty:	Difficult.
Traffic:	Moderate.

Elevation gain:	6,128 feet.
Maps:	Morningstar Mountain, Swift Reservoir, Fish Lake, Gateway Pass, Gooseberry Park USGS quads.
For more information:	Rocky Mountain Ranger District, 1102 Main Ave. NW, P.O. Box 340, Choteau, Montana 59442, 406-466-5341.

Finding the trailhead: The trail begins and ends at the Swift Dam trailhead. From U.S. Highway 89, follow the road to Swift Reservoir, which departs from a rest area just north of Dupuyer. This road runs west for 20 miles to reach the trailhead at the foot of the dam.

Key points:

Note: The road along the north side of Swift Reservoir is closed, and this may add about a mile to your hike.

0.0	Haywood Creek.
0.1	Junction with the South Fork Birch Creek Trail (105). Stay right.
0.7	Trail makes two fords of the North Fork of Birch Creek.
1.5	Trail crosses Hungry Horse Creek.
1.6	Junction with the Hungry Man Trail (122). Keep going straight.
2.2	Trail crosses Killem Horse Creek.
2.7	Junction with the Blind Tommie Trail (171). Bear right.

Bighorn Mountain rises above the headwaters of the South Fork.

Gateway Pass Loop

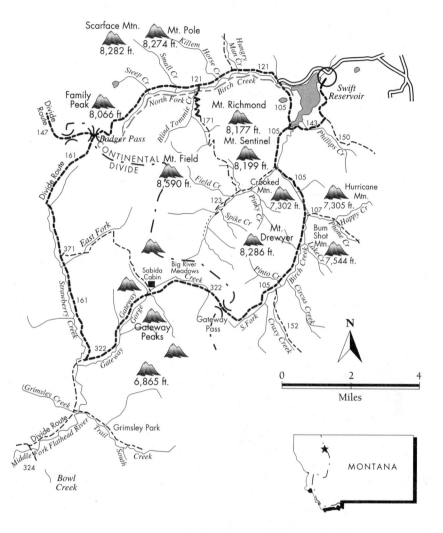

3.8   Trail crosses Small Creek.

4.7   Trail fords Steep Creek and begins to climb.

6.7   Trail crosses the divide into the Badger Creek drainage.

7.9   Junction with the South Fork Badger Creek Trail (104). Stay left.

8.1   Badger Pass. Junction with the Strawberry Creek Trail (161). Turn left.

Note: This is the starting point for the Crucifixion Loop Option.

12.0   Junction with East Fork Strawberry Creek Trail, stay right.

15.0   Junction with Gateway Gorge Trail, turn left.

16.4	Trail enters Gateway Gorge.
16.7	Trail exits Gateway Gorge.
17.0	Trail fords Gateway Creek.
17.2	Junction with East Fork of Stawberry Creek Trail. Stay right for Gateway Pass.
18.1	Big River Meadows.
19.3	Gateway Pass.
20.8	Junction with the Corrugate Ridge Trail (152). Keep going straight for Gateway Pass.
20.9	Trail crosses Pinto Creek.
23.6	Junction with the North Fork Teton Trail (107).
24.2	Trail fords the South Fork to reach its east bank.
24.3	Trail crosses Post Creek.
25.3	Junction with the Middle Fork Trail (123). Turn right after fording Birch Creek.
26.8	Junction with the South Fork Birch Creek Trail (105). Bear left.
26.9	Trail makes a ford of Birch Creek.
27.5	Trail crosses Phillips Creek.
27.8	Junction with the Walling Reef Trail (150). Bear left.
28.4	Hellroaring Spring.
29.6	Swift Dam trailhead.

The hike: This trail penetrates some of the most spectacular scenery of the Bob Marshall Wilderness Complex, crossing two high mountain passes over the Continental Divide and following several rushing streams. It also includes a section of the Continental Divide National Scenic Trail along Strawberry Creek.

It starts through a rather open valley flanked by sheer rock pinnacles on its way over the divide and into the Badger–Two Medicine country to Badger Pass, from which the trail descends into the Strawberry Creek drainage. The pass below Family Peak is generally free of snow from June on. Access to the trail is a bit tricky, because the trail around the northern shore of Swift Reservoir crosses the Blackfeet Indian Reservation and is currently closed to the public. Therefore, it is necessary to traverse the southern shore of the reservoir, then turn north along the South Fork Birch Creek Trail (105) to reach the North Fork trail.

From Haywood Creek, an old dirt road climbs onto a hilltop, where it reaches an intersection with the South Fork trail. Mounts Poia and Morningstar rise to the north, marking the eastern rim of the valley. To the west, Mount Richmond towers above the rushing stream. Bear west as the old road descends to the creek bed and is replaced by a narrow trail. After several hundred yards of creekside travel, the trail completes two fords of the North Fork. These fords are marked by rock cairns and can be avoided by nimble-foot travelers by skirting the foot of a large Cut Bank. The trail then climbs into a forest of Douglas-fir and lodgepole pine, interspersed with numerous openings that allow ever-expanding views of the surrounding mountains.

The trail soon climbs to avoid a small gorge created by the erosion of the stream through a rising incline of rock. The vantage point at the top of the rise shows off the jagged northern spur of Mount Field, as well as the more massive summit of Family Peak beyond it. These peaks provide a constant backdrop as the trail ducks in and out of the forest for the next several miles. The trail crosses Hungry Horse Creek and then passes an old and faint trail to the high plains (122). In short order, Killem Horse Creek is crossed. Below the trail, the North Fork frolics through a series of small waterfalls as it passes through a ledge of unyielding bedrock. Aspen and spruce begin to dominate the scattered forest as the trail makes its way along the bottomland to reach the next trail junction.

Here, a trail running up the Blind Tommie Valley veers off to the left, while the North Fork trail hugs the hillside and begins to climb across a slope of loose talus. To the south, the glorious north face of Mount Field towers above the Blind Tommie Valley like a reigning monarch. The trail climbs into the forest for a time, then wanders out onto the gravel bars along the creek on its way to a crossing of Steep Creek. The pointed top of Scarface Mountain becomes briefly visible as the trail fords this stream and then wanders through the clearing on its far bank. The trail then begins a modest but steady climb as it crosses an avalanche slope within sight of a small waterfall. After another stretch of forest, the trail climbs purposefully through a much larger open slope, high above the creek. This slope overlooks a tumbling cascade, with the northern buttresses of Mount Field looming close around the head of the valley.

The trail then climbs into the high, open cirque behind Family Peak, where bighorn sheep can sometimes be spotted as they feed on alpine grasses and forbs. The trail increases its grade as it climbs the headwall of the valley to reach a high pass. Far to the west, the distant peaks of the Trilobite Range rise on the western skyline, while the peaks of the Badger Creek country march away to the north. From the pass, the trail descends steeply for a time, then turns southward to curl around the headwaters of the South Fork of Badger Creek. Just before the trail reaches the trees, look north for a view of Goat Mountain and the other high peaks surrounding the lower reaches of Badger Creek. After entering the trees, the trail splits. Both trails run to Badger Pass; the lower fork is more direct but is boggy in wet weather, while the trail to the left sticks to higher, drier ground. The trail passes a junction with the South Fork Badger Creek Trail (104) just before reaching a major trail junction at Badger Pass. Here, the trail to Strawberry Creek and the Middle Fork of the Flathead (161) runs south. Note: Badger Pass is the end of route to Crucifixion Loop, see Crucifixion Loop Option following this hike.

Strawberry Creek Trail (161) receives lots of traffic and is easy to follow. From the tree-covered Badger Pass (6,278 feet) head south on Strawberry Creek Trail 161, a level path that soon emerges into a big meadow covered with wild strawberries and Indian paintbrush. Several peaks loom above the treeline on the basin's east side, dominated by a pyramidal summit streaked with snow and scree.

Gateway Rock looms above Gateway Creek.

Stay on the main trail on the gradual descent, avoiding several side-routes to the left that disappear into boggy areas. Boulder-hop Strawberry Creek near a campsite and then ford it again above Gateway Creek. At 15 miles, reach the junction with Gateway Gorge Trail and turn left, heading east for Gateway Pass.

The next section of trail from Strawberry Creek Trail 161 provides a route from the valley of the Middle Fork to the rugged Birch Creek country via a low pass over the Continental Divide. Along the way, it passes such scenic attractions as Gateway Gorge and Big River Meadows. Because of the relatively low elevation of Gateway Pass, this route is passable even in early summer, when the higher passes are still clogged with snow. However, rock slides in Gateway Gorge often make passage difficult for stock parties early in the season.

From the trail junction on Strawberry Creek, the Gateway Gorge trail climbs moderately for 1.5 miles through the trees, with occasional mud hazards during wet weather. After crossing a tributary stream, the trail breaks out abruptly onto a grassy slope, with the massive buttes flanking Gateway Gorge rising dead ahead. As the trail climbs into the gorge, take a few backward glances as the peaks of the Trilobite Range reveal themselves in succession through the window formed by Gateway Gorge. The towering cliffs that flank the creek dwarf trees and travelers alike, and their size and ancient age provide an instructive yardstick for measuring the importance of man's best efforts. Note also the intricate network of bighorn sheep trails in the talus below the far wall of the gorge. These cliffs have provided a home for mountain sheep for millennia. The trail climbs across slopes of loose talus as it passes through the gorge, then descends again as it approaches the far end.

The trail continues eastward beside the creek for a short distance before making a knee-deep ford to reach its south bank. Several hundred yards farther, the trail reaches a junction with the trail that runs north to Sabido Cabin and the East Fork of Strawberry Creek. Stay right for Gateway Pass, as the trail climbs a wooded hillside that offers a few final glimpses of the mountains that surround the gorge. After a brief but steady ascent, the trail runs out into the western fringe of Big River Meadows, a broad expanse of grass dissected by tiny, willow-choked streamlets. To the north, an eroded tailbone of the Sawtooth Range stands guard over the valley, the multicolored bands of sediment showing in its washed-out slopes. The trail crosses the full 1.5-mile length of the meadows, braiding out into a number of channels as it does so. Subalpine fir begins to crowd in as the trail makes its final ascent to Gateway Pass. The pass itself has little scenic value, but the country beyond it contains some of the most awe-inspiring scenery in the Rockies.

The final section from Gateway pass to Swift Dam travels down the rugged valley of the Birch Creek's South Fork, an open, windswept basin rimmed with towering peaks. From Gateway Pass, descend through a shallow wooded ravine into a valley of virgin forest. Pass under the towering ramparts of Bighorn Peak and its northern spur. After descending some more, the trail passes through a number of boggy spots. Next, pass above a nameless waterfall on the South Fork and continue northeast to the junction with Corrugate Ridge Trail (152) in the meadows opposite Crazy Creek. After passing the broad gravel fan of Pine Creek, the trail crosses grassy slopes, opening up to reveal Mount Patrick Gass rising majestically above the Circus Creek Valley. Then, the trail passes through a vigorous forest of aspen and lodgepole pine, and makes its way down into the sinuous cleft of a twisting canyon, continuing on the South Fork Trail.

Next, several hunters' trails descend to the creek bottoms on their way to the Lake Creek Valley. After passing the sight of another narrow gorge, the trail climbs back out of the trees. Looking southward up the valley of Phone Creek, an unnamed spire towers above the timber to the east. After emerging on grassy slopes, the trail reaches a rather confusing junction with the North Fork Teton Trail (107), which descends to a ford of the creek, while the main trail turns northeast, sticking to the higher ground. After a muddy slog through timber, the trail crosses the South Fork, a knee deep ford, and then Post Creek, before climbing northward, as the tilted slabs of Mount Patrick Gass reveal themselves. This peak, one of the most impressive reefs in the area, was named in honor of a member of the Lewis and Clark expedition.

The trail makes its way beneath the slickrock face of a nameless reef, sporting small waterfalls that descend from hidden basins. The rugged face of Crooked Mountain looms across the creek, while a forward glance yields fine views of Mount Sentinel. Bum Shot Mountain dominates the valley to the south. From a grassy hilltop above the South Fork, the trail then works its way down a muddy gulch. After a thigh-deep ford just below the confluence of the Middle and South Forks, it will be necessary to turn right at the junction with the Middle Fork Trail (123). Next, hike northeastward through arid country for about a mile.

Soon afterward, the trail reaches a junction with the South Fork Birch Creek Trail (143); turn right here. Next, the trail makes a tricky thigh-deep ford of the rushing stream. The trail climbs over a low rise from Birch Creek to ford Phillips Creek and climbs toward a junction with the lightly-maintained Walling Reef Trail (150). The trail climbs to a high point, then descends passing Hellroaring Spring. Finally, the trail follows the shores of Swift Reservoir revealing vistas of Major Steel Backbone, Mount Richmond, and Mount Sentinel. Hike down the access road south of the dam to reach the trailhead.

17 Crucifixion Loop Option from Badger Pass on the Gateway Pass Loop

General description:	An extended trip to the lower reaches of Badger Creek's South Fork from Badger Pass.
Distance past Badger Pass:	12.4 miles round trip.
Difficulty:	Moderate.
Traffic:	Moderate between Badger Pass and Beaver Lake; otherwise light.
Elevation gain:	1,222 feet.
Maps:	Morningstar Mountain USGS Quad.
For more information:	Rocky Mountain Ranger District, 1102 Main Ave. NW, P.O. Box 340, Choteau, Montana 59442, 406-466-5341.

Finding the trail: This trail begins and ends at Badger Pass. The most direct route to the pass is via the North Fork of Birch Creek.

Key points:
- 0.0 Badger Pass. Bear west on Trail 147.
- 0.9 Trail crosses the Cox Creek drainage divide and enters the Bob Marshall Wilderness.
- 1.6 Trail crosses the outlet of Beaver Lake.
- 1.7 Junction with the Muskrat Creek Trail (147). Turn right.
- 2.3 Unmarked junction with the cutoff trail that follows the north shore of Beaver Lake. Turn left.

2.7	Muskrat Pass. Trail leaves the Bob Marshall Wilderness.
3.6	Blue Lake.
4.5	Junction with the Muskrat Creek Cutoff Trail (146). Bear right.
5.3	Trail crosses Crucifixion Creek.
6.3	Junction with the South Fork Badger Creek Trail (104). Turn right.
6.35	Trail crosses Crucifixion Creek.
6.8	Trail fords the South Fork of Badger Creek to reach its east bank.
8.5	Trail returns to the western bank of the South Fork.
10.4	Trail makes its final ford of the South Fork of Badger Creek.
12.2	Junction with the North Fork Birch Creek Trail (121). Turn right to complete the loop.
12.4	Badger Pass.

The hike: The Crucifixion Loop trail offers a day hike for travelers who find themselves in the Badger Pass vicinity. From Badger Pass, follow Trail 147 west toward Beaver Lake. After passing through subalpine forest for a short distance, the trail crosses a series of marshy openings. The trail then crosses the wilderness boundary and becomes much drier on its descent to the shores of Beaver Lake. This marshy pool is surrounded by grassy meadows and is overlooked by rounded hills. In early morning, white-tailed deer emerge from the forest to graze in the lakeshore meadows. After crossing the lake's outlet stream, the trail reaches a junction with the Muskrat Creek Trail (147).

Turn right onto this narrow path, which winds around the western shore of the lake on wooded bluffs. Upon reaching the head of the lake, the trail descends to the edge of the surrounding meadows and passes an isolated beaver pond. Far to the east, the craggy summit of the Mount Field's northern spur rises above the trees. After passing the beaver pond, the trail reaches an intersection with a cutoff trail that skirts the north side of the lake. Turn left and continue up the valley as the trail passes through grassy meadows dotted with occasional clumps of low-growing willows. The trail reaches Muskrat Pass about 0.67 mile northwest of the lake. If the pass was not marked by signposts, it would be impossible to tell that one is crossing the Continental Divide.

After crossing the pass and leaving the Bob Marshall Wilderness, the trail descends imperceptibly through more open meadows at the headwaters of Muskrat Creek. After dipping down through the woods to reach the creek, the trail climbs onto a level terrace overlooked by the twin humps of a nameless hill to the east. The trail passes above Blue Lake, another shallow, marshy pond surrounded by forest. The trail stays high on the hillside as the Muskrat Valley drops away below it, and after a mile, it reaches the next trail junction. The rather faint Muskrat Creek trail descends to the left toward Lost Horse Camp, while the Crucifixion Loop trail bears right, bearing the name "Muskrat Cutoff Trail 145."

This trail crosses yet another imperceptible drainage divide, then settles into a gentle descent beside Crucifixion Creek. This tiny tributary of the South Fork of Badger Creek is overlooked by the small but rocky point of

Crucifixion Loop Option from Badger Pass on the Gateway Pass Loop

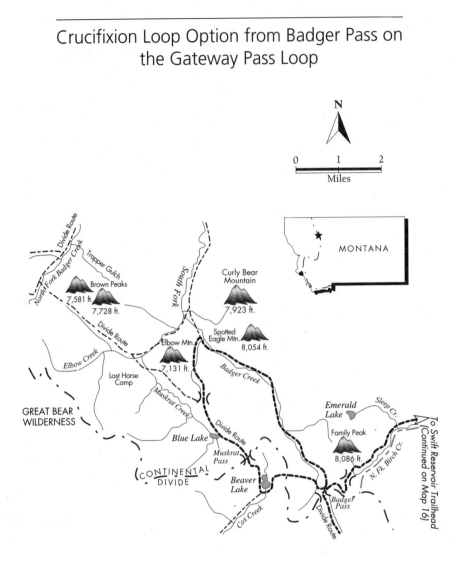

Elbow Mountain. To the northeast, the broad shield of Goat Mountain rises in the distance. Upon reaching a slight bend in the course of the valley, the trail dips down to cross the creek and then climbs the bare knoll beyond. All at once, the twin summits of Curly Bear and Spotted Eagle mountains tower to the east while Half Dome Crag rises in the distance. The trail switchbacks frequently as it descends through the timber, passing a cutoff trail that bears north toward the lower reaches of Badger Creek. Upon reaching a marked junction with the South Fork Badger Creek Trail (104), turn right.

This trail runs southeast as it crosses Crucifixion Creek at the foot of a pleasant waterfall. The trail soon descends to the bank of the South Fork of Badger Creek, which it crosses at a calf-deep ford. On the open slopes of the east bank, a glance to the northwest reveals the bedrock arc of Goat Mountain, while the peak-lined canyon of the South Fork runs southeast toward Badger Pass. Views continue to be good as the trail crosses the open slopes cleared by avalanches born on the heights of Spotted Eagle Mountain. The trail then wanders out onto the gravel bank of the creek and becomes a bit faint. Subalpine fir replaces lodgepole pine as the dominant tree as the trail fords the creek for a second time, then climbs onto a grassy ledge above the west bank. Look north for a final view of Spotted Eagle Mountain; hereafter, the trail alternates between forest and pocket-sized openings that offer little in the way of scenery.

The forest pulls itself around the creek like a cloak, and the trail passes a minor waterfall as it continues its gentle ascent up the valley. Shortly thereafter, the route crosses what appears to be a substantial tributary; in reality, this is the main body of the South Fork of Badger Creek. Fallen logs are on hand for hikers who want to keep their feet dry. The next mile or so is pocked with boggy seeps, until the trail finally climbs out of the valley bottom and onto the slope to the east. After a brief but vigorous ascent, the trail crosses a small tributary and wends its way through subalpine parkland to reach a junction with the North Fork Birch Creek Trail (121). Turn right and descend the short distance to Badger Pass to complete the loop.

View of Half Dome Crag from Crucifixion Creek.

18 West Fork of the Sun River Route to Pearl Basin and White River Pass

General description:	A backpacking trip from Benchmark to Indian Point Meadows, from which you have two extended trip options along the Continental Divide: Pearl Basin and White River Pass.
Distance:	10.5 miles.
Difficulty:	Moderate.
Traffic:	Heavy.
Elevation gain:	679 feet.
Maps:	Benchmark, Pretty Prairies, Prairie Reef USGS quads.
For more information:	Rocky Mountain Ranger District, 1102 Main Ave. NW, P.O. Box 340, Choteau, Montana 59442, 406-466-5341.

Finding the trailhead: From Augusta take the Benchmark Road westward. At the junction with the Willow Creek road, turn left and follow the road as it enters the mountains and bends north. The trail begins at the South Fork Sun River trailhead, beyond the airfield and at the end of the road.

Key points:

0.0	South Fork Sun River trailhead.
0.2	Pack bridge over the South Fork of the Sun River.
0.25	Junction with the South Fork Sun River Trail. Bear right for the West Fork.
0.7	Trail crosses Burned Creek.
1.5	Trail fords Deer Creek.
3.6	Unmarked junction with the Bighead Creek Trail (242). Bear left.
4.9	Pack bridge over the West Fork of the Sun River.
5.1	Junction of the South (202) and West (203) Fork Sun River trails. Turn left.
9.1	Trail crosses Reef Creek.
9.6	Junction with the Prairie Reef Lookout Trail (224). Keep going straight for Indian Point Meadows.
10.5	Trail enters Indian Point Meadows.
10.6	Junction with the Pearl Basin-Camp Creek Pass Trail (209). Eight miles to Camp Creek Pass.
10.9	Indian Point Cabin. 4.5 miles to White River Pass.

The hike: This route begins at the Benchmark entry point, the most heavily used access point for the Bob Marshall Wilderness. It follows the heavily-traveled Sun River Trail (202) for the first several miles, then turns west along the less frequently traveled West Fork of the Sun. This latter portion

Looking down on the West Fork Valley with the peaks of Nineteen Ridge rising beyond.

of the route offers scenic delights of its own, as well as providing an important access route to travelers bound for the Chinese Wall, the Pearl Basin, and White River Pass.

From the South Fork trailhead, follow the trail northward to a pack bridge that spans the South Fork of the Sun River. On the far side of the bridge is a trail junction, turn right and follow the main trail northward. This wide path crosses lodgepole pine benchlands above the river for the first mile or so, then turns inland. After crossing Deer Creek, the trail slogs through a spruce swamp of incredible bogginess. Trail maintenance has improved this section. After the trail crosses the wilderness boundary, it returns to the drier lodgepole forest, and soon reaches a junction with the rather substantial Bighead Creek Trail (242). Stay left for the West Fork of the Sun. The trail then descends as it bends around to the west, rounding the corner of Deadman Hill as it does so. The going gets muddy again as the trail passes through one last spruce stand before reaching a pack bridge over the West Fork of the Sun River.

Once the north bank of the West Fork has been reached, the West Fork Trail (203) bends westward, crossing the rolling prairies that border the riverbank. As the trail mounts a shoulder of Prairie Reef, it reveals in a first

West Fork of the Sun River Route to
Pearl Basin and White River Pass

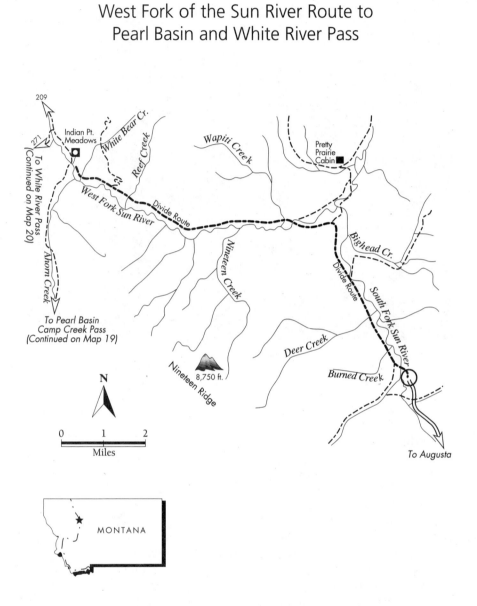

glimpse the gunmetal spires atop Nineteen Ridge. As the trail continues its riverside trek, open meadows allow ever-expanding vistas of the sharp spires that cap the verdant shoulders of Nineteen Ridge like the teeth of a saw blade. The trail then enters a low-elevation forest for the next several miles, emerging briefly at isolated glades. After crossing Reef Creek, the trail climbs onto the grassy slopes of Prairie Reef, allowing the first views of Red Butte far to the west. The trail passes the Prairie Reef Lookout Trail (209), then descends across grassy benches to reach Indian Point Meadows. In the interest of site rehabilitation, pack and saddle parties may not camp in these meadows; however, there are plenty of suitable sites both up- and downriver from these meadows. The junction with the Camp Creek Pass Trail (209) marks the end of this trip. Two options below continue this hike to Camp Creek Pass and White River Pass.

19 Pearl Basin–Camp Creek Pass Option from West Fork of the Sun

General description:	An extended trip from Indian Point Meadows to the Pearl Basin.
Distance:	5.5 miles to the Pearl Basin, 8 miles to Camp Creek Pass, one way.
Difficulty:	Difficult.
Traffic:	Light.
Elevation gain:	1,935 feet.
Maps:	Prairie Reef, Trap Mountain USGS quads.
For more information:	Rocky Mountain Ranger District, 1102 Main Ave. NW, P.O. Box 340, Choteau, Montana 59442, 406-466-5341.

Finding the trailhead: This trail departs from the West Fork Sun River Trail (203) at a marked junction in Indian Point Meadows as described in the previous hike.

Key points:
- 0.0   Indian Point Meadows.
- 0.1   Trail fords the West Fork of the Sun River and enters the Ahorn Creek Valley.
- 2.0   Trail fords Ahorn Creek to reach its east bank.
- 3.2   Junction with the Grizzly Basin Trail (225). Stay right and ford the East Fork of Ahorn Creek.
- 3.4   Trail returns to the west bank of Ahorn Creek.
- 5.5   Trail enters the Pearl Basin.
- 8.0   Camp Creek Pass.

The hike: This lightly-used trail connects the West Fork of the Sun River with the basin on the banks of Danaher Creek. On its way, it passes through the Pearl Basin, noted for its spectacular scenery. This high basin is an important summer range for elk, and these magnificent beasts can sometimes be seen from the trail during June and July.

Pearl Basin–Camp Creek Pass Option from West Fork of the Sun

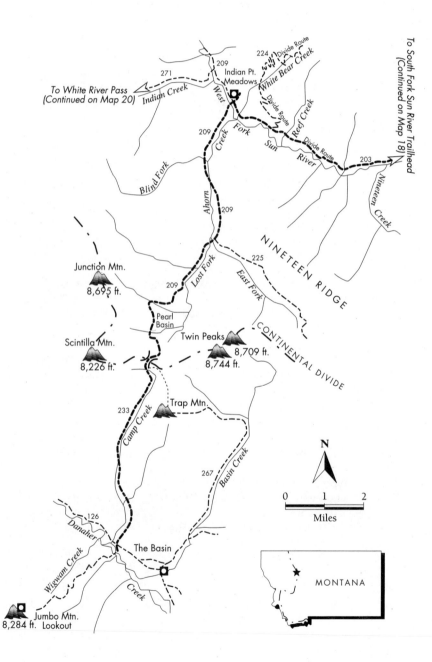

To White River Pass
(Continued on Map 20)

To South Fork Sun River Trailhead
(Continued on Map 18)

271

209

224 Divide Route

Indian Pt. Meadows

White Bear Creek

Indian Creek

West

Creek

Fork

Divide Route

Reef Creek

Sun

River

Divide Route

203

Blind Fork

Ahorn

209

Nineteen Creek

N I N E T E E N

225

Junction Mtn.
8,695 ft.

Lost Fork

East Fork

R I D G E

209

Pearl Basin

Twin Peaks
8,709 ft.

C O N T I N E N T A L

Scintilla Mtn.
8,226 ft.

8,744 ft.

D I V I D E

233

Trap Mtn.

Camp Creek

267

Basin Creek

N

0   1   2
Miles

Danaher

126

The Basin

Wigwam Creek

Creek

MONTANA

Jumbo Mtn.
8,284 ft. Lookout

From the signpost at the northern end of Indian Point Meadows, the trail runs southwest into the trees that flank the West Fork of the Sun. Look for blazes as the rather faint trail enters the trees. The path becomes more distinct as it hopscotches across a shallow side channel of the river to reach the main ford. The crossing is knee-deep, but there are plenty of logjams on the upstream side for a dry-footed crossing. Once on the far bank, follow the cairns upstream for 30 yards from the original fording point to reach the spot where the trail ducks through a gap in the willows and enters the forest beyond. From this point on, the trail is quite distinct and hard to miss.

The forest bordering the north bank of Ahorn Creek is dominated by lodgepole pine and is underlain by a sparse cover of pine grass and snowberry. The trail climbs in fits and starts along the slope bordering the western bank of the creek. Upon reaching a crossing of the Blind Fork of Ahorn Creek, the forest becomes a much richer bottomland community of spruce and fir. Half a mile later, the path reaches a shallow ford of the main body of Ahorn Creek. It then begins to climb gently along the dry hillside overlooking the eastern side of the valley. The forest community on this slope is a loose-knit forest of subalpine fir, underlain by clumps of beargrass. This community is not usually found at such a low altitude; it is more typical of timberline areas. The trail descends briefly to reach a marked trail junction

The alpine meadows of Pearl Basin below Twin Peaks.

with the Grizzly Basin Trail (226). This junction has been submerged by the overflowing waters of Ahorn Creek's East Fork.

After a 30-yard wade across the flooded trail bed, the route crosses a strip of dry land before reaching another ford of Ahorn Creek. The trail bends southwest as it passes inland, climbing gently through forested bottomlands on its way to a nameless tributary. After a shallow ford, the trail begins to climb a bit more briskly as it passes along the crest of a series of low hummocks. Upon reaching a clearing created by periodic avalanches, the trail begins to ascend in earnest, and the opening in the forest canopy allows the first of many unobstructed views of the Twin Peaks. After a number of switchbacks, the trail runs southwest along a rocky sidehill. It then zigzags upward to crest the eastern rim of the Pearl Basin.

Entering the basin, the trail passes into a long, narrow dale overlooked on the east by a scalloped finger of rock that projects from the main mass of Junction Mountain. The trail passes around the head of this miniature valley and turns south beneath overhanging cliffs to reach the next spur ridge. Meadows abound as the trail makes its way through fir parkland into the next basin, which is overlooked by a lofty southern spire of Junction Mountain. The trail then runs southeast, climbing gently through a brushy subalpine forest to reach the southern edge of Pearl Basin. The pocket-sized glades found here are shaded by dark forests, and marshy country prevails in the intervening depressions. The trail turns west again as it makes a short but brisk climb to reach Camp Creek Pass. The pass is low and wooded as it crosses the Continental Divide, but a steep descent brings the traveler to an overused camping spot among stout subalpine fir and meadows of the upper Camp Creek Basin.

20 White River Pass Option from West Fork of the Sun

General description:	An extended trip from the West Fork of the Sun to the White River.
Distance:	9.2 miles.
Difficulty:	Difficult.
Traffic:	Moderate.
Elevation gain:	2,186 feet.
Maps:	Prairie Reef, Haystack Mountain USGS quads.
Finding the trailhead:	This trail departs from Trail 203, 1 mile north of Indian Point Meadows.
For more information:	Rocky Mountain Ranger District, 1102 Main Ave. NW, P.O. Box 340, Choteau, Montana 59442, 406-466-5341.

White River Pass Option from West Fork of the Sun

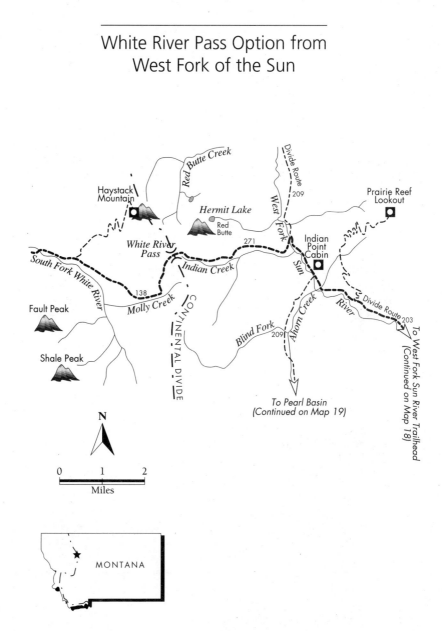

Key points:

 0.0   Trail fords the West Fork of the Sun River
 4.5   White River Pass.

The hike: This popular route across the Continental Divide connects Indian Point Meadows with the valley of the White River. Although this route does not offer views of the Chinese Wall, it does reveal stunning vistas of the Flathead Alps and Haystack Mountain.

From the shores of the West Fork of the Sun, this trail makes a crossing of this swift, knee-deep river then climbs through the lodgepole pine forest along the north bank of Indian Creek. Crossing the high benches above the stream, the trail runs westward toward the pass. Straight ahead, the blood-colored crags of Red Butte rise above the surrounding hills. The trail climbs steadily as it passes below a talus slope punctuated by scattered groves of aspen.

Upon reaching the southern slopes of Red Butte, the trail crosses a tiny stream that makes its way down from the rugged wastelands above. The path then crosses an open slope above a slender waterfall on Indian Creek. A second tributary lays the bedrock bare, and the stone reveals its origin: ripple marks have been preserved in the mudstone from the time long past when the rock was a shallow seafloor. The trail continues its moderate ascent across meadowy slopes, climbing into a high basin that was recently laid bare by a forest fire. Subalpine fir are beginning to recolonize the moister depressions, while the drier slopes above harbor only beargrass. As the valley doglegs to the north, the trail crosses it and climbs steeply along its

Looking through White River Pass from the east.

western wall. The rounded western shoulders of Red Butte frame the mottled patterns of timber and grassland on the shoulders of Prairie Reef. The trail then turns west to climb through the narrow defile of White River Pass.

Travelers approaching the pass from the east will be immediately confronted by the massive white monolith that rises beyond the pass. Looking northwest from the pass, the folded ridges of the White River Syncline can be seen on the far side of the White River Valley. The trail sidehills to the south, reaching another high saddle at the foot of the limestone edifice. Haystack Mountain rears its tilted plane of rock to the north, and a similar limestone stratum juts skyward to the south. Beyond it lie the pointed teeth of the Flathead Alps.

THE CONTINENTAL DIVIDE IN SOUTHERN MONTANA

Southwestern Montana is probably better known for its fishing than its hiking, with many hikers heading for areas around Glacier and Yellowstone National Parks, but the area features the first crossing of the divide by non-Indian explorers at Lemhi Pass, where Lewis and Clark first made it across into present-day Idaho.

This area also features one of the most complete sections of the Continental Divide National Scenic Trail (CDT), especially in the Anaconda–Pintler Wilderness Area where the trail is well marked and frequented often. In addition, the section from Lemhi Pass to Monida Pass is a good choice for exploring a remote section of the CDT route.

21 Rainbow Lake

General description:	An ideal hike for campers willing to undertake a difficult out-and-back to a high lake in the heart of the Anaconda–Pintler Wilderness, 30 miles southwest of Anaconda.
Distance:	7 miles.
Difficulty:	Difficult.
Traffic:	Moderate to Heavy.
Elevation gain:	2,675 feet.
Maps:	Warren Peak USGS Quad, the Beaverhead–Deerlodge National Forest Map and the Anaconda–Pintler Wilderness Map.
For more information:	District Ranger, Philipsburg Ranger District, Deerlodge National Forest, P.O. Box H, Philipsburg, Montana 59858, 406-859-3211.

Rainbow Lake

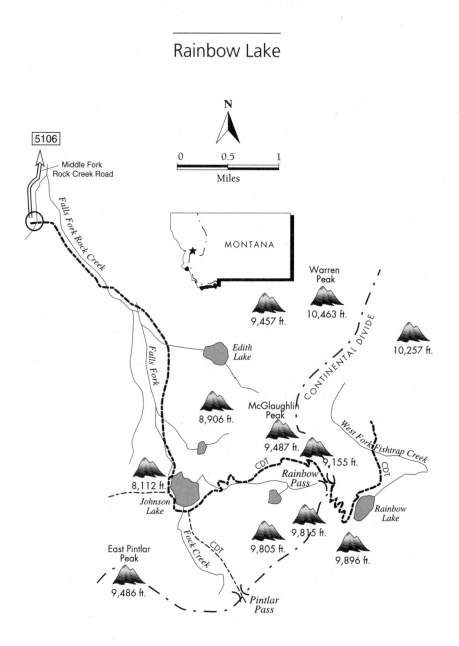

Finding the trailhead: Take Montana Highway 1 south of Philipsburg for 6 miles to Montana Highway 38. Turn west on MT 38 for 9 miles to Middle Fork Road #5106. Then take the Middle Fork Road and follow it south until it ends 17 miles later.

The hike: Ever want to set up camp in an alpine clearing where a diversity of peaks surround a small, deep lake loaded with trout? This spot may not be a secret, but it is still special, especially to those who share its natural gifts. Rainbow Lake, since it was first published in *Hiking Montana,* has increasingly been a popular destination of local hikers and vacationers. Be especially carefull to maintain a Leave-No-Trace ethic when visiting this lake as years of use have trampled vegetation and reduced wood supply. Fires are not recommended.

Start on Falls Fork Trail 29. It's a 4.5-mile uphill grind to Johnson Lake (elevation 7,720 feet). Hike along the west shore of this lake to a trail junction at the south end, and take the left-hand fork to the east to Continental Divide Trail 9. Turn left and climb a 2.5-mile stretch with moderate switchbacks to 9,040-foot Rainbow Pass.

The snow usually clings to this high land until at least late June, so mid-July or later is best for this hike. There is plenty of water along the trail except for the stretch between Johnson and Rainbow Lakes. Giardia can be found in the waters of the Anaconda-Pintler Wilderness, so filter or chemically treat all drinking water.

Rainbow Pass is a great place to relax and enjoy the surroundings. To the east is the ominous, broad pyramid of 10,793-foot West Goat Peak, highest in the Pintler Range. To the south are slopes covered with rare alpine larch. And right below you is your destination—Rainbow Lake. You can see the trail twisting down to the 8,215-foot elevation lake.

The lake has several good camping spots, with a popular one at the outlet. The rainbow trout are especially active in the morning and evening. Firewood may be scarce so consider going without fire. There are trails to explore and peaks to climb in all directions.

The geology of this area is striking. The range is made up mainly of typical Montana sedimentary rock, but with granitic intrusions, which account for all the odd-looking granite boulders strewn about in unexpected places. This phenomenon is especially evident on the trail to Warren Lake.

—Pat Caffrey

---

22 Pioneer and High-Up Lakes

General description:	A fairly strenuous overnight round trip (well-suited for a three-day trip) to a small lake just below the Montana–Idaho border. Located on the east slope of the Continental Divide in the Beaverhead National Forest, 15 miles southwest of Jackson and 65 miles west of Dillon.
Distance:	10 miles.

Difficulty:	Difficult.
Traffic:	Moderate.
Elevation gain:	2,400 feet.
Maps:	Goldstone Mountain USGS Quad and Beaverhead– Deerlodge National Forest Map.
For more information:	Wisdom Ranger District, Beaverhead National Forest, P.O. Box 238, Wisdom, Montana 59761, 406-689-3243.

Finding the trailhead: Drive 0.5 mile south of Jackson on Montana Highway 278 and turn right onto a gravel road near the top of a hill. Follow Forest Road 181 (Skinner Meadows Road) south and west to Van Houten Lake Campground, crossing many of the upper tributaries of the Big Hole River on narrow bridges. At the South Van Houten Campground, continue straight ahead for approximately 1.5 miles along Forest Road 181 (Bloody Dick Road) to the Jahnke Creek trailhead. Two-wheel-drive vehicles with adequate clearance can go up the Forest Road 7328 (Jahnke Creek Trail) for about 0.5 mile to its intersection with Overland Trail 36. At this point, you should park your vehicle and continue on foot.

The hike: The Overland Trail 36 goes downhill and joins Pioneer Creek Trail 479 just before the creek crossing. Shortly after this crossing is the junction with Trail 442, which continues along the south side of Pioneer Creek as a primitive vehicle track. This track is very pleasant to walk along as it winds among parks and groves. Watch for moose in the willow bottoms by the creek.

Panoramic views from the Continental Divide in the Italian Peaks. Rosemary Rowe photo

The trail climbs slowly and crosses the creek again about 4 miles in. Just past this crossing, the trail branches; the shortest route continues along the creek, while the right-hand trail climbs the hill to an old miner's cabin and eventually rejoins the main trail. After this intersection, the trail is closed to motor vehicles. The trail starts to climb more steeply as you approach the high peaks along the Continental Divide. Even at this high elevation (7,000 to 8,000 feet), there are large spruces and firs growing close to Pioneer Creek.

The last part of the route is a regular hiking trail. It crosses the north branch of Pioneer Creek and cuts across a slope to the south branch of the creek. This section of the trail away from the stream may be confusing, so consult your map and watch for faint blazes. Pioneer Lake lies about a mile farther (roughly 8 miles in). It offers some good camping spots and a close-up look at the Continental Divide.

Pioneer and High-Up Lakes

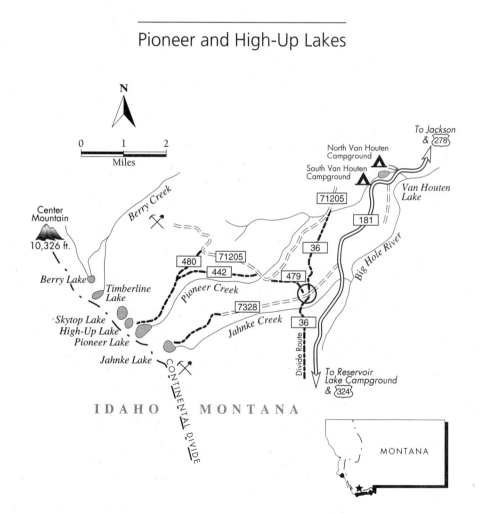

If you are ambitious, you may want to try a short climb up the hill west of Pioneer Lake on faint animal paths to High-Up Lake, actually a pair of alpine jewels just below the divide. There is a good campsite on the east end of the lake with a fine view back down the valley you just labored up. A third lake, Skytop, lies over the next ridge, but its shores are rockier. Off-trail side trips require good routefinding skills.

Try to catch the sunrise above the Big Hole Valley over the high peaks of the East Pioneer Mountains. A moonrise is also worth staying up for—ghostly light silhouettes the limbs of dead whitebark pine surrounding the lake. Pine beetles killed these trees decades ago, but this treeline forest is renewing itself.

High-Up Lake is a great place to spend an extra day exploring. The Continental Divide is a short climb on steep talus above the south end of the lake. On top of the divide one commonly sees mountain goats among the crags. The west slope of the divide is gentler than the steep glacier-carved east wall, and it is possible to walk north and south along the crest amid wild scenery. Center Mountain rises 3 miles to the north along the ridge. It can provide a moderate, nontechnical climb, but use caution among its loose slide rock. To the west are the rugged Big Horn Crags in the great wild area of central Idaho, the River of No Return Wilderness.

Both Pioneer and High-Up Lakes have small cutthroat, but neither are noted for fishing. The Big Hole and its surrounding mountains are notorious for their mosquitoes. Plan a late summer hike or bring plenty of repellent. The trail along Pioneer Creek stays close to water most of the distance. Anglers and less ambitious hikers will enjoy ambling along the willow-bordered stream on the lower portion of the trail. High-Up Lake and most of the Pioneer Creek Valley are within the 76,600-acre West Big Hole proposed wilderness.

—*Fred Swanson*

23 Deadman and Nicholia Creeks

General-description:	A three- or four-day backpacking trip for experienced hikers in the seldom-visited Italian Peaks proposed wilderness, just 20 miles southwest of Lima. The hike features a huge glacial cirque of Italian Peak, high on the Continental Divide.
Distance:	23 miles round trip from Nicholia Trailhead.
Difficulty:	Difficult.
Traffic:	Light.
Elevation gain:	2,760 feet.
Maps:	Scott Peak USGS Quad and the Beaverhead National Forest Travel Plan Map.

For more information: Dillon Ranger District, Beaverhead National Forest, 420 Barrett Street, Dillon, Montana 59725, 406-683-3960.

Finding the trailhead: The trailhead is remote but easy to find using the Beaverhead National Forest Map. Turn off Interstate 15 at the Dell Exit 23, 45 miles south of Dillon. Follow the gravel road that parallels the interstate's western side for 1.5 miles south, where a road turns westward up Big Sheep Canyon on Forest Road 257. After 18 miles the road branches; take the left branch toward Nicholia–Deadman. In 2.25 miles, Forest Road 3922 branches again. Continue to the left on Forest Road 657 up the broad valley of Nicholia Creek.

Another 4.5 miles will bring you to a creek crossing, 0.5 mile inside the National Forest boundary and a good place to start the hike. If you have two vehicles, take one with high clearance over the road to Deadman Lake toward the southeast; if not, walk 6.8 miles to Deadman Lake on the Continental Divide National Scenic Trail (CDT).

The hike: The following description starts from Deadman Lake, reached by four-wheel-drive, but you can also follow the CDT from the Nicholia Creek Trailhead. Few hikers visit this remote, isolated mountain range in the far southwestern corner of the state, but its spectacular alpine scenery is sure to make it more popular in years to come.

Deadman Lake, which offers some cutthroat fishing, is a small pond lying in a steep, V-shaped valley. Trail 91 heads south up the right side of the lake, the trail (such as it is) enters the proposed wilderness area and leaves the rough jeep track behind.

The trails in this region receive little use and have a tendency to fade away in the many grassy meadows along the track. A few tips are in order: Do not trust the trail as shown on the Scott Peak USGS Quad. It is very old, and inaccurate to boot. Do trust the blazes on the trees, which look like upside-down exclamation points. The trail stays close to the stream except in places where the trail is built above to avoid avalanche debree.

For 4 miles the trail follows Deadman Creek, frequently fording the small stream to avoid the little lakes formed by avalanches and mudslides coming off the high, nameless ridge to the west. Even in late July, snow may remain at the base of these avalanche chutes, which can easily be avoided by remaining on the eastern side of the stream.

The valley at this point begins to take on a more alpine character, showing signs of the glaciers that once carved the U-shaped upper canyon. The pretty meadows here are a good place for the first night's camp. Or, if you have the energy, you can hike up to Divide Lake. This lies in a rocky depression just a few yards on the Idaho side of the Continental Divide and is perfectly invisible from the Deadman Creek side. The old trail used to climb the grassy slope up to a broad saddle on the divide to the lake, but it is now grown over. Use your topo map, and there should be no problem.

Deadman and Nicholia Creeks

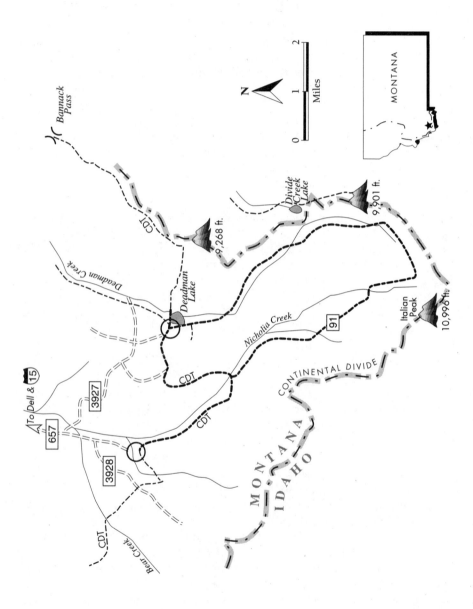

The advantage of camping at Divide Lake is that you may catch a few cutthroat for dinner (Idaho fishing license required). The disadvantage is having to climb the 400 feet up to the lake and back down again to continue the hike.

The trail climbs gradually through the alpine meadows of the upper Deadman drainage, with the steep rocky ridge of the Continental Divide looming overhead to the left. At one point, a huge geological formation, called a breach anticline, forms a cliff along the divide, resembling a meteor impact crater. About 4 miles from the Divide Lake turnoff, the trail reaches the pass between the Deadman and Nicholia Creek drainages. Here at 9,400 feet, the alpine scenery is spectacular, with the knife-edge ridge of the divide rising up to the 10,998-foot summit of Italian Peak. Keep your eyes peeled for bighorn sheep and goats up on the high slopes.

The trail switchbacks down a steep talus slope into the alpine meadows at the base of the north wall of Italian Peak. A snowfield lingers year-round on Italian Peak's north wall, perhaps aspiring to become a glacier. This alpine basin makes a perfect second night's campsite and may convince you to spend an extra day exploring the meadows and talus slopes of this huge cirque. This is the southernmost point in Montana, and surely, it is one of the prettiest.

Going northward, the trail descends the broad, green valley of Nicholia Creek, staying on the western side of the stream just above the bogs in the creek bottom. Again, the trail tends to disappear in some of the meadows; look for blazes through the forested parts. This part of the Nicholia Creek drainage is considered a segment of the recently completed, 60-mile Continental Divide National Scenic Trail. At one large meadow, about 3 miles from the cirque basin, the route is marked by a series of f 5-foot-high posts.

Past this meadow, Trail 91 enters the lower reaches of Nicholia Creek and becomes very well defined, especially after it crosses to the eastern bank of the stream. For 6 miles, the route follows an old, grass-grown jeep track through the sagebrush flats. Be sure to turn around frequently to see the changing views of Italian Peak and Scott Peak over in Idaho. Some 8.5 miles after leaving the cirque at the base of Italian Peak, you reach your waiting car.

Although there are several fresh springs in both the Deadman and Nicholia valleys, you should be prepared to treat your water, since cows graze the meadows along most of the route. The bugs can be bad as well, so bring lots of insect repellent.

The high pass between Nicholia and Deadman Creeks is usually clear of snow by the Fourth of July, but check local conditions with the Forest Service before you start. The Forest Service has proposed wilderness status for the Italian Peaks area.

—*Ed Madej and Rosemary Rowe*

The Continental Divide in Wyoming

Over 500 miles of the Continental Divide run through Wyoming. Starting in the Greater Yellowstone Ecosystem, the divide winds through Yellowstone National Park before winding through the Teton and Bridger Wilderness Areas, on to the dry open Wyoming landscape near the Ferris Mountains, and finally to the Huston Park Wilderness. Although the Continental Divide trail in Wyoming, and especially south of the Wind River Range, is far from finished, there are still many spectacular places along the divide to visit. This chapter includes selected hikes from Yellowstone National Park (permits required) and hikes along the divide throughout Wyoming.

THE CONTINENTAL DIVIDE IN YELLOWSTONE NATIONAL PARK

Here are a few important things to remember about Yellowstone:

In many other national parks and wilderness areas, you can go anywhere anytime—not in Yellowstone. The National Park Service manages Yellowstone for natural regulation in general and for the preservation of large predators like grizzly bears and wolves in particular. In some areas of the park, bear management affects hiking. Some areas are closed permanently, for part of the season, or have limited hours. In addition, any hazardous situation that develops often brings temporary closures that protect both bears and people.

The abundant wildlife of Yellowstone adds a spectacular element to the hiking experience, but when you see bison on or near the trail, do not be nonchalant. Bison look tame and docile, but the opposite is true. Always give bison a wide berth.

The mosquito populations of Yellowstone are infamous. In June and July, and even occasionally in August, the clouds of mosquitoes seem like they could block out the sun, so come prepared with plenty of repellent and netting. You can also wait until August or September when most mosquitoes die off.

Hiking many trails in Yellowstone involves fording large rivers. If this is not your strength or interest, be sure to research your hike in advance to avoid a ford.

Normal weather patterns (if there are such things) in the summer create clear mornings with thundershowers (or "rollers" as they're called locally) in the mid-afternoon, followed by clear, cooler evenings. This means early morning hikers usually enjoy better weather, and they more often get their tents set up before it rains. But it can snow any day of the year in Yellowstone, so always be prepared for that possibility.

Note: Campsites are rated on a five-star basis, with a five-star site featuring views, water access, tent sites, and privacy. A one-star campsite may have difficult access to water and lack privacy and views.

24 Shoshone Lake

General description:	Multi-day loop backpacking trip to Shoshone Lake.
Difficulty:	Difficult.
Distance:	28.3 miles.
Elevation gain:	Overall minimal elevation gain, but several short, steep hills around the lake.
Maps:	Trails Illustrated Old Faithful and Craig Pass, Shoshone Geyser Basin, Lewis Falls USGS quads.
For more information:	Backcountry Office, P.O. Box 168, Yellowstone National Park, Wyoming 82190, 307-344-3160.

Shoshone Lake.

Finding the trailhead: Drive 8.4 miles west of West Thumb Junction (0.25 mile past the DeLacy Creek Picnic Area) or 8.6 miles east of Old Faithful and park in a pull out on the south side of the road.

Key points:

The hike: A three-night, four-day trip with an easy first day which leaves time for driving to the trailhead. Camp the first night at 8S2 or 8S3, second night at 8R5 or 8T1, and the third night at 8S1 (preferred) or 8M1 or 8M2.

Shoshone Lake is one of the most popular backpacking destinations in Yellowstone. In addition, paddlers come up the Lewis River and camp at the lake which actually has more boat-access-only campsites (not covered in this book) than trail-access campsites. If you want to avoid an overpopulation of mosquitoes, wait until late August to go to Shoshone Lake.

Shoshone Lake is a huge, deep lake (8,050 acres and up to 205 feet deep) in shadow of the Continental Divide near Craig Pass. The trail starts out just east of Craig Pass with a small descent into DeLacy Creek and then follows the stream grade about 200 feet down to the lake. The first mile goes through unburned forest right along the creek. Then, the creek widens into a slow-moving, marshy stream and the trail opens up into a series of meadows. The trail to the lake is in great shape and stays dry, distinct, and easy to follow all the way to the lake.

When you reach the Shoshone Lake Trail (assuming you chose the counterclockwise route described here), take a right (west). You walk along a beach for a short distance and ford DeLacy Creek before you go into the timber and to 8S2 and 8S3 where you probably want to spend your first night.

The trail stays near the lake for another mile or so after the campsites

Shoshone Lake

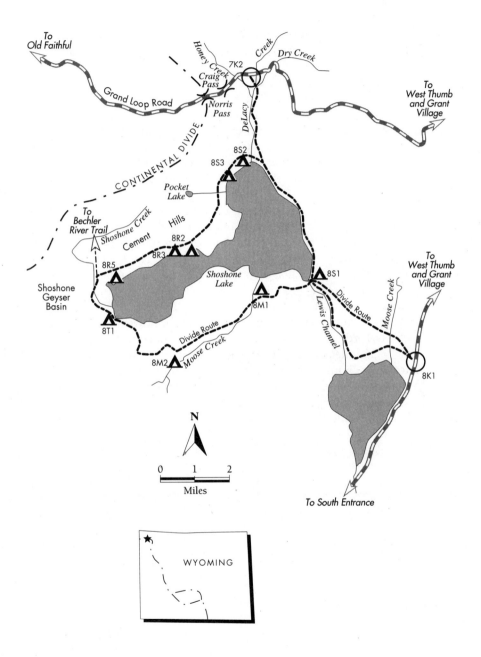

To Old Faithful

Honey Creek
7K2
Creek
Dry Creek
Craig Pass
Norris Pass

Grand Loop Road

DeLacy

To West Thumb and Grant Village

CONTINENTAL DIVIDE

8S2
8S3

Pocket Lake

To Bechler River Trail

Shoshone Creek

Hills

Cement

8R2
8R3

8R5

Shoshone Geyser Basin

Shoshone Lake

8S1

To West Thumb and Grant Village

Moose Creek

8M1

Lewis Channel

Divide Route

8T1

Divide Route

Moose Creek

8M2

8K1

N

0   1   2
Miles

To South Entrance

★
WYOMING

before heading away from the lake for about 3.5 miles, climbing over several small but sometimes steep ridges until you come back to the lakeshore around 8R2 and 8R3 and the patrol cabin. Although well-defined, this section of trail gets rocky in places.

After the patrol cabin, the trail goes out of sight of the lake again and stays there until you reach the junction with the trail to Lone Star Geyser and Old Faithful. Again, the trail goes up and down over several small ridges and stays in unburned timber.

At the junction, turn left (south), and the trail opens up into Shoshone Geyser Basin which has dozens of interesting thermal features. In the basin, you face two marshy fords of an unnamed creek and Fall Creek and near the end of the basin, one more ford of Cold Mountain Creek. In July, the entire basin stays marshy which is probably one reason horses are not allowed in the basin. About halfway through the basin, you will see the horse by-pass trail comes in from the right (west). Keep going straight (south) along the lake.

Just after the Cold Mountain Creek ford, the trail gets faint. Watch for markers on the end of the timber, and once you get in the trees, the trail is well-defined. From here, the trail climbs steeply up 300 feet to a ridge above the lake and then drops steeply into Moose Creek. The trail then follows Moose Creek (with one ford just before 8M1) all the way to the Lewis Channel, going over two small ridges just before reaching the channel.

The Lewis Channel (the outlet of Shoshone Lake) is a big stream and fording it can get your pulse rate up. In late season, however, it is less difficult. After the ford, go 0.25 mile along the lakeshore to the junction between Lewis Channel Trail and Dogshead Trailhead. Go left (north) here and in another 0.25 mile, you reach the patrol cabin and 8S1.

From here, it is 4 miles to the DeLacy Creek Trailhead where you came in. This section of trail goes right along the lakeshore the entire way, even dipping down to walk on the rocky beach in several places. You get terrific views of the lake all along this stretch of trail. At DeLacy Creek, take a right (north) and retrace your steps to the trailhead.

Options: You can take this trip in reverse with the same degree of difficulty. You can also reach Shoshone Lake from the Fern Cascades, Lone Star Geyser, and Dogshead trailhead and still make a loop (but a longer loop) out of the trip.

25 Bechler River

General description:	A multi-day backpacking adventure into one of the most remote and beautiful sections of Yellowstone, including a pass over the Continental Divide. Shuttle required.
Difficulty:	Difficult because of length, but easy otherwise.
Distance:	30.3 miles.
Traffic:	Light with the exception of the section around Lone Star Geyser, which receives heavy traffic.
Elevation gain:	980 feet.
Maps:	Trails Illustrated Old Faithful, and Old Faithful, Shoshone Geyser Basin, Trischman Knob, Cave Falls and Bechler Falls USGS quads.
For more information:	Backcountry Supervisor, Bechler Ranger Station, P.O. Box 168, Yellowstone National Park, Wyoming 82190, 307-646-7313.

Finding the trailhead: Drive east of Old Faithful, 3.5 miles, and park at the Lone Star Trailhead (OK1). Leave a vehicle or arrange to be picked up at the Bechler River Ranger Station in the far southwestern corner of the park.

You can reach the ranger station by two routes. The rough, scenic route goes from Flagg Ranch just south of the park on the Ashton-Flagg Road, past Grassy Lake Reservoir. Watch for signs for a signed junction where you turn right (north) to the Cave Falls Road and right (east) again when you reach the Cave Falls Road. After about 2 miles on an unpaved section of Cave Falls Road, you reach a junction where the pavement starts and you can turn left (north) to the to the ranger station.

You can also get to the Bechler Ranger Station from the west from either Ashton, Idaho, or West Yellowstone, Montana, by getting on Idaho State Highway 47 and turning on the Cave Falls Road.

Key points:

1.6	Junction with Spring Creek Trail.
2.4	Lone Star Geyser and end of paved trail.
2.7	Junction with trail to Fern Cascades Trailhead and Old Faithful.
3.0	Campsite OA1. ★★★
3.5	OA2. ★★★
4.0	OA3. ★★★
7.0	Grants Pass (Continental Divide).
7.5	Shoshone Lake Trail and 8G1.
9.8	9D4. ★★★
11.6	9D3. ★★★
12.1	Douglas Knob.
13.9	Twister Falls and 9D2. ★★★
15.2	Three River Junction, Ragged Falls and 9D1. ★★★

15.7	9B9. ★★★
16.7	9B8. ★★★
17.8	9B7. ★★★
18.4	9B6. ★★★
19 .0	Treasure Island.
19.2	Iris Falls.
19.4	9B5. ★★★
19.6	Colonnade Falls.
21.7	Ranger Lake and 9B4. ★★★
22.6	First cutoff trail to Bechler Meadows Trail and 9B2. ★★★
25.6	Junction with Mountain Ash Creek Trail.
26.5	Rocky Ford of Bechler River, junction with the second cutoff trail to Bechler Meadows and 9C1. ★★★
29.3	Junction with Bechler Falls Trail.
30.3	Bechler Ranger Station

The hike: Along with the Thorofare and Gallatin Skyline, the Bechler River ranks among the best backpacking trips in Yellowstone. Wild and remote and not too difficult (good trail with no monster hills), it also offers great fishing, and matchless scenery.

This is one of the few sections of Yellowstone that escaped the fires of 1988, perhaps the only 30-mile hike you can take without walking through a burned landscape. You can usually find water along this trail, so unlike many long hikes, you do not have to carry that extra water bottle. Be forwarned—mosquitoes can be vicious in July. If you plan to fish, be sure to get a park fishing permit and remember all of the Bechler River Valley is catch-and-release only.

Plan for a five-day trip staying at OA1 or OA3 the first night. This allows time for a leisurely drive to the trailhead on the first day as well as fishing the Upper Firehole or a side trip to Shoshone Geyser Basin. Spend the second night at 9D4 or 9D3, the third night at 9B7 or 9B6 and the fourth night at 9B2 or 9C1.

The first leg of this backpacking adventure to Lone Star Geyser is as easy as it gets—2.4 miles on a flat, paved trail. Lone Star is a well-known and heavily visited geyser—so popular that the NPS has paved the trail and opened it to mountain bikers. Even though you might see a few bikers and more than a few hikers on this section of trail, it is still a pleasant hike along the Upper Firehole River.

At the 1.6-mile mark, stay right (south) at the junction with the Spring Creek Trail, continuing on the paved path. The pavement ends about 100 feet before the geyser and is blocked by downed trees to discourage bicycle traffic beyond this point.

Lone Star Geyser was named for its isolated location (5 miles south of Old Faithful with no other geysers in the neighborhood). The name has nothing to do with Texas, the Lone Star State. It has a great castle and erupts 30 to 50 feet every two to three hours or so for about ten to fifteen minutes and makes gurgling sounds between eruptions.

Bechler River

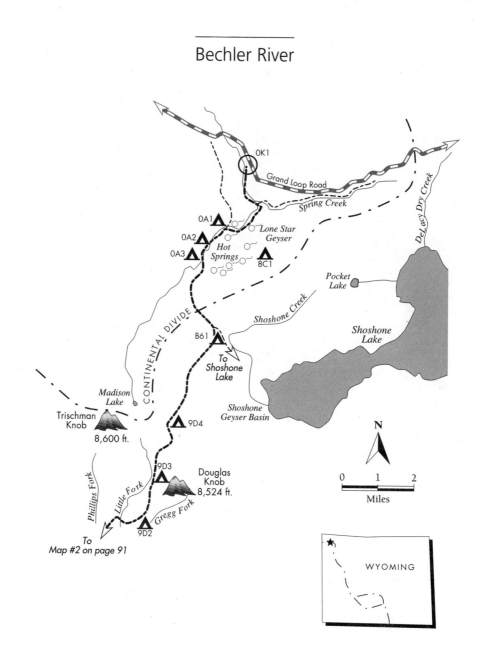

Some maps show a little loop north of the geyser, but that loop really doesn't exist on the ground. Follow the unpaved but excellent trail past the geyser for less than a 0.25 mile before turning left (south) on the main trail to the Bechler River. You could have skipped the paved section and added a mile to your trip by starting at the Fern Cascades Trailhead near Old Faithful and getting to the same point.

Bechler River.

From here, the trail crosses (on a foot bridge) and then continues along the Upper Firehole River for about 2 miles before veering off to the left and climbing about 300 feet up to the Continental Divide at Grants Pass. The pass is heavily forested, effectively blocking the view.

After the pass, the trail drops only slightly (about 150 feet) down to the junction with the Shoshone Lake Trail. The trail through this section is in great shape and is well-defined and marked.

At this junction, stay right (south) and head for the Bechler River. Before you drop down to the river, you get to go over the Continental Divide again. Once more, the climb is gentle, hardly in line with popular images of the Great Divide, but still a Category III, 600-foot climb over about 3 miles of trail.

After crossing the Divide, head downhill for the next 20 miles. Hike gradually downhill into the Littles Fork, passing Douglas Knob on your left (south) at about the 12-mile mark and then over a small ridge into the Falls Fork and to Twister Falls which is farther downstream on the Falls Fork than

Bechler River

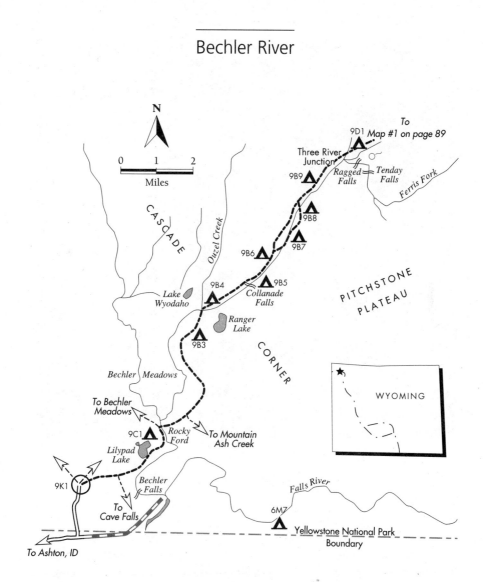

shown on the maps. Twister Falls makes an unusual twist as the water drops. Not visible from the trail, take a short spur trail to a viewpoint.

Douglas Knob is forested and visible, but not as notable as its namesake, one of the most colorful and famous rangers in the early days of Yellowstone. Witness this: In 1921, Douglas tried to walk across Yellowstone Lake from West Thumb to Lake. Two miles into his trip, he fell through the ice, but crawled out, stripped off his clothes in thirty-below-zero weather, wrung out the water and redressed himself in frozen-stiff garments. Then, a tough decision—go 2 miles back to West Thumb or 15 miles to Lake. He hiked the

Colonnade Falls on the Bechler River.

15 miles, and when somebody asked him why he didn't take the 2-mile option, he replied, "They'd have kidded me to death."

Another 2 miles brings you to Three Rivers Junction, a flat floodplain where three forks (Ferris, Gregg, and Phillips) merge to form the Bechler River (named after the chief topographer of the Hayden survey). Ragged Falls is off to your left (south) on Ferris Fork. There is also a patrol cabin not marked on the topo maps.

You are now in the Bechler River Canyon which is lined with cliffs, thermal areas, hot springs, cascades, waterfalls, and generally outstanding scenery. You follow the canyon for another 7 miles. You may see anglers casting for the wily rainbow inhabiting the scenic waterway.

The trail continues to be in great shape, well-defined and well-marked, but a little rocky in a few places. Most tributary streams have foot bridges to keep your feet dry. There are more berries (huckleberries, thimbleberries, strawberries, and others species, too) in this area than most parts of Yellowstone which means there are bears, too, so be alert.

While in the canyon, you ford the Bechler River twice. The first ford (at about the 16.5-mile mark by 9B8) is easy and knee-deep, but the second (at about the 18-mile mark just before 9B7), is hip-deep (even in August) with a fairly fast current. Kids might have a tough time with the second ford.

When you get to Colonnade Falls, be sure to take a break and hike the short side trip (less than 0.25 mile) to see the magnificent double falls.

You cannot see Ranger Lake from the trail, but if you watch the map, you can take a 0.5-mile, off-trail walk to see the forest-lined, 56-acre lake. You might also try to outsmart the rainbow trout living there.

After Ranger Lake, you leave the canyon behind and head out into the incredible flat piece of wild real estate called Bechler Meadows. You basically stay on the same contour line for the last 8 miles of the hike. At the junction with the first cutoff trail to the west over to Bechler Meadows Trail, you can go either way, but this trail description follows the Bechler River Trail, so go left (south).

From the junction, the trail stays on the east side of the massive Bechler Meadows where the Bechler River splits up into several channels. In about 3 miles, you come to the junction with the Mountain Ash Trail. Go right (south). In another mile or so, you reach the Rocky Ford of the Bechler River. If you cross right where the trail meets the river, you will need dry underwear on the other side. If you cross about a 100 feet downstream, it is only knee-deep. The rocks are moss-covered and slippery, so a sturdy walking stick might prevent an embarrassing flop into the icy water.

After the ford, its an easy 3.8 miles to the ranger station. After four nights out, you might be thinking about a shower and a big steak, but you still should hang your pack for a few minutes and take the short out-and-back side trip over to see Bechler Falls, a huge cascade on the Bechler River with a nice steady roar to add an extra touch to the end of your adventure in Bechler River Country.

Options: This trip could, of course, be done in reverse if the shuttle logistics are more convenient, but it would be uphill most of the way.

You can finish you hike by going by the falls if you left your vehicle at the Cave Falls Trailhead instead of the ranger station. This would only shorten the hike by about a quarter mile or so. You could also shorten your trip by taking the Bechler Meadows Trail instead of staying on the Bechler River Trail, but you'd miss Rocky Ford and Bechler Falls.

Unlike many other areas of Yellowstone, there are many options for creatively building a backpacking adventure for the Bechler River area. For example, this hike can also be started or finished at the Fern Cascades, DeLacy Creek, Dogshead, Cave Falls, Fish Lake, Cascade Creek, or Grassy Lake trailheads.

Side trips: If you have the time, you could hang your pack and take a rewarding, 2.5-mile round trip to Shoshone Geyser Basin on the west end of Shoshone Lake. Near the end of the trip, tack an extra hour on your last day with the short side trip to see Bechler Falls.

26 Pitchstone Plateau

General description:	A long day hike or overnighter through some of the wildest country in Yellowstone National Park. This hike requires a shuttle.
Difficulty:	Difficult.
Distance:	20.2 miles.
Traffic:	Light.
Elevation gain:	963 feet.
Maps:	Trails Illustrated Old Faithful and Lewis Canyon and Grassy Lake Reservoir USGS quads.
For more information:	Backcountry Supervisor, Snake River Ranger Station, P.O. Box 168, Yellowstone National Park, Wyoming 82190, 307-242-7209

Finding the trailhead: About 2 miles south of the park on U.S. Highway 287 and just before Flagg Ranch, turn west on what is called the Ashton–Flagg Road. This also goes to Flagg Ranch Village. After about 0.5 mile, turn right (west) as the left fork goes to the campground. The road stays paved for about 2 more miles before turning into a gradually worsening gravel road. The trail starts at Grassy Lake Trailhead (9K5) just after crossing under the spillway at the west end of Grassy Lake Reservoir which is just south of the park 10 miles west of Flagg Ranch. At the east end of the trail, leave a vehicle or arrange to be picked up at the Phantom/Pitchstone Trailhead (8K4) which is 14 miles south of West Thumb or 6 miles north of the South Entrance. The 8K4 trailhead is a pull out on the south side of the road barely big enough for about three vehicles.

Key points:

1.0	Junction with Cascade Creek Trail and Falls River Ford.
1.2	9C5 ★★★★ and junction with Union Falls Trail.
13.0	8P1 ★★★ and 8P2. ★★★
14.2	Phantom Fumarole.
20.2	South Entrance Road.

The hike: This hike traverses some of the greatest scenery in Yellowstone, but it is not for beginning hikers. Pitchstone Plateau is a rugged hike requiring route-finding skills. Be sure to take plenty of water because reliable sources are scarce late in the summer.

If you start at Grassy Lake Reservoir, the first mile is partly on an old roadbed—flat and very easy hiking. It follows the stream that leaves the reservoir and then the Falls River. At the 1.0-mile mark, you have to ford the Falls River. This is a long ford, but only knee-deep in August. Try this trail in mid-July at the earliest, because the Pitchstone Plateau gets lots of snow. If snow covers the cairns, the route can be hard to find.

Pitchstone Plateau

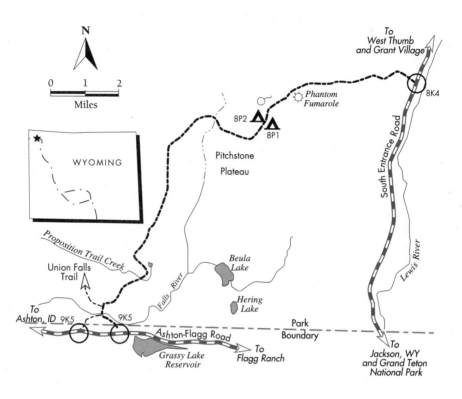

Right after the ford, you will see 9C5 and then a few feet later the trail to Pitchstone Plateau, both on your right. The trail you are on (which goes to Union Falls) is much better, so be careful not to walk by this junction.

From this junction to the Pitchstone Plateau, the trail becomes indistinct for several miles, but it is marked fairly well with cairns and orange markers. It goes through burnt forest for about 3 miles and then unburned timber on a more defined trail for another 3 miles to the plateau.

When you get up on Pitchstone Plateau, the trail disappears, but frequent cairns show the way. This section of trail goes through a series of gorgeous, high-altitude meadows with spectacular views in all directions, including a choice view of the Tetons off to the south. The name "Pitchstone" means glassy black igneous rock that resembles a hardened pitch, and this will be easy to observe. The Pitchstone Plateau is one of the most recent examples of volcanic flows in the area, and the black volcanic rock is strewn everywhere across the plateau.

From the campsites, the trail continues as a chain of cairns, mostly through open country. About a mile past the campsites, you go by impressive Phantom Fumarole, a colorful and quite active mudpot that puts out lots of steam. It earned its name because it was hard to find except on cold days when early explorers could spot the steam cloud above it. From here, you then hike back into the timber for the last 3 miles before reaching the South Entrance Road. This section of trail was heavily burned in 1988.

Footnote: the signs at opposite ends of the trail have discrepancies in the mileages, but it looks like the longer distance is more correct.

Options: The shuttle can be done from either direction depending on what logistics are most convenient. At the south end, you can start or end at the Cascade Creek Trailhead (9K5). This is a slightly shorter route, but it involves half a mile on a four-wheel-drive road which starts 1.5 miles east of the dam at Grassy Lake Reservoir. If you do not have a four-wheel-drive vehicle and have to walk the road, it is shorter to start or end at Grassy Lake Reservoir. Also, the Grassy Lake Reservoir trailhead is easier to find.

Side trips: Because of the open terrain, you can hike off-trail on the Pitchstone Plateau, but you should talk to rangers about your plans and make sure you are proficient with map and compass.

27 Riddle Lake

General description:	Probably the easiest hike in America that crosses the Continental Divide and goes to a beautiful mountain lake.
Difficulty:	Easy.
Distance:	4.6 miles, or 7.4 miles round trip.
Traffic:	Moderate.
Elevation gain:	Minimal.
Maps:	Trails Illustrated Yellowstone Lake and Mount Sheridan USGS quad.
For more information:	Backcountry Supervisor, Lake Ranger District, P.O. Box 168, Yellowstone National Park, Wyoming 82190, 307-242-2402.

Finding the trailhead: Drive 4.1 miles south of West Thumb and turn into the parking area for the Riddle Lake Trailhead (7K3) on the east side of the road.

The hike: This ranks as one of the easiest hikes to a backcountry lake in the park. Just over 2 miles and flat as a pool table, this must be close to the flattest 2 miles in all of Yellowstone Park.

The trail is in great shape and passes through unburned forest and past several small meadows. Watch for elk and moose in the meadows. Some of

Riddle Lake

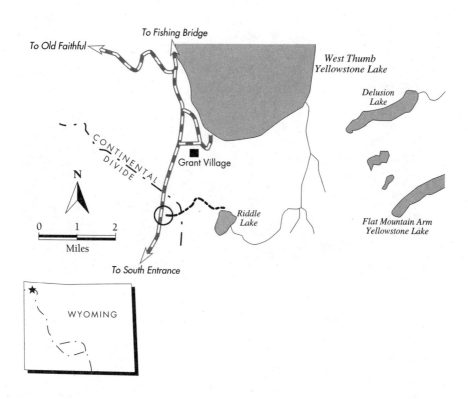

the meadows stay marshy until July, so you might get your feet wet if you go before July—although some of the small stream crossings have foot bridges.

Riddle Lake gets its name because early on in the park's history, it was believed to be a "two-ocean lake" sitting right on the Continental Divide with outlets flowing both east and west. This turned out to be an early mapping error. The lake is actually about 2 miles east of the Divide where the trailhead is located.

The lake has a huge marshy meadow on its southwest corner, and in late summer lilypads float on the surface. The trail goes along the north edge of the lake to a small beach where it officially ends. You get a great view of the Red Mountains from the lake.

Riddle Lake.

28 Heart Lake

General description:	A long out-and-back day hike or a moderate backpacking trip with several interesting side trips.
Difficulty:	Moderate.
Distance:	16 miles round trip.
Traffic:	Moderate.
Elevation gain:	345 feet.
Maps:	Trails Illustrated Yellowstone Lake and Mount Sheridan and Heart Lake USGS quads.
For more information:	Backcountry Supervisor, Lake Ranger District, P.O. Box 168, Yellowstone National Park, Wyoming 82190, 307-242-2402.

Finding the trailhead: Drive 5.2 miles south of Grant Village Junction and park at the Heart Lake Trailhead (8H1) on the east side of the road.

The hike: Although a strong hiker can easily hike to Heart Lake and back in a day, it would be a shame not to spend more time there. I recommend a three-day trip, staying two nights at the lake and climbing Mount Sheridan on the second day. If you want to spend four days, use the extra day to hike around the lake.

Heart Lake • Mount Sheridan
Heart Lake Loop • Two Ocean Plateau

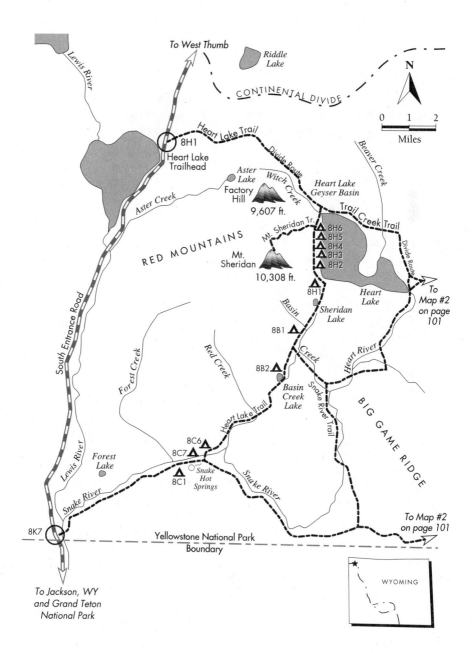

To Map #2
on page
101

To Map #2
on page 101

Heart Lake looks like the big heart of Yellowstone, but it was not named for its shape. It is named after Hart Humey, an old trapper who frequented the area before the park was created. Through the years, Hart Lake became Heart Lake.

Regardless of the name, this is one of the spots you really should see if you plan on hiking much in Yellowstone. This is a uniquely large and beautiful mountain lake in the shadow of stately Mount Sheridan. Anglers love the healthy population of large cutthroat and lake trout here. Watch for eagles and loons from the lakeshore, and scan the slopes of Mount Sheridan for the mighty grizzly.

Heart Lake has become a popular destination for hikers, so do not plan on having the lake or the trail to yourself. The trail is in great shape all the way, with bridges over all streams. It climbs through unburned forest interrupted here and there by small meadows for the first 5 miles. Then, the trail passes through a burn from the 1988 fires to a great viewpoint of the lake, Factory Hill, and also Witch Creek, which was probably named for the numerous hot springs and steam vents that line most of its course. At this viewpoint, it seems as if you are closer to the lake because it is so large, but you actually have more than 2 miles to go.

From this point on, the trail goes through open terrain with great scenery as you drop down into the Witch Creek drainage. It is tempting to stop and investigate thermal areas. If you do, be careful not to disturb delicate ecosystems or burn yourself. On a cold day, the thermal areas kick up so much steam that it clouds views of the lake. Factory Hill (named for the steam vents that resemble smoke stacks) partly blocks the view of Mount Sheridan despite its high elevation, just before you reach the lake and the junction with the Trail Creek Trail. The Heart Lake Patrol Cabin is visible off to the left. A ranger stays there most of the summer.

If you are staying overnight or climbing Mount Sheridan, turn right (south) at the junction. The trail follows the shoreline through the Witch Creek bottomlands and by overflow of Rustic Geyser and several hot pools off to your right. Again, these thermal areas are fascinating to explore, but be cautious. At the first junction, the left fork goes to 8H6. You go right to the other campsites and to the Mount Sheridan spur trail, about 200 yards farther down the trail.

If you are staying overnight, you probably want one of the six campsites on the west side of the lake. If you are day hiking, do not spend too much time exploring the lake or fishing because it is an 8-mile hike (including a climb out of Witch Creek) back to the trailhead.

Options: Heart Lake can be part of several long backpacking trips in the southeastern section of the park.

Side trips: The obvious (and spectacular) side trip is the trail up Mount Sheridan. Refer to the Mount Sheridan hike for details.

Heart Lake • Mount Sheridan
Heart Lake Loop • Two Ocean Plateau

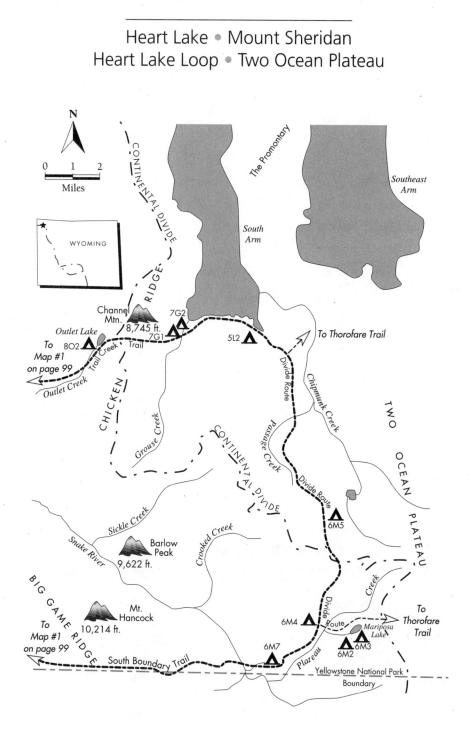

29 Mount Sheridan

See map on pages 99 and 101

General description:	A strenuous but short out-and-back day hike or side trip to an incredible vista where you can look down on the Continental Divide far below.
Difficulty:	Difficult.
Distance:	6 miles round trip.
Traffic:	Moderate.
Elevation gain:	2,700 feet.
Maps:	Trails Illustrated Yellowstone Lake and Mount Sheridan USGS quad.
For more information:	Backcountry supervisor, Lake Ranger District, P.O. Box 168, Yellowstone National Park, Wyoming 82190, 307-242-2402.

Finding the trailhead: Drive 5.2 miles south of Grant Village Junction and park at the Heart Lake Trailhead (8H1) on the east side of the road. This trail starts on the west shore of Heart Lake.

The hike: The hike up to the lookout on 10,308-foot Mount Sheridan is one of the (if not, the) most scenic mountain top hikes in the park. It definitely rivals the climbs up Mount Washburn and Mount Holmes for scenery. It might seem better, though, because it takes more effort to get here. When you add the Heart Lake Trail, your hike covers 11 miles one-way from the South Entrance Road to the summit.

Taking a deserved break on the top of Mount Sheridan.

The trail starts out through some large meadows before going into burned lodgepole pines and a series of large switchbacks. The switchbacks soon give way to a steeper, winding trail up the north ridge of the mountain. This is the steepest part of the climb. At the 2-mile mark, the trail breaks out above the treeline and the slope gets slightly more gradual as the trail loops around to the west side of the mountain. But more gradual does not imply gradual. This is a tough Category I climb all the way, covering 2,700 feet in only 3 miles.

Be sure to bring water because there is none on the mountain (unless you go early enough to catch a few snowbanks before they disappear). A good time to try this hike is after mid-July, to avoid running into too many snowbanks.

Plan on spending an hour or so on the summit to identify all the mountains and lakes you can see. Take a good look at the Grand Teton to the south and the seldom-seen Delusion Lake to the north. Even from up here, Heart Lake looks big.

30 Heart Lake Loop

See map on pages 99 and 101

General description: A moderate loop backpacking trip around Heart Lake, one of the largest mountain lakes along the Continental Divide.

Difficulty: Moderate.

Distance: 33.9 miles.

Traffic: Moderate with the heaviest use on the west shore of Heart Lake.

Elevation gain: Minimal.

Maps: Trails Illustrated Yellowstone Lake and Mount Sheridan and Heart Lake USGS quads.

For more information: Backcountry Supervisor, Lake Ranger District, P.O. Box 168, Yellowstone National Park, Wyoming 82190, 307-242-2402.

Finding the trailhead: Drive 5.2 miles south of Grant Village Junction and park at the Heart Lake Trailhead (8H1) on the east side of the road.

Key points:
5.0   Viewpoint down Witch Creek to Heart Lake.
7.8   Heart Lake Patrol Cabin.
8.0   Trail Creek Trail Junction.
8.2   Rustic Geyser.
8.3   Trail to 8H6. ★★★★
8.7   Trail to 8H5 ★★★★ and spur trail to Mount Sheridan.
9.0   Trail to 8H4. ★★★★

Heart Lake with Mount Sheridan as a scenic backdrop.

9.5	Spur trails to 8H3 ★★★★ and 8H2. ★★★★
10.5	8H1. ★★
11.5	Sheridan Lake.
13.0	8B1. ★★★★
13.5	Basin Creek Trail Junction.
15.6	8B5. ★★★
16.0	Junction with Snake River Trail.
16.9	Ford the Snake River.
18.2	Ford the Snake River.
18.3	8C5. ★★★★
18.4	Junction with Heart River Trail.
19.0	Ford the Heart River.
21.5	Ford the Heart River and Outlet Creek.
21.7	Junction with Trail Creek Trail and 8J4 (3Y)
22.0	8J6. ★★★★
24.2	8J1. ★★★★★
25.7	Junction with Heart Lake Trail.
25.9	Heart Lake Patrol Cabin.
33.9	Heart Lake Trailhead.

The hike: I recommend a five-day trip with two nights on the west shore of Heart Lake (using the extra day to climb Mount Sheridan), the third night at 8B2, 8B5 or 8C5, and the last night at 8J4, 8J6 or 8J1. This is a superb, moderately difficult backpacking trip especially suited for anglers—and one of the few backpacking trips in Yellowstone for which an annoying vehicle shuttle is not required.

The first section (8 miles) is a pleasant, mostly level walk into Heart Lake, as described in the Heart Lake hike.

If you have taken the counterclockwise route for the loop around the lake, turn right (south) at the junction just past the patrol cabin and stay at one of the six campsites on the west side of the lake. If you plan on hiking up to the summit of Mount Sheridan (and you will be sorry if you do not), reserve the campsite for two nights.

The hike along the west side of the lake climbs slightly away from the lakeshore after 8H6 and then drops back to the shoreline before 8H1. You climb a little hill when leaving the lake before dropping into Sheridan Lake, a small, marsh-lined lake off to your right (west). In the spring, the trail gets boggy in spots near the lake.

The trail continues through mostly open terrain and meadows along Basin Creek. At the junction with the Basin Creek Trail, go left (southeast) and continue following Basin Creek through mostly burned timber until you see the Snake River and the junction with the Heart River Trail. The trail through this section is well-defined with frequent stream crossings.

Here, turn left (northeast) and hike along the Snake River through a big meadow for about a mile until you reach the ford. The trail is a little rocky, but in fair shape. Early in the year, the ford might be hazardous, but after mid-July, it is only knee deep.

Fording the Snake River.

After fording the Snake, the trail angles away from the river into a heavily burned area until you reach the junction with the trail going south to the headwaters of the Snake. You ford the Snake River again just before the junction, now an even smaller stream because the Heart River has not joined yet. Turn left (north) and head toward Heart Lake on the Heart River Trail.

This section of trail is in good shape as it closely follows the Heart River and passes through lightly burned forest most of the way to Heart Lake. About halfway to the lake you ford this river once and then again (along with Outlet Creek) just before reaching Heart Lake. All of these fords are easier than the Snake River ford.

When you reach the Trail Creek Trail, go left (west), and finish your circle of Heart Lake back to the junction at the patrol cabin. The trail is in great shape through this section, but it stays in the timber much of the way and offers only rare glimpses of the lake. From here, retrace your steps to the Heart Lake Trailhead.

Options: You can take the loop in either direction with no increased difficulty.

Side trips: The Mount Sheridan hike is almost a must-do side trip, but you can also take short hikes to Basin Creek Lake and Outlet Lake.

31 Heart Lake and Two Ocean Plateau

See map on pages 99 and 101

General description:	A long, strenuous loop backpacking trip through the most remote corner of Yellowstone National Park.
Difficulty:	Difficult.
Distance:	62.3 miles.
Traffic:	Light with the exception of the area around Heart Lake.
Elevation gain:	1,498 feet.
Maps:	Trails Illustrated Yellowstone Lake and Mount Sheridan, Heart Lake, Mount Hancock, Snake Hot Springs, Alder Lake, Trail Lake, Crooked Creek, and Badger Creek USGS quads.
For more information:	Backcountry Supervisor, Lake Ranger District, P.O. Box 168, Yellowstone National Park, Wyoming 82190, 307-242-2402.

Finding the trailhead: Drive 5.2 miles south of Grant Village Junction and park in the trailhead parking area on the east side of the road at the Heart Lake Trailhead (8N1).

Key points:

5.0	Viewpoint down Witch Creek to Heart Lake.
7.8	Heart Lake Patrol Cabin.
8.0	Trail Creek Trail Junction.
9.5	8J1. ★★★★★
11.7	8J6. ★★★★
12.0	8J4 ★★★ and junction with the Heart River Trail.
12.3	8J3. ★★★
15.0	8O2 and Outlet Lake.
17.8	7G1. ★★★★
18.2	7G2.
18.4	Bushwhack to 7N4 and 7N2.
20.9	5L2. ★★★
21.3	Junction with Two Ocean Plateau Trail.
22.7	Junction with cutoff trail to Trail Creek Trail.
28.0	6M5. ★★★
32.3	6M4 ★★★, junction with South Boundary/Mariposa Lake Trail.
35.8	6M7 ★★★ and the Fox Creek Patrol Cabin.
36.0	Trail going south out of park.
36.4	Ford the Snake River.
36.5	Junction with Snake River Trail.
38.5	8C9. ★★★
47.0	Junction with Heart River Trail to 8C5 (4Y).
50.3	8J4 ★★★ and junction with the Trail Creek Trail.

50.6	8J6. ★★★
52.8	8J1. ★★★★★
54.3	Junction with Heart Lake Trail.
54.5	Heart Lake Patrol Cabin.
62.3	Heart Lake Trailhead.

The hike: This trip goes through some of the most remote and infrequently visited parts of Yellowstone—i.e. for prepared and self-reliant hikers only. To make it more difficult, the campsites are farther apart which means 3 to 5 miles more per day. Also, because of high water at the fords and heavy bear use, most campsites do not open until July.

The distance between campsites makes this loop trip most suitable for serious hikers who can cover up to 12–14 miles in a day. I recommend a six-day trip with preferred (and alternate) campsites as follows:

First night–8J1 (8J6, 8J4); Second night–5L2 (7G1, 7G2, 7N4, 7N2); Third night–6M2 (6M5, 6M4); Fourth night–8C9 (6M7); Fifth night–8C5 (8J4, 8J6).

Refer to the Heart Lake and Heart Lake Loop hikes for more details, but the first leg of the trip to Heart Lake is an easy hike on a great trail with a nice view of Heart Lake, Factory Hill, and the thermal features of Witch Creek along the last 3 miles. The junction with the Trail Creek Trail is right on the shoreline of Heart Lake just past the patrol cabin (where you can usually find a ranger in July and August).

If you have chosen the clockwise route (as described here), take a left at this junction and circle around the north side of the lake where you prob-

On the Continental Divide east of Mariposa Lake on the Two Ocean Plateau.

ably want to spend your first night out. This section of trail offers a terrific view of the lake with massive Mount Sheridan as the backdrop. (If you started early enough and have time for a hike up Mount Sheridan, hang your packs near this junction and enjoy this ultra-scenic side trip.)

On the east side of Heart Lake, turn left (east) at the junction with the Heart River Trail going south (from whence you will return four days later). From here to South Arm, the trail goes through mostly burned forest. Trail conditions worsen from the heavily used trail around Heart Lake, especially one seriously boggy section about a mile after leaving the lake. You follow Outlet Creek, gradually climbing up to Outlet Lake just before crossing the Continental Divide on Chicken Ridge (most likely named for the high grouse population in the area). Outlet Lake is a beautiful jewel in the forest with open shoreline, but no fish.

After leaving Outlet Lake, a short hill goes up to a gentle pass over the Continental Divide (only about 7,900 feet here) where the forest opens up into a huge meadow. From the Divide to the South Arm, the trail is not well marked and gets faint in places, especially near Grouse Creek. The trail generally follows the creek and crosses it near 7G1. Around the South Arm, the trail improves.

Two Ocean Plateau near the Continental Divide.

Along the Continental Divide between Southeast Arm and Mariposa Lake.

At the junction with the Two Ocean Plateau Trail, go right (south). About a mile later, take another right (south) at the cutoff trail to the Southeast Arm. From here, the trail follows the Chipmunk Creek bottomlands for about a mile before going over a small divide into Passage Creek. Then, it climbs more steeply up to the Continental Divide. Crossing the Divide here takes much more work than the crossing back on Chicken Ridge. The last 0.5 mile is a Category II climb.

The trail from the Divide down toward the South Boundary Trail goes through open terrain with outstanding scenery of the Two Ocean Plateau country. The trail gets inconspicuous in several places on both sides of the Divide, so watch carefully for trail markers—which you might not be able to see because of the clouds of particularly nasty mosquitoes.

The section of trail from South Arm to the South Boundary Trail is a long day, so you might not have the energy to take the side trip up to Mariposa Lake, which is only a mile but steep. If you stay at 6M4, you can hike it after dinner or early the next morning.

From this junction, the trail follows Plateau Creek through unburned timber past the Harebell Patrol Cabin to the headwaters of the Snake River. Some maps may indicate that the junction is on the east side of the river, but it is actually on the west side. At this junction, go right (northwest) and hike through the meadows lining the river. Be extra alert not to get diverted onto one of the many game trails in this area. Lots of elk go through here, and in many cases, their trails are better than the official trail. Mud slides have also taken out a few sections of trail. You ford the Snake just past 8C9, which can be an easy crossing after mid-July.

At the junction with the Heart River Trail, go right (north) unless you plan to stay at 8C5 or take the long route back to Heart Lake. You face two easy fords the Heart River before reaching the Trail Creek Trail. From this junction, retrace your steps back to the trailhead.

Options: The loop can be done in reverse with no extra work. You can extend the trip and make a larger loop by going west on the Heart Lake Trail to the Basin Creek Trail and then north along the west side of Heart Lake to hook up with the Trail Creek Trail at the Heart Lake Patrol Cabin. This avoids retracing your steps around the north side of Heart Lake, but it adds 6.5 miles to your trip.

Side trips: If you get an early start on the first or last day of your trip (or for some reason want more exercise), take the 8-mile (round trip) climb up to the summit of Mount Sheridan. Even if you choose not to camp at Mariposa Lake (6M2), you would be rewarded by hanging your pack and taking the 2-mile (round trip) side trip to this scenic, high-altitude lake.

THE CONTINENTAL DIVIDE THROUGH THE WIND RIVER RANGE

In 1964, the year of passage of the National Wilderness Act, congress designated the Bridger Wilderness. The area is roadless and unspoiled; a 99-mile length nestles against a portion of the Continental Divide whose sheer ruggedness truly exemplifies the term "backbone of the nation." Approximately 500 miles of intersecting trails leave little of this wilderness inaccessible to hikers, yet cross-country treks to isolated peaks, neighboring creek drainages, and untrailed lakes are easily possible. Please tread lightly across the high-altitude environments if you leave the trail. More than 1,300 lakes (2,300 if you count nameless little lakes and ponds) dot the wilderness landscape.

The Pinedale Ranger District has implemented some wilderness-wide rules for the Bridger Wilderness Area. There are no campfires allowed above timberline and no usage of any "standing tree," meaning dead, or alive, or alive with dead branches, for firewood. In other words, only downed wood can be used for fires. Groups are limited to 15 people, permits are required for organized groups, and camping is prohibited in a location visible from any lake or trail unless that location is more than 200 feet from that lake or trail. There is also a 16-day stay limit in the wilderness. Follow these rules throughout the Teton, Fitzpatrick, and Bridger Wilderness Areas.

The absolute best trail and topo map of the Wind River Range is published by Earthwalk Press, 2239 Union Street, Eureka, California 95501. They carry a northern and a southern Wind River Range Hiking Map and Guide Series, each one condensing 15 or more 7.5 minute USGS quadrangles into a single 1:48,000 overview map. Topography is not lost while large overviews of the country are gained. Trails are highlighted, so trip planning is made easier. These maps are available at all sporting goods stores in towns around the range. Again, Falcon Publishing's *Hiking Wyoming's Wind River Range* is also well mapped.

32 Jade Lakes

General description:	A short and easy hike to two exceptionally pretty high-country lakes, located 26 miles northwest of Dubois in the northwestern corner of the Shoshone National Forest. The lakes feature towering stratified cliffs and fair fishing. Expect fees at Brooks Lake Campground and a trailhead register.
Distance:	2.5 miles.
Difficulty:	Easy.
Traffic:	Moderate.
Elevation gain:	370 feet.
Maps:	Shoshone National Forest north half map, or USGS Togwotee Pass and Dundee Meadows quads.
For more information:	Wind River Ranger District, Masonic Building, 1403 West Ramshorn, P.O. Box 186, Dubois, Wyoming 82513, 307-455-2466.

Finding the trailhead: Approximately 27 miles west of Dubois on U.S. Highways 287 and 26, or 7.8 miles east of the Togwotee (To-GWUH-tee) Pass crest, the well-signed Brooks Lake road jogs north. This graveled main road is easy to follow for the 5.2 miles to the Brooks Lake Campground. Just before the Brooks Lake Lodge, turn north at the campground sign, but not into the camping area. Stay west and drive the short distance to the signed trailhead near the southern shores of Brooks Lake.

The hike: US 287 west of Dubois climbs into an enticing section of southern Absaroka high country. As you drive the road, you'll notice that these somewhat wild and unusual stratified layers of volcanic cliff keep bobbing into greater and greater view. Upper and Lower Jade Lakes offer an easy 2.5 mile (one way) hike that places you both directly under the desired cliffs and beside emerald lakes that reflect the majesty of the surrounding country. Jade is the official stone of the state of Wyoming.

The first 0.5 mile follows the Brooks Lake/Cub Pass trail. Here, a sign points northwestward to Jade Lakes, and you can see five or more eroded, parallel trails cutting up a hillside. Follow one of these trails up the steep slopes for 0.5 mile. Then the walk mellows out for the final 1.5 miles as the trail—now coalesced to a single path—wanders through a gentle and more open forest.

The tiny, stagnant pond at 1.5 miles, although green in color, is not one of the Jade Lakes. Continue along the trail for another 0.5 mile and descend into a depression holding the beautiful, greenish, deep waters of Upper Jade Lake. Here, those layered grayish blue, brownish and white cliffs tower over and reflect off the waters of the lake. Excellent camping is found near the southwestern shore of the lake and at its northern shore by the creek outlet.

Lower Jade Lake lies a steep downhill 0.5 mile farther along the trail. It forms the big cousin of Upper Jade, but does not carry the reflection or offer many camping opportunities. Both lakes receive excellent fishing reports.

At the extreme northwest corner of the lower lake, a horse/hunting trail cuts to the north. It appears to be an ancient Forest Service trail that they are trying to forget, and my advice is to help the Forest Service along and stay off it. When last I ventured on it, I lost the path, along with my sense of direction, within several miles. Twelve hours later, I staggered back to Brooks

Absaroka beauty at Upper Jade Lake.

Jade Lakes

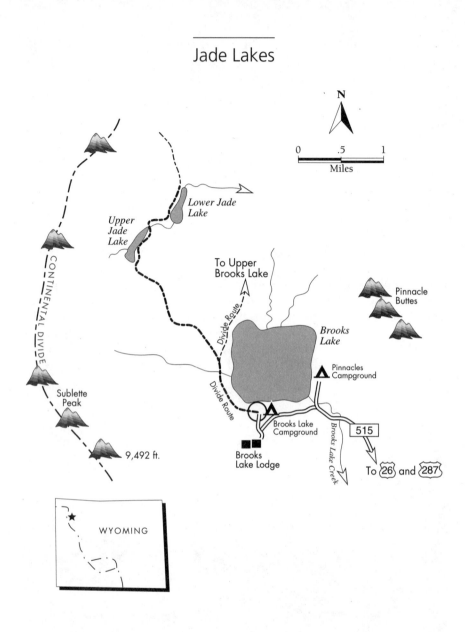

Lake, having somehow traversed the untrailed Clear Creek Drainage of the Teton Wilderness, an entirely different forest and drainage away. It was a most humbling lesson on how even an experienced hiker can easily get confused and turn a simple hike into a lost-and-found situation.

33 Lake Louise

General description:	A shorter day hike to pretty and serene, cliff-encompassed Lake Louise (8,600 feet). Overnight camping is an enjoyable option. The lake offers excellent fishing in a deep lake. A hot fire charred the valley above this lake in 1976, and the natural forest regeneration is interesting to witness. The hike is located approximately 14 miles southeast of Dubois, in the northeast section of the Wind River Range.
Distance:	3 miles, one way.
Difficulty:	Moderate.
Traffic:	Moderate.
Elevation gain:	1,000 feet.
Maps:	Shoshone National Forest south half visitors map, Torrey Lake, Simpson Lake USGS quads. Also, Earthwalk Press's Northern Wind River Range.
For more information:	Wind River Ranger District, 1403 West Ramshorn, P.O. Box 186, Dubois, Wyoming 82513, 307-455-2466.

Finding the trailhead: The sign is not very big, 3.8 miles east of downtown Dubois along U.S. Highway 287/26, so watch carefully for it on the southern side of the road. It notes a Wyoming Game and Fish Department fish hatchery location. As you turn off the highway to the south, the road immediately forks, the right or west fork journeying to the fish hatchery and the left or southeast branch following another small sign that points to a conservation camp. Follow this second route toward the camp, and enjoy the ensuing 2.5 miles of washboard gravel road. At the Wyoming Game and Fish Department sheep range sign, the road again forks. The conservation camp sign you want to follow points eastward, and the next 3.5 miles of driving becomes the worst road in America that a two-wheel-drive rig can still negotiate. The private property owners have not graded this rock garden of a road since its birth, and it will truly test your driving and your patience.

At the conservation camp, almost 6 miles after leaving the highway, the road forks again. Go right or northwest, following the Glacier Trail sign. Another 2 miles places you in a huge Fitzpatrick Wilderness Trailhead parking area. The Glacier Trail, the Whiskey Mountain Trail, and the Lake Louise Trail begin as one path at the western end of this lot.

The hike: This little hike often serves as a primer to the long Glacier Trail hike (Hike 34). It allows folks to test their boots or firm their muscles a bit before undertaking a rather colossal mountain trail. But Lake Louise also offers a great introduction to and an escape into the rocky northern-most corner of the Wind Rivers.

Lake Louise

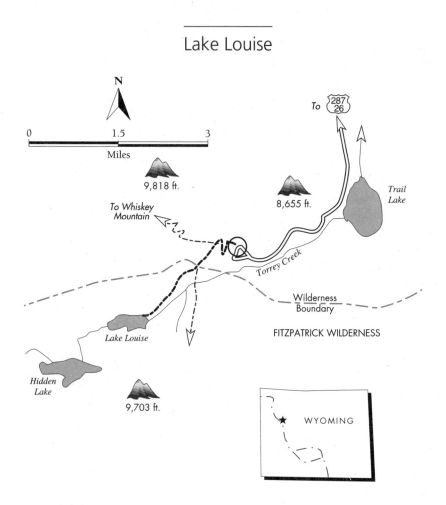

Short does not necessarily mean easy. The first 0.4 mile of trail switchbacks steeply uphill. Here the Whiskey Mountain Trail branches to the northwest. Continue along the Glacier Trail for another 0.2 mile and a sign will direct you westward toward Lake Louise.

The next 2 miles of trail are easy to follow but somewhat breathy to walk as the trail wanders into, over, and around these impressive waves of rosy-colored granite rock. It weaves into meadow and forest microenvironments located between the rock-wave troughs. In addition, it passes beside some incredible Torrey Creek cascades. The last several hundred yards leading to the lake is granite shelf walking.

The deep waters of Lake Louise are completely imprisoned by restricting granite cliffs. One can traverse the lake's distance by either crossing the log jam at the foot of the lake and circumventing the southern shores, or by picking a way around the northern cliffs of the lake. Both routes require some scrambling and a little climbing. The southern shore option contains some excellent campsites and is a bit easier.

Cliff-immured Lake Louise.

In 1976, a fire burned the forested area between Lake Louise and its upstream counterpart, Hidden Lake. Rejuvenation has been slow due to the sterile and rugged environment. However, a cross-country journey between the lakes and along Torrey Creek is possible, albeit exacting. For the dedicated angler, it may be worth the effort. Hidden Lake has been known to boil like a pot of tea during a hatch-induced feeding frenzy.

34 Glacier Trail

General description: A rugged, five to eight day (or longer) hike to the largest glacial area and highest peak in Wyoming, located approximately 15 miles southeast of Dubois, in the northeast section of the Wind River Range. The area offers the biggest glaciers, the highest peaks, the deepest, cliff-encased valleys, and the most beautiful blue-green glacier-milk creek weaving a channel through it all.

Distance: 28 miles, one way.
Difficulty: Strenuous.
Traffic: Very heavy.

Mountainous country west of Gannett Peak. Paul Donharl photo

Elevation gain:	5,145 feet.
Maps:	Shoshone National Forest southern half visitor's map, Torrey Lake, Inkwells, Fremont Peak North, Gannet Peak, Downs Mountain USGS quads. Earthwalk Press's Northern Wind River Range hiking map.
For more information:	Wind River Ranger District, 1403 West Ramshorn, Dubois, Wyoming 82513, 307-455-2466.

Finding the trailhead: Access via vehicle is exactly the same including the super rough road as the Lake Louise trailhead access (Hike 33). The trailhead is located at the west end of the parking lot.

The hike: The Fitzpatrick Wilderness, 198,838 acres of high-elevation, mountainous rock wonder, was designated in 1976 from what was originally named the Glacier Primitive Area. The area encompasses the northern portion of the Wind Rivers east of the divide. Tom Fitzpatrick was a contemporary of Jim Bridger, and naming agencies decided to place the wilderness appellations of the two trail blazes side-by-side.

The Glacier Trail forms a 28-mile (one way) adventure. Numerous additional side trails and cross-country explorations are possible in this region, and anyone hiking in for less than a week's time can expect to miss a great deal of adventure and scenery. This is a most popular and sometimes crowded

Glacier Trail

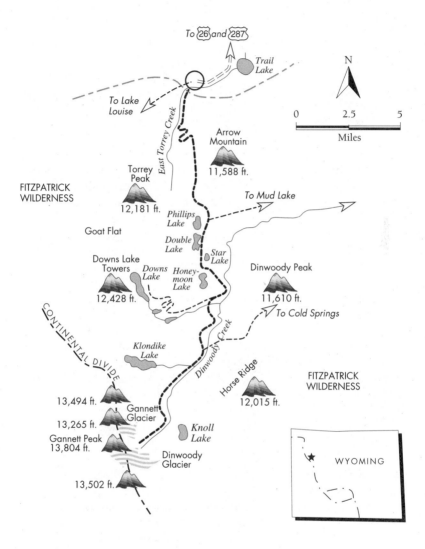

To ⟨26⟩ and ⟨287⟩

Trail Lake

N

0   2.5   5
Miles

To Lake Louise

East Torrey Creek

Arrow Mountain
11,588 ft.

Torrey Peak
12,181 ft.

FITZPATRICK WILDERNESS

Phillips Lake

To Mud Lake

Goat Flat

Double Lake

Star Lake

Dinwoody Peak
11,610 ft.

To Cold Springs

Downs Lake Towers

Downs Lake

Honey-moon Lake

12,428 ft.

Dinwoody Creek

Klondike Lake

Horse Ridge

FITZPATRICK WILDERNESS

CONTINENTAL DIVIDE

13,494 ft.

12,015 ft.

Gannett Glacier

13,265 ft.

Knoll Lake

Gannett Peak
13,804 ft.

Dinwoody Glacier

13,502 ft.

WYOMING

trail. Count on viewing many overused campsites and on encountering many other hikers as you travel. The land, though, still seems large enough to swallow all that enter it.

Older maps will show the trail beginning with a sinuous switchback up the southern sides of Arrow Mountain. In 1976, a massive rockslide wiped out a large section of that mountainside. You can still see the scar if you look south-southwest from the parking area. The next year the Forest Service built the current parking facilities and rerouted the trail up the eastern side of East Torrey Creek. This proves to be a less steep, less waterless, and less taxing beginning than the old trail. The original route tended to desiccate and annihilate first-time and out-of-shape hikers.

A lot of elevation gain accompanies the first 7 or 8 miles of the hike. From a 7,600-foot creek bottom beginning to a 10,895-foot pass above Burro Flat, new trail or not, it is a huffer-and-puffer. Hikers need to be aware that beyond those of Burro Flats, additional water and campsites lie another 4 miles, around the Phillips and Dinwoody Lakes area. Above Burro Flat, around what is called Williamson Corrals, water and tree shelter vanish. The open alpine is amazingly beautiful and quite exposed. Because it forms such a first-day respite after miles of hard hiking, this second camping area from Upper Phillips to and including Star Lake, really shows the scars of overuse. Livestock camping and campfires are now prohibited in this area.

From Double Lake southward, the trail begins a rugged descent into the Dinwoody Creek drainage. Downs Fork Meadows serves as the introduction to the exceptionally colored, milky-green creek that will be a companion much of the rest of the journey. Camping is a wherever, whenever choice from now on as long as you are 100 feet from trails and streams. At Big Meadows, a few miles beyond the Downs Fork Trail intersection, the huge granite monoliths and castles begin to encase the milky-creeked valley. After you pass the Ink Wells Trail intersection, close to 20 miles into the hike, the forests part and the high peaks of Gannett (13,804 feet) and Woodrow Wilson (13,503 feet) begin to rule the western skyline. It all gets bigger and better, more open and more deeply encased, the farther you hike. Although you are continually loomed over, towered above, and tucked in a yawning valley, you still tend to feel you are on top of the world.

The Glacier Trail is well signed and maintained its entire distance. Some of the side hikes—Inkwells, Downs Fork, and Klondike Lake—may not be, although the old Downs Fork Bridge was finally replaced in 1996. Good topographic maps are necessary on this trip.

Beyond Floyd Wilson Meadows, which contains the last stands of diminishing trees, the trail continues climbing a few miles along the northern banks of a southern branch of Dinwoody Creek. Then it ends as Dinwoody Glacier moraine becomes too unpredictable to build on. One can continue over Dinwoody Glacier to what is labeled Glacier Pass and drop into the Titcomb Lakes Basin in the Bridger Wilderness. This trek is close to a fourth-class scramble over the most rugged of rocky country and may require an ice axe to safely climb the huge glacier. Ascending Gannett Peak is also an option, but there are a few technical spots, and it tends to transcend the scope of a hiker's guide.

35 Green River Lakes to Summit Lake

General description:	A multi-day, adventurous backpacking trip into the rocky headwaters of the Green River, located approximately 50 miles north of Pinedale, in the northern section of the Bridger Wilderness. The area offers breath-taking country that promotional bureaus photograph for their "Visit Wild Wyoming" brochures and wild vistas of the Gannett Peak area. Expect fees at Green River Lakes Campground of $8 to $10 per night.
Distance:	16 miles, one way.
Difficulty:	Strenuous.
Traffic:	Moderate to heavy.
Elevation gain:	2,230 feet.
Maps:	Bridger–Teton National Forest Pinedale Ranger District visitor map; Green River Lakes, Squaretop Mountain, Gannett Peak USGS quads; Earthwalk Press's Northern Wind River Range Hiking and Guide.
For more information:	Pinedale Ranger District, 29 Fremont Lake Road, Pinedale, Wyoming, 82941, 307-367-4326.

Alpine splendor at Alpine Lakes. PAUL DONHARL PHOTO

121

Finding the trailhead: From Pinedale, drive six miles west on U.S. Highway 191 to a Bridger Wilderness Green River Access sign. This is also Wyoming Highway 352, and it wanders northward for 26.4 miles before the pavement ends and the road transforms into graveled Forest Road 091. Another long 20 miles of this road brings you to the Green River Lakes Campground. Just before driving into the fee campground area, a large sign directs hikers to a wilderness parking area.

The hike: So many hiking options exist here, so much outstanding and spectacular beauty abound that a week will barely allow you to see and feel the country. Take at least five days, but ten days is better. This is not country you want to rush through. The Green River Valley offers awesome views and settings. Let Summit Lake be a basecamp from which to expand into the surrounding peaks, glaciers, and alpine lakes, but not a final goal.

You can begin this trail by journeying around Lower Green River Lake via either the southwestern or the northeastern shores. The bridge over Clear Creek has been replaced more than once, so check with the Pinedale Ranger District before assuming it is there. The Lakeside Trail is indicated at the hiker's parking lot.

The first 2.5 miles of this level Lakeside Trail skirt the shore of the lake, but the forest hides the surrounding views. After you walk across the meadow at the head of Lower Green River Lake, cross the quite large bridge spanning the Green River, and hike a total of 3 miles to Upper Green River Lake. Here the limitless panoramas begin, and they never end. This area is actually one of the most photographed scenes in Wyoming. Towering Squaretop Mountain creates a magnificent backdrop to this scenic lake. For 2.5 miles beyond the upper lake, large and open meadows rule the valley bottom. Squaretop Mountain grows from a distant centerpiece to a looming overhead projection.

After 6 miles of level hiking, the meadow ends and the trail becomes typical Wind River valley hiking. Thick forests and rocky trails sneak beneath the shear and towering granite faces of surrounding cliffs. You must cross the river back to the west side at 9.8 miles. This may be quite a crossing. The Forest Service has removed the wired-together, bobbing-log bridge over the swift waters, and plans to build a more permanent structure in 1998. NOTE: This will be the sixth replacement of the bridge in this area. With increasing numbers of wet years happening, they cannot guarantee a bridge will be there when you hike this country. If the bridge is out, one option is to backtrack about 0.3 mile down trail and wade the river at a stock crossing trail. Use common sense here, and do not take a chance if the waters seem too deep.

You'll reach Three Forks Park 1.5 miles after the river crossing—a glorious breath of meadow country that affords no camping opportunities. Be advised that with the 200-foot camping restriction regulation, it can be hard to find suitable camping locations in the first 12 miles of this trail. Up to Three Forks Park, the 11 miles of the trail has been mostly level. Beyond

Green River Lakes to Summit Lake

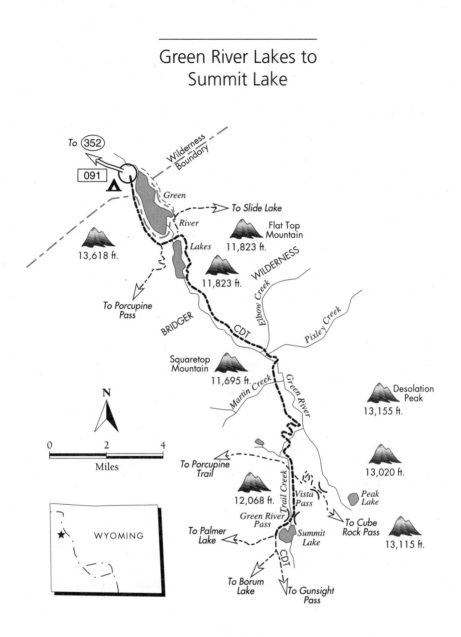

Three Forks, it begins a steep switchbacking climb for 2 miles. Here you encounter Trail Creek, a too-wide-to-jump gush of crystalline water. No bridge guarantees on this one either.

About a mile beyond the Trail Creek crossing, a signed intersection offers a route westward to the Porcupine Trail. You have hiked over 13 miles to this point, and the high, jagged, and spectacular country is just beginning. There are now numerous options and decisions to consider. Great camping exists in this Trail Creek Park area. In fact, so many people camp here you might consider cutting way off the trail to set up a base camp from which to explore. To the south, the 3-mile hike to Green River Pass and Summit Lake is mostly above timberline. At the lake the land is wide, flat, open and above it all. Along the way, a wild trail jogs westward to Vista, Cube Rock, and Shannon Passes. Every step of this trail places you in the western shadows of the highest Wind River Peaks. In tune with the mode of the country, there can be no guarantee that this trail exists during any given year. The area is highly prone to slides and avalanches, and as often as the Forest Service rebuilds it, the trail is annihilated.

Be sure and carry a good map for an overview of all the hiking options in this grandest of mountain high country.

36 Alpine Lakes

General description:	A six to ten day, very rugged trek for experienced hikers into the heart of the Wind River high country, located about 25 miles northeast of Pinedale, in the central part of the Wind River Range. The area offers alpine peaks, cross-country glacier walks, and seldom-visited terrain. Expect fees at Trails End Campground of $8 to $10 per night.
Distance:	45 miles for the loop.
Difficulty:	Difficult.
Traffic:	Heavy near trailhead, lighter as you get further in.
Elevation gain:	4,050 feet.
Maps:	Bridger–Teton National Forest Pinedale Ranger District and Shoshone National Forest south half visitors maps; Fremont Peak South, Bridger Lakes, Horseshoe Lakes USGS quads.
For more information:	Pinedale Ranger District, 29 East Fremont Lake Road, Pinedale, Wyoming 82941, 307-367-4326, and Wahsakie Ranger District, 333 East Main Street Lander, Wyoming 82520-3499, 307-332-5460.

Finding the trailhead: The trailhead starts at Elkhart Park, 14 miles northeast of Pinedale. Take Sublette County Road 134 (prominently signed for Fremont and Half Moon Lakes) east out of Pinedale. The paved road dead-ends at the Trails End Campground. The trailhead is located at the northeast corner of the parking lot, between the campground and the ranger's station.

The hike: Little Sandy Lake and Sweetwater Gap receive little use. Now look at an awesome area starting at the highest usage trailhead in the Bridger Wilderness. The parking lot itself is designed to accommodate 120 cars.

This is a rugged 45-mile loop into the central section of the Wind River Range. It crosses the Continental Divide twice and follows a high glacial valley. It is best to give yourself a minimum of 6 days of travel due to the nature of the terrain and the unpredictability of the weather.

Begin on the Pole Creek Trail, which heads east through the woods following Faler Creek for 1 mile. It then turns northeast and reaches Miller Park after 4 miles. Here a trail to Miller Lake cuts off to the right. Pole Creek Trail re-enters the woods for about a mile and comes out on Photographers Point, which affords spectacular views of Gorge Lake and the Continental Divide to the east.

Another meadow appears in 0.5 mile where the Sweeney Lake Trail cuts to the right. The main trail rounds a knob and drops down to Eklund Lake. At the north end of the lake, Pole Creek Trail turns right and heads east. The Seneca Lake Trail, your new route, turns left and drops down around the west side of Barbara Lake. This trail then descends several switchbacks and climbs back up to Hobbs Lake.

About one-half mile beyond Hobbs Lake, the trail crosses Seneca Creek, which must be forded farther upstream during high water in the early part of the season. The trail passes several small lakes in the next mile and drops into a small basin before climbing up to Seneca Lake. You're now about 8 miles from Elkhart Park. Fremont and Jackson Peaks dominate the eastern skyline. With the 200-foot camping limitation, there are very few campsites in this area.

From here, the Seneca Lake Trail continues along the shoreline of the western side of the lake. High water early in the season may force a higher route by scrambling over the rocks above the shore. At the north end of the lake the Lost Lake Trail heads left and the Seneca Lake Trail continues to Little Seneca Lake, beyond which it ascends to meet the Highline Trail.

The Highline Trail runs north and south at about timberline for the entire length of the Wind River Range. Follow this trail north up a series of switchbacks to a saddle where the Highline Trail continues north and the Indian Pass Trail, your new route, turns east toward Island Lake.

You'll reach Island Lake in about 1.5 miles. This is a most popular area, with many campsites on the southeastern shore. The Indian Pass Trail skirts the southern shore and then starts a gradual climb for 0.75 mile to the cutoff for Titcomb Basin. Titcomb Basin is always over-crowded, with up to 75 camps at a time (way beyond the original wilderness management plan). Indian Pass Trail turns right here, and it is just over 3 miles to the pass (the sign says 6).

Indian Pass Trail climbs about 200 feet in the first mile to Indian Basin. Here there are suitable campsites around the several lakes in the basin. However, the weather is very unpredictable at this elevation, with frequent afternoon showers, lightning, hail and possibly snow. The trail climbs over 1,000 feet in the next two miles, passing under the bases of Fremont (13,745 feet) and Jackson (13,517 feet) peaks. At Indian Pass, 12,100 feet, the trail ends.

Alpine Lakes

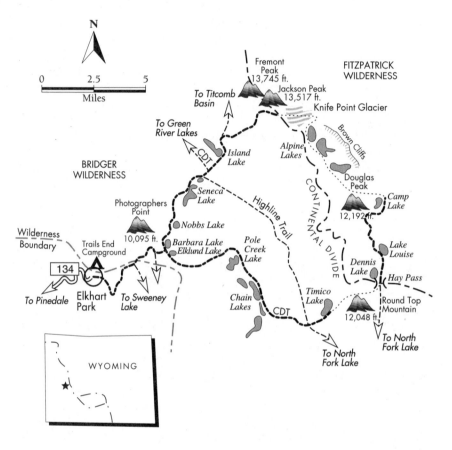

Beyond Indian Pass, cross-country and wilderness adventure begins. Knowledge of cross-country and glacier travel with appropriate equipment is a prerequisite for this part of the journey. Descend east onto Knife Point Glacier. An ice axe is necessary, and crampons are highly recommended. Journey east past the large rock knobs and then turn southeast toward a looming 12,860-foot unnamed peak. After a mile of glacier crossing, begin a steep ascent to a saddle, which lies at 12,120 feet. Maps label this Alpine Pass.

From the top of this saddle, it is a steep descent to the highest of the three Alpine Lakes. There is a good area for a campsite at the north end of this lake. The Brown Cliffs rise almost 1,500 vertical feet on the east, as does the Continental Divide on the west.

From the north end of the lake, climb up the western wall to just below the snout of an ice field and stay high above the lake for the next two miles. Be prepared to scramble over some "Volkswagen" sized boulders on the way.

At the north end of the lowest Alpine Lake, some maps show a suggested route, which follows the eastern shore. This will result in a 100-foot walk through the lake and in chest-deep water. An alternative is to follow the western shore for about 0.75 mile to the drainage from a lake at the base of Douglas Peak. Go to the lake and turn east, climb about 100 feet to a small saddle, and descend, following the drainage to the three small and unnamed lakes just above Camp Lake.

A real trail appears on the eastern shore of Camp Lake. Follow this trail south and begin a 600-foot climb to two small but deep lakes at the southern base of Douglas Peak. Cross the saddle and descend into the Middle Fork of the Bull Lake Creek drainage, which contains Upper Golden, Louise, and Golden Lakes respectively. The trail follows the northern shores of these lakes and begins a 700-foot climb to Hay Pass.

At Hay Pass, 10,960 feet, the trail drops into the North Fork of Boulder Creek and eventually meets the cutoff to the Timico Lake Trail. A many-mile-saving alternative to this route is to bushwhack around the northern slopes of Round Top Mountain from Hay Pass. Head southwest from the lake west of Hay Pass to the meadows at 11,000 feet and follow this elevation around to the saddle where you rejoin the trail to Timico Lake. Keep and eye out for bighorn sheep. At Timico Lake, there are several good campsites, both at the northern end and away from the eastern shores.

The trail crosses the Fremont Trail about a mile west of Timico Lake. At the signpost, head almost due west on the Bell Lakes Trail which drops down to Chain Lakes in 3 miles. At Chain Lakes the trail junctions with the Highline Trail. Follow the Highline Trail north about 2 miles to the lower ford of Pole Creek. About 0.25 mile past this ford, the Pole Creek Trail is reached. Eklund Lake lies about 3.5 miles west on this trail, which passes several small lakes, including Mary's Lake. Mary's Lake boasts but a few campsites, but the meadows and ponds east of it supply great camping. Once at Eklund Lake, Elkhart Park is but six more miles west.

—*Paul Donharl*

37 Middle Fork Popo Agie River/ Tayo Park Loop Trail

General description:	A rugged, five-day or longer backpacking trip into high country lakes surrounded by majestic peaks. The hike begins approximately 12 miles southwest of Lander and offers astonishing vistas of panoramic peaks and alpine lake settings. Rumors indicate Deep Creek Lakes may contain Golden Trout.
Distance:	45 miles, round trip.
Difficulty:	Strenuous.
Traffic:	Heavy.
Elevation gain:	3,500 feet.
Maps:	Shoshone National Forest south half visitors map. Fossil Hill, Cony Mountain, Sweetwater Gap USGS quads. In addition, Earthwalk Press has an excellent overview topography and trail map of the Southern Wind Rivers available at local sporting goods and outfitting stores.
For more information:	Washakie Ranger District, 333 East Main, Lander, Wyoming 82520, 307-332-5460.

Finding the trailhead: Wyoming Highway 131 (the Sinks Canyon State Park Road) leaves Lander at Fifth Street, and the entire 11 miles west to the trailhead is paved. Just past the Bruce Picnic Area, the road turns south and crosses the Middle Fork of the Popo Agie River. South of and across the bridge is a several acre parking lot geared to accommodate the many hikers, packers, and horse packers that now use the trail.

The hike: 1971 marked the first time I traveled this major access trail into the then Popo Agie Primitive Area. Then, a grimy little dirt road out of Lander led to an unmarked and obscure trailhead. A few horsepackers and a survival school named NOLS were practically the only users of the wilderness. For five weeks, we traveled these mountains, meeting almost no people and experiencing wild beauty beyond comprehension. Gone are the days. This is now a bustling trailhead.

The Middle Fork trail not only serves as a gracious introduction to the Wind Rivers, but it forms the major access route into the entire Popo Agie Wilderness. A map posted on the trailhead sign shows a system of 28 different trails, with this one trailhead as the gateway to all. Bear in mind that the hike to Popo Agie Falls, the first mile of the trail, is the goal of over half the people using the trail.

The steep and rocky beginning, in 1 mile, takes you 600 feet higher to where a short side trail journeys off for a view of the impressive Popo Agie

Middle Fork Popo Agie River/ Tayo Park Loop Trail

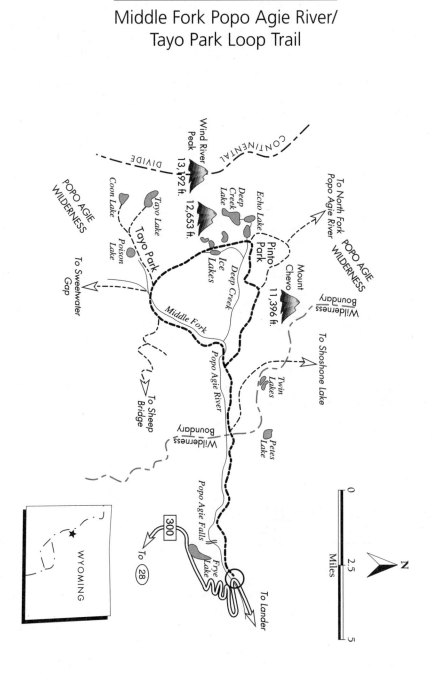

Falls. Periodic decisions need to be made, if you haven't pre-planned your trip, on which side trails to take. I present this hike as a journey up the Middle Fork to Three Forks Park, a jog along the Pinto Park Trail, a slice over to the Deep Creek and Ice Creek Lakes, a journey into Tayo Park, and a loop back down the Popo Agie Middle Fork, again to Three Forks Park and out the main trail. Nevertheless, this itinerary forms a basic introduction, and many other possibilities present themselves along the route.

The wilderness boundary begins about 6 miles after the trailhead. This wilderness has a "no camping within 200 feet of trail, lakes and streams" rule, and between that and the extremely rugged, rocky, and timbered countryside, it is another 4 miles to good camping at Three Forks Park. The trail is well signed from here to Pinto Park. Four more miles and the Deep Creek Cutoff Trail jogs south, and the rewards for your long hiking efforts begin. The Deep Creek Lakes, the Ice Lakes and upper Tayo Park are set in almost dreamlike high alpine meadows that lie beneath the base of giant peaks and shear granite cliffs.

Wind River Peak, at 13,192 feet, offers a challenging cross-country peak climb without any technical gear required. Its gentle ridges are accessible from the southern shores of the upper Deep Creek Lakes. Be aware that there are several creek crossings between the Echo Lakes and Tayo Park, and a major creek crossing occurs on the Middle Fork Trail before you re-enter Three Forks Park from the west. These waters are swift and icy. In fact, Ice Lakes can still be frozen solid in mid-July. Wind River Peak may be a snow climb up to that time, and an ice axe can be useful.

It would take a book-length description to do justice to the vast beauty encompassed by this hike. It is an excellent first taste of the southern Wind Rivers and will surely pique your adventure buds into wanting more. The trail intersections are well signed, but a topo map is still advisable. Signs do have a habit of disappearing.

38 Little Sandy Lake

General description:	A day hike or easy overnighter to a spectacular lake setting, located approximately 50 miles northeast of Farson or 60 miles southeast of Pinedale, in the extreme southeastern corner of the Bridger Wilderness. The area offers one of the shortest hikes granting access to the spectacular peak and lake country of the southern Wind Rivers. Can be used as a jump-off point for longer ventures into the deep wilderness.
Distance:	4.5 miles.
Difficulty:	Moderate.

Traffic:	Light.
Elevation gain:	1,400 feet.
Maps:	Bridger–Teton National Forest Pinedale Ranger District map; Sweetwater Needles, Sweetwater Gap, Temple Peak USGS quads.
For more information:	Pinedale Ranger District, 29 East Fremont Lake Road, P.O. Box 220, Pinedale, Wyoming 82941, 307-367-4326.

Finding the trailhead: One half mile east of South Pass on Wyoming Highway 28, signs for the Sweetwater Gap Ranch, Bridger Wilderness Big Sandy Entrance, and the Lander Cutoff Road direct you onto the Lander Cutoff Road. Drive 15.4 miles northwest along the rolling hills of this graded road. Here, at the first graded road heading northward, a Bureau of Land Management sign points to the Juel Ranch and to Sweetwater Gap. Follow this road north, but do not take the BLM road jutting to the west after 3.5 miles of travel. Continue northward for another 2.5 miles until another BLM sign directs you left (north) to the Bridger National Forest. At 8.5 miles along this road, a Forest Service sign falsely notes that it is still 6 miles to the Bridger Wilderness. Turn left (west) at this road junction, which immediately becomes a jeep road. My little two-wheel-drive truck made it up some serious grades in the road's 2-mile distance, but a lesser clearance vehicle will require you to park and hike these couple miles. At the road's end, a sign points north to the trail and east to a tiny parking lot.

The hike: In 1988, a massive forest fire swept through several thousand acres of the southeastern corner of the Wind Rivers. The burn generated a heat so intense it actually sterilized the soil, creating a condition of extreme erodablility. The beginnings of this route to Little Sandy Lake and to the Sweetwater Gap area provide excellent on-site fire ecology lessons. The earth is just now beginning plant successions that will ultimately reforest the area. This particular trail is a much more lightly used pathway to Little Sandy Lake than the popular trail from the Big Sandy access. It is also one of the shortest hiking accesses into the heart of the high peak country.

In but a 0.1 mile distance, beside a wilderness registration sign, the trail forks. There may be no direction sign at this fork, but the Little Sandy Lake Trail heads left while the Sweetwater Gap Trail goes right. After a short downhill wander into a meadow, the Little Sandy Trail almost vanishes. The trick here is to cut straight northwest across the meadow (sometimes, it is a swamp). A cairn marks the trail's meadow exit, and the track of the trail visibly cuts into the burned forest above the grassy and open area.

The next mile forms an intense experience in fire-transformed landscapes. Near the Bridger Wilderness boundary, the burn stops. One step has you hiking a used-match forest and the next places you beneath a green bower, as if no burn ever occurred. The trail is gentle for the first 1.5 miles. Then it remembers it has a pass to climb, and the next 2 miles ascend a steep grade. Take time to view the surrounding lodgepole forests. Some amazing burls

Little Sandy Lake

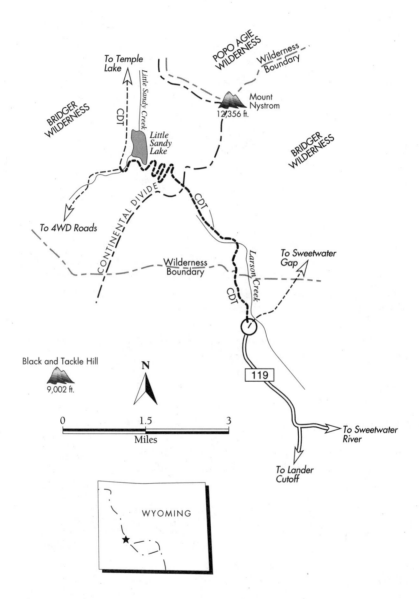

have formed on these trees. The Continental Divide crossing into the Little Sandy drainage is thickly forested and unspectacular, but the now descending trail's occasional views of the striking walls, cliffs, and high pinnacles of the peaks towering over the lake make up for that. A little over a mile of steep downhill switchbacking places you in a Wind River scenic wonderland by the lake.

Camping spots are a bit sparse beside Little Sandy Lake. The trail leading into the high peak heart of this area skirts the southern shores of the lake and crosses Little Sandy Creek before venturing north. If you hike this trip as a day hike, remember the climb and return distance you have yet to cover before day's end.

39 Sweetwater Gap

General description:	A long but quite enjoyable day hike (or a leisurely overnighter) to a high pass that accesses the Popo Agie Wilderness from the south, located approximately 60 miles southeast of Pinedale, in the extreme southeastern corner of the Bridger Wilderness. The area offers wonderful stream fishing, pretty meadow camping and incomparable views.
Distance:	7 miles, one way.
Difficulty:	Moderately strenuous.
Traffic:	Light.
Elevation gain:	1,620 feet.
Maps:	Bridger–Teton National Forest Pinedale Ranger District Bridger Wilderness map; Sweetwater Needles, Sweetwater Gap USGS quads.
For more information:	Pinedale Ranger District, 29 Fremont Lake Road, P.O. Box 220, Pinedale, Wyoming 82941, 307-367-4326.

Finding the trailhead: Directions are identical to those in the Little Sandy Lake Trail (Hike 38).

The hike: Sweetwater Gap is a fun adventure into the headwater beginnings of that untamed river. After hiking the initial 0.1 mile from the registration sign, be certain to take the right (east) fork at the trail intersection. Like its counterpart to the west, this trail also journeys through the blackened landscape of a recent forest fire. The first 1.3 miles to the Bridger Wilderness boundary is quite a charred-wood experience. Beyond that, green forest dominates the scenery, and so do the gentle pools and still pockets of the rapidly forming Sweetwater River. Several peaceful meadows dress the forest and offer ideal camping and stream fishing spots.

Sweetwater Gap

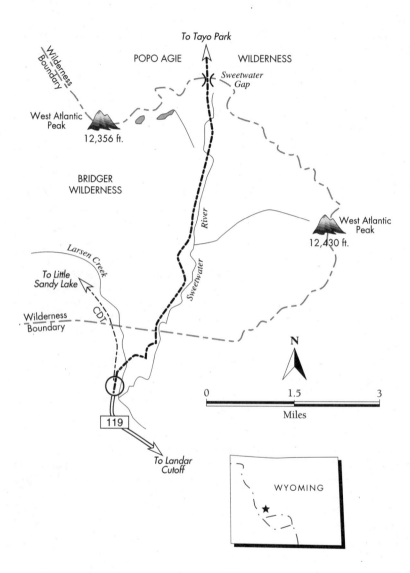

The trail wanders gently uphill for over 5 miles. Then the lodgepole pine turns to limber pine, and the sub-alpine spruce claims hillside dominance. The final 2 miles to Sweetwater Gap become a moderate climb. The pass itself is a large and broad meadow with excellent views northwest toward Wind River Peak.

This trail is a most typical Wind River trail, in that you hike and hike, mostly over rocky path and through obscure lodgepole forests. Occasional glimpses of large peaks present themselves, but the views rarely last more than a moment. Then, near the summit, the mountain world explodes into stunning views. Sweetwater Gap, from this approach, offers a shorter and less-used access into the Tayo Park/Ice Lakes high country of the southern Popo Agie Wilderness. Fine camping spots are available the entire length of the trail, including in and around the open meadows near the pass.

With little hiker usage, both the Sweetwater Gap and the Little Sandy Lake trails are rarely maintained, so you might be climbing over a few logs, especially in the burn areas.

THE CONTINENTAL DIVIDE
SOUTH OF THE WIND RIVER RANGE

South of the Wind River Range the divide drops into arid desert and scrubland, much of it on private land or BLM managed areas. Work on the CDT has been slow in this area. It does not fit the traditional forested alpine setting most people think of as the divide. Your companions may be cattle and coyotes, but solitude is probably more likely in the Ferris Mountains or the Huston Park Wilderness than anywhere in the popular Wind Rivers.

40 Ferris Mountains

General description:	A trail-less, virtually unknown mountain range in the Ferris Mountains Wilderness Study Area, located approximately 45 miles north of Rawlins, near a high desert pass and small settlement called Muddy Gap. The area offers unpopulated hiking; unknown deep canyons; high mountain ridges and peaks and all of it is untrailed.
Distance:	Varies.
Difficulty:	Expert hikers only.
Traffic:	Light.
Elevation gain:	Varies, up to 2,400 ft.
Maps:	BLM BAIROIL 1:100,000 surface management map; Spanish Mine, Young's Pass, Muddy Gap USGS quads.
For more information:	BLM Rawlins District, 1300 North Third Street, Rawlins, Wyoming 82301-0670, 307-328-4200.

Finding the trailhead: Driving north from Rawlins on U.S. Highway 287 for 45 miles places you at the one-gas-station town named Three Forks or Muddy Gap. South and east of this highway junction area lies the unknown range called the Ferris Mountains.

Currently it takes a real bloodhound to nose out the legal byways into this range. The only legal access into the Ferris Mountains at this time is via county and offshoot BLM roads on the north side of the range. In several places even the county roads have no signs, but they seem to be the more gravelly ones that intersect the main highway with stop signs. The BLM roads are primitive, high clearance, and barely maintained. One person driving on a road when it is too wet can leave rut damage and make it less passable for others. The map accompanying this area describes road access as it stands in 1998, but the recreation director's major recommendation is that persons contact the Rawlins BLM office before heading into the Ferris Mountains.

The hike: The absolute hardest chore a guidebook author faces is deciding whether or not to reveal to the hiking crowd the biggest secret he has discovered. The Ferris Mountains form a BLM wilderness study area of 22,245 acres, one of the largest untouched areas the BLM owns. Forested peaks up to 10,000 feet hide from view the shrub-covered and unforested slopes, the grassy meadows and riparian zones that are present in the many open parks of this range. The mountains are rugged, quite steep, and essentially roadless. Wildlife abounds here, as does unusual geology.

The greatest joy of the Ferris Mountains is that they exemplify wilderness as wilderness used to be. They are not only unscathed by roads, they also contain no trails. The hiking experience of the Ferris Mountains is one of driving to the area, parking near the scenery or landscape that attracts you the most, and just wandering anywhere the calling takes you. I cannot draw a map of a specific hike because there is none. This area is a vast playground without any of the confines (i.e. trails) we've allowed to dominate most other hiking playgrounds. Variety and surprising beauty rule this country. I wandered aimlessly for a day in the northeastern corner of the range and experienced vast, untrammeled valleys, crystal creeks, sandstone hogback ridges, flowers beyond comparison, juniper/pinyon forests and snow-dappled forested mountaintops sporting incomparable views in all directions.

A trip into the Ferris Mountains is recommended for those who have strong map and compass skills. It is not for the novice hiker. The place offers you both the chance to grab a topo and test your orientation skills and the chance to test your luck at wandering into something new and surprising. (Note: There are some private lands in the mountains. Permission should be obtained from private landowners before using their lands).

The water in these mountains is good, which is to say that it is not alkali, as is most of the water in this section of Wyoming. However, many cattle roam this country. Also, be aware that if it rains and your rig is off the

Ferris Mountains

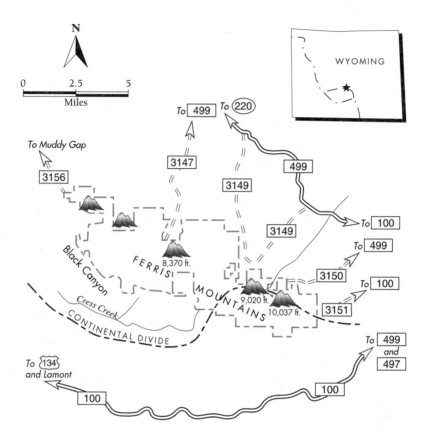

N

0   2.5   5
Miles

WYOMING

To Muddy Gap

To 499   To 220

3147
3156
3149
499

To 100

3149
To 499

FERRIS 8,370 ft.

3150   To 100

Black Canyon

MOUNTAINS
9,020 ft.
10,037 ft.   3151

Cress Creek

CONTINENTAL DIVIDE

To 499
and
497

To 134
and Lamont

100
100

country road, where you are will be home until the sun shines for a few hours.

The Ferris Mountains area has been recommended for wilderness classification by the BLM and the President. It now must gain similar approval from our "wilderness-loving" Republican Congress. Letters and loud voices are needed if this wild land is to remain that way.

41 Baby Lake Trail

General description:	A generally secluded trail through forests and mountain meadows. Offers a chance to tie into the Continental Divide National Scenic Trail. Located approximately 20 miles west of Encampment, in the northern section of the Huston Park Wilderness. Expect fees of $6 to $9 per night at area campgrounds.
Distance:	6 miles, one way.
Difficulty:	Moderately strenuous.
Traffic:	Moderate.
Elevation gain:	1,250 feet.
Maps:	Medicine Bow National Forest visitor's map; Bridger Peak, Red Mountain USGS quads.
For more information:	Brush Creek/Hayden Ranger District, Medicine Bow National Forest, 204 West Ninth Street, Encampment, Wyoming 82325, 307-327-5481.

Finding the trailhead: Drive west from Encampment on Wyoming 70 for approximately 20 miles. On the way, you will cross the Continental Divide at Battle Pass (9,916 feet). This spot, and a location 1 mile south at the Huston Park Trailhead, are good places to park a vehicle if you want to make a 9 mile, one-way hike on the Baby Lake Trail. Approximately 6 miles farther, a few hundred feet before the Lost Creek Campground, turn left (south) onto Forest Road 811. After 300 feet make another left turn onto a more primitive road and travel about 0.75 mile south to the trailhead. If you are driving a low-clearance vehicle, you should park along the gravel just off the highway.

The hike: The Baby Lake Trail is a scenic hike through lodgepole forests and high mountain meadows. Although easily completed in one day, there are numerous campsites along the way. The trail gets its name from the fact that it follows Baby Lake Creek. It does not specifically go to Baby Lake.

On foot from the parking lot, continue south and downhill on a primitive road to the Huston Park Wilderness boundary. The road pre-dates the wilderness designation of the area. In 0.5 mile, it descends 400 feet to an old sheep bridge across Battle Creek.

The bridge and the Baby Lake Trail are legacies of sheep grazing on national forest lands. Reconstructed in 1962 to provide access for sheep grazing, it now provides access for hikers and backpackers. Sheep use of the Baby Lake area was discontinued in 1986. While hiking this area, notice that most of the trees are relatively young. Huge fires, on the scale of the recent Yellowstone conflagration, killed many of the trees in the Sierra Madre Mountains between 120 and 140 years ago. For about 100 years after these

Baby Lake Trail

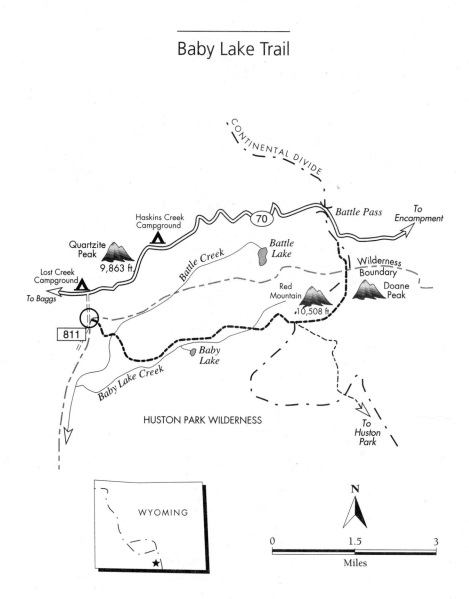

fires the area was relatively open, meaning the trees were small and there was room between them for grass and shrubs to grow. Over the past several decades, as the trees have grown larger, they have shaded out more of the ground. This shading has gradually decreased the amount of grass and forbs for livestock and wildlife.

After crossing the bridge, bear left up a short hill. Blazes and cairns mark the trail from this point on. For the next hour or so, your hike will be through lodgepole pine forests. In about 2 miles, the trail begins to parallel Baby Lake Creek. Out of sight of the trail, the creek is evident by the murmur it makes behind a screen of alder and willows. Baby Lake is located about 0.8 mile south of the trail in a large meadow. The term "lake" is generous.

In a short time, the vegetation begins the transition from heavy forest to an area of mixed forest and mountain meadows. The trail across these meadows is often overgrown with lush grass. Be alert for blazes on trees at the far end of the meadow. Cairns and posts also mark the route. These meadows are a favorite bedding ground for the many deer and elk in the area.

After traveling through several meadows, the trail gradually steepens until it reaches the continental divide at the low saddle just south of Red Mountain. This can be a turnaround point, or you can continue and turn south onto the Continental Divide National Scenic Trail and into alpine Huston Park. Looking back, you get a great view of the Snake River Valley. Ahead are lush meadows at the head of Long Peak.

For those who left a vehicle near Battle Pass, continue on and slightly downhill for another 0.25 mile to the junction with the Huston Park Trail. Turning north, it is a short 3 miles to the highway at Battle Pass.

Forty-five miles of the CDT cross the Brush Creek/Hayden District of the Medicine Bow National Forest. About 13 miles of the CDT follow the continental divide in the 31,000-acre Huston Park Wilderness. These miles of trail have recently been remarked and maintained.

—*Mike Murphy*

The Continental Divide in Colorado

The divide in Colorado separates major river drainages on the east (the Arkansas and the Platte) from drainages flowing to the Pacific on the west by way of the Colorado River. Well known for its 14,000-foot peaks, Colorado carries the divide through Rocky Mountain National Park and the Indian Peaks, Hunter–Frying Pan, Holy Cross, Never Summer, and Weminuche Wilderness Areas, some of the most spectacular high-alpine hiking in North America. Snow clings to the high country even late into summer, but Colorado divide trails offer adventure from late spring through early fall every year.

42 Parkview Mountain

General description:	A day hike to the summit of Parkview Mountain, the high point of the Rabbit Ears Range.
Difficulty:	Moderate.
Distance:	5 miles, one way.
Traffic:	Light.
Elevation gain:	2,796 feet.
Maps:	Parkview Mountain and Radial Mountain USGS quads; Arapaho National Forest Map, Trails Illustrated Rand Map.
For more information:	Arapaho National Forest, Sulphur Ranger District, 62429 US Highway 40, Box 10, Granby, Colorado 80446, 970-887-4100.

Finding the trailhead: Drive south from Walden (or north from Granby) on Colorado Highway 125 to the summit of Willow Creek Pass, which is on the Continental Divide. Proceed south over the pass for about 0.6 mile to the second timber road on your right. You can park or drive on, but the road becomes increasingly rough and steep as you proceed, and it may not be suitable for passenger cars. Your hike will be longer if you park here, but the walking is easy up this old road.

The hike: An imposing and aptly named landmark in northern Colorado, Parkview Mountain is the high point of the Rabbit Ears Range, which separates North and Middle Parks. A hike to its summit offers beautiful alpine wildflowers, herds of elk, and spectacular views of the surrounding mountains and mountain parks.

Begin your hike by crossing a small stream and make a right and then a left turn at the two forks you encounter as the road climbs in the first 0.25 mile.

Looking northeast from the summit of Parkview Mountain to the Never Summer Range.

From here keep to what is obviously the main road, as it switches back many times for about 2 miles through old timber sales on the lower slopes of Parkview Mountain.

This area was once clearcut and has since been reseeded. As you climb, you can use this opportunity to observe the reestablishment of a new forest. At the upper end of the timber sale the road steepens and switches back several times more until it crosses a steep bowl and avalanche chute below timberline. Just past this point, you have a choice of two routes leading to the summit.

One possibility (and the easier of the two) is to climb to your right directly up the ridge from the road. This route climbs steadily through scattered timber to timberline. From here it is a short, but steep, climb to the long ridge leading west and then south to the summit. This route provides beautiful views of North Park along its length. Look for elk on the broad grassy slopes on the north side of the mountain.

An alternate route begins another 0.5 mile along where the road ends in a beautiful glacial cirque below the peak. From this point you can see the small lookout shelter on the summit. Set out around the cirque and intersect

Parkview Mountain

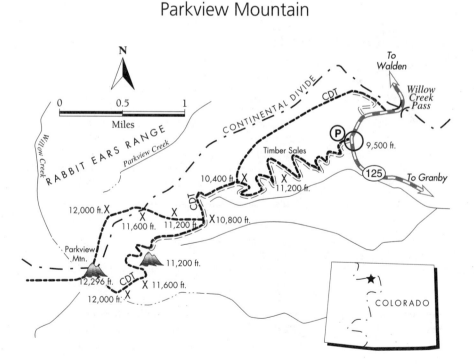

the ridge on the south side. Take time to notice the wildflowers here: American bistort, columbine, Indian paintbrush, and many more. The climb is very steep here to the summit ridge, but the last quarter-mile is nearly level. Keep an eye out for the tiny alpine flowers which thrive in this harsh environment including blue forget-me-nots.

Once at the summit, sign the register and enjoy the view. To the north is the beautiful green expanse of North Park, bordered on the west by the Park Range and the Mount Zirkel Wilderness Area and on the east by the Medicine Bow Mountains and the Rawah Wilderness Area. On a clear day you should be able to discern the outline of the sand dunes of North Park, which lie at the base of the Medicine Bow Mountains, a much smaller version of those found at Great Sand Dunes National Monument. To the east is the Never Summer Range, and beyond it, to the southeast, are Longs Peak, the Indian Peaks, and Berthoud Pass. To the south lies Middle Park and to the southwest are the Gore Range and the Flat Tops. To the west you may be able to discern the distinct shape of Rabbit Ears Peak, marking the end of the Rabbit Ears Range at Rabbit Ears Pass. From this one point you can see most of the course of the Continental Divide throughout northern Colorado.

—*Caryn, Peter and Crystal Boddie*

43 Baker Gulch

General description:	A day hike or backpacking trip beginning in Rocky Mountain National Park and following Baker Gulch to Baker Pass in the Never Summer Range and Never Summer Wilderness, just 6 miles from the west entrance in Rocky Mountain National Park. The hike offers beautiful views from Baker Pass; good fishing in Baker Gulch Creek; lots of wildlife; including bighorn sheep and blue grouse.
Difficulty:	Moderate.
Distance:	6 miles, one way.
Traffic:	Light to moderate.
Elevation gain:	2,300 feet.
Maps:	Bowen Mountain and Mount Richtofen USGS quads; Arapaho National Forest Map, Trails Illustrated Rocky Mountain National Park.
For more information:	Arapaho National Forest, Sulphur Ranger District; 62249 U.S. Highway 40, P.O. Box 10, Granby, Colorado 80446, 970-887-4100.

Finding the trailhead: Enter Rocky Mountain National Park at the west entrance and follow Trail Ridge Road for 6.4 miles to the Bowen-Baker trailhead. Park in the picnic area parking lot and hike up the road 0.5 mile to the "Baker Trailhead" sign. Go right at the fork.

The hike: The Baker Gulch Trail takes you from Rocky Mountain National Park into the Never Summer Wilderness and up to Baker Pass, where you will have beautiful views in all directions.

Rising from the Kawuneeche Valley through lodgepole pine, the trail follows Baker Gulch at a moderate grade. Up the trail 1.3 miles, a worn spot to the right indicates the way to a large beaver pond that fishermen will find inviting. The trail then continues through an area of deadfall and follows several switchbacks (and stops for raspberries) before leveling off to cross a boulder field. As you cross the boulders, look for the small mammals that make this boulder field their home. The marmots are relatively easy to spot, but not so for those little, squeaky picas. You will also pass the Grand Ditch Road carved into the steep south-facing slope above the trail. The ditch, built in the 1890s, provides the eastern plains with runoff water for irrigation.

After switching back through stands of aspen, the trail passes through a lush meadow alive with wildflowers, particularly columbine and the unusual American bistort. Look for Longs Peak to the east here and for the cliffs of Bowen Mountain above Baker Gulch to the southwest. You can also see the green of the Kawuneeche Valley below.

Shortly after leaving the meadow, the trail crosses the Grand Ditch service road. There is a wooden bridge across the ditch itself, and then you enter a forest of Engelmann spruce and subalpine fir. Four miles from the trailhead you will meet a stream, which becomes difficult to cross during spring runoff. On the opposite bank is a sign marking the Parika Lake turnoff. Follow the Baker Gulch Trail, which continues north and to the right, crossing several small streams and meadows where deer and elk can frequently be seen grazing. The large barren mountain to the right is Baker Mountain (12,397 feet). Rock cairns mark the last 0.5 mile of the hike, which follows a gentle slope through marshy alpine meadows (a fragile environment) to the saddle of Baker Pass (11,253 feet) on the Continental Divide.

To the east are the Cloud Mountains of the Never Summer Range, which form the boundary between Routt National Forest and Rocky Mountain National Park and along which goes the divide. The southernmost of these is Mount Stratus, named after low altitude horizontal clouds. Looking north of Mount Stratus is Mount Nimbus. Farther to the north is Mount Cumulus. Mount Cirrus, named after high altitude clouds, is the highest of the cloud mountains with a summit of 12,797 feet. Between Cirrus and Cumulus is Howard Mountain, said to have been named after Luke Howard, the man who first classified cloud forms. North of the Cloud Mountains is Mount Richthofen, at 12,940 feet, the highest mountain in the Never Summer Range.

Another trail from Baker Pass leads southwest, traversing the slope just

Baker Gulch

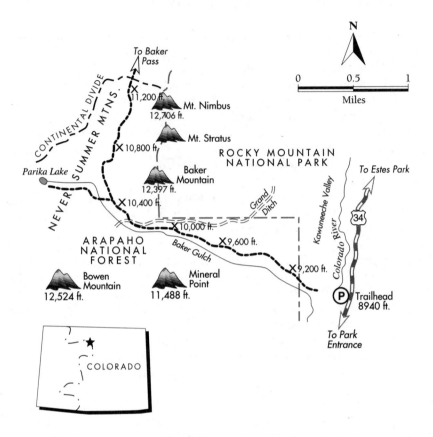

below the Continental Divide to Parika Lake. You can also continue on into the Routt National Forest along the Michigan River Trail and the Jack Creek Trail, known as Baker Pass Trail. Otherwise, return as you came once you have enjoyed this beautiful view. Be sure to watch for wildlife, including bighorn sheep and blue grouse as you return.

44 Hell Canyon

General description:	A rigorous day hike or overnighter into Hell Canyon, a steep glacial valley in the Indian Peaks Wilderness, near the southern edge of Rocky Mountain National Park.
Difficulty:	Difficult.
Distance:	9 miles, one way.
Traffic:	Light.
Elevations gain:	3,000 feet.
Maps:	Monarch Lake and Isolation Peak USGS quads; Arapaho National Forest Map, Trails Illustrated Indian Peaks and Rocky Mountain National Park.
For more information:	Arapaho National Forest, Sulphur District, 62429 U.S. Highway 40, P.O. Box 10, Granby, Colorado 80446, 970-887-4100.

Finding the trailhead: To reach Hell Canyon, take U.S. Highway 34 northeast from Granby towards Rocky Mountain National Park and Shadow Mountain National Recreation Area. About 6 miles north of Granby, take a right on Arapaho Bay Road which follows the southern shore of Lake Granby. Go on past Lake Granby to the road's end at Monarch Lake. Here a large parking lot serves as the trailhead for both the Arapaho Canyon and Cascade Creek Trail systems.

The hike: Hell Canyon is very aptly named, a fact that becomes clear to anyone hiking up the unmarked trail that climbs to a saddle leading into Rocky Mountain National Park. Still, this is a hike well worth taking. Hell Canyon, as it rises above Buchanan Creek, cuts deeply into the landscape of this semi-primitive area where wildlife abounds.

Follow the Cascade Creek Trail along the northeastern shore of Monarch Lake past the Forest Service cabin, then southeast to the trail register at the east end of Monarch Lake. From the register continue 2 miles along Buchanan Creek to the intersection with the first major drainage from the north. This is Hell Canyon. The trail begins about 100 yards before a bridge. This spot, marked by an old charred tree stump, is where you want to leave the Cascade Creek Trail to head up the unmarked Hell Canyon Trail.

Rumor has it that a USGS party was caught in the canyon during a mid-November snow storm while surveying. They were forced to bushwhack for several days in order to make good their retreat through fresh snow and over ice that made travel precarious at best. The party demanded that the canyon be named Hell Canyon when they finally reached their headquarters.

No doubt, you will understand how the canyon earned its reputation as you make the long, steep climb to Long Lake some 2.5 miles from Buchanan

Hell Canyon

Creek. Fishing in the lake is good and Mount Irving Hale, which rises some 1,500 feet above the lake, provides a magnificent setting. You may be tempted to make this your destination, but you will find it worthwhile to continue on beyond Long Lake. The terrain becomes less steep (but remains challenging) and the trail becomes a rough foot path, as Forest Service maintenance is provided only to Long Lake. Crawford Lake, 0.5 mile farther up the canyon, is worth pushing on for, set as it is in a large and unexpected meadow. The terrain beyond becomes very interesting as you approach Stone Lake and timberline. Boulders as large as houses dot the landscape, and trees give way to grasses and shrubs.

From Stone Lake you climb a final 600 feet to the saddle that is your destination. The Continental Divide it just to the east. A sign marking the southern boundary of Rocky Mountain National Park indicates the top of Hell Canyon. Travel north takes you into the park and Paradise Park. After enjoying this beautiful area, return as you came.

—*Doug Crocker*

Monarch Lake. FOREST SERVICE PHOTO

45 Mount Nystrom Trail

General description:	An easily accessible day hike along broad ridgetops above timberline near Berthoud Pass, just 45 miles west of Denver. This hike offers easy access to timberline and the Continental Divide, great views, and wildflowers.
Difficulty:	Easy to moderate.
Distance:	From 2 to 8 miles, one way.
Traffic:	Light to moderate.
Elevation gain:	1,350 feet.
Maps:	Berthoud Pass, Fraser and Byers Peak USGS quads; Arapaho National Forest Map, Trails Illustrated Rollins Pass.
For more information:	Arapaho National Forest, Sulphur Ranger District, 62429 U.S. Highway 40, P.O. Box 10, Granby, Colorado 80446, 970-887-4100.

Finding the trailhead: To reach Berthoud Pass, take Interstate 70 west to U.S. Highway 40 and follow it to the summit of the pass. Park at the ski lodge on the east side.

To begin your hike, cross the highway and climb the ski slopes to the top of the chairlift. For an easier start of your hike, you can take the chairlift when it is operating most weekends and holidays during the summer.

From the top of the chairlift, follow the ridge west to its intersection with another broad ridge from the north. Here you should be able to locate the Mount Nystrom Trail, marked with rock cairns.

The hike: The Mount Nystrom Trail follows a long and broad ridge of the Continental Divide and a side ridge from Mount Nystrom to the Mary Jane Ski Area. This route provides beautiful views of the surrounding mountains and a chance to see the spectacular wildflowers of this alpine environment. An easy access to this trail, which also provides the least elevation gain, is from Berthoud Pass. From this point you have options for short or extended day hikes and an extended backpack, as well.

From the Mount Nystrom Trailhead, your hike will be an easy walk in either direction. To the right the trail follows the ridge for about 7 miles to the Mary Jane Ski Area. You can shuttle a car to the parking lot there. To the left the trail follows the Continental Divide about 2 miles to Stanley Mountain and another 6 miles to Mount Nystrom.

This area is part of the Vasquez Mountains and is characterized by broad, rolling ridgetops with steep-sided, glacial cirques carved into them. In general, the larger cirques are found on the eastern sides of the ridges where the prevailing winds have deposited snow to form the glaciers. This pattern is repeated over and over again here.

Mount Nystrom Trail

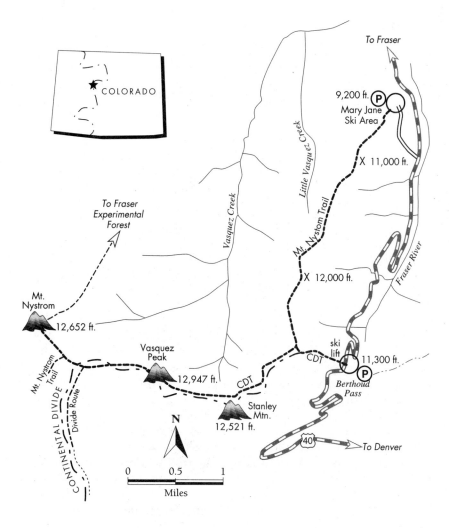

From Berthoud Pass, Stanley Mountain (12,521 feet) is a short day hike of about 3.5 miles one way, with an elevation gain of about 1,200 feet. From the top of the mountain you can look directly south and down the path of the famous Stanley Slide, a huge avalanche chute. This is one of the most dangerous chutes in the Front Range because it crosses US 40 in two separate places and can bury the highway under as much as 20 feet of snow.

From Stanley Mountain you can continue on towards Mount Nystrom (12,652 feet) and beyond to intersect with trails to St. Louis Peak and the

Fraser Experimental Forest, or you can return as you came. Whatever you choose to do, be sure to keep an eye out for signs of impending thunderstorms, as this is no place to be caught unaware.

—Brian Dempsey

46 Monte Cristo Gulch

General description:	A short day hike from beautiful Blue Lakes above timberline into a historic mining area, located about 10 miles southwest of Breckenridge.
Distance:	About 1.25 miles, one way.
Difficulty:	Moderate.
Traffic:	Light to Moderate.
Maps:	Breckenridge USGS Quad; Trails Illustrated Breckenridge South; Arapaho National Forest Map.
For more information:	Arapaho National Forest, Dillon Ranger District, 280 Blue River Parkway, P.O. Box 620, Silverthorne, Colorado 80498, 970-468-5400.

Finding the trailhead: To reach your starting point at Blue Lakes, drive south on Colorado Highway 9 from the Bell Tower Mall in Breckenridge 7.9 miles. Turn right on Blue Lakes Road (Number 850) and look for the sign that says 2 miles to Blue Lakes. You will pass a number of cabins in the beginning. Drive up to the dam where there is a big turnaround for parking. These are the Blue Lakes.

Begin your hike on the north end of the dam (right hand side as you face up valley). While you are on the dam look to your right for a rock cairn. Then look uphill for a couple of brown rock outcroppings. Head up toward them. More cairns mark the way and the trail will become clear near the outcroppings.

The hike: This short hike above timberline in Monte Cristo Gulch in the Tenmile Range is an easily accessible introduction to the rugged glaciated terrain above timberline and the mining history of Colorado. The trail takes you from two beautiful lakes along the southern flank of fourteener Quandary Peak (14,265 feet) to a mining site in the shadow of the mountain. Along the way and at your destination you will see old mine relics, gaining a sense of the mining history of this area while enjoying beautiful views and wildflowers. You may see snow along the trail even in midsummer. Warning: It is never a good idea to get too close to the old mines or to enter them. You never know how stable or unstable they are. Never let children explore around mines.

Monte Cristo Gulch

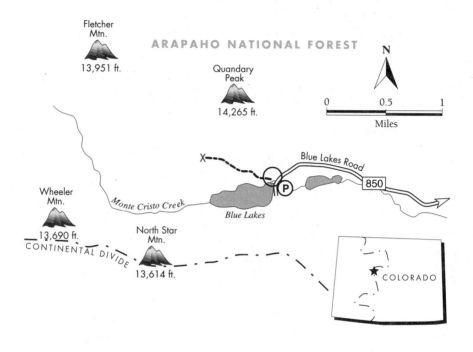

Follow the trail along the southern flank of Quandary Peak and through willows, meadows, and tundra. Some of the flowers you may see along the trail are American bistort, chiming bells, buttercups, and harebells. You will be heading toward a pass between Quandary and Fletcher Mountain to the northwest. In fact, from the end of the valley it is possible to extend this hike into a climb of Fletcher Mountain (13,951 feet). However, before climbing other thirteeners in the Tenmile Range or fourteener Quandary Peak, it would be a good idea to consult one of the good books on climbing the thirteeners and fourteeners.

In a little more than 0.5 mile you will come upon two old cabins from mining days gone by. Summit County, along with Park County to the south and Lake County to the west, saw extensive mining activity in the nineteenth century. In fact, gold was discovered here in Monte Cristo Gulch in 1860.

If you have a topo map with you, it is fun to look and see the names of some of the mines: Monte Cristo, Magnolia, Russia, Moose, Dolly Varden, Sweet Home, Security, Paris, Buckskin Joe, and so on. Some of these mines had particularly rich lodes of gold—also zinc, silver, lead, copper, and more—and had mills associated with them. Of course, there are many mines on the topo without names denoted simply as "Mine." Still, each one had a story in the people who came to claim, work, and then leave them, whether they left with or without riches.

About 0.5 mile past the cabins there once was a mine. Relics remain today, otherwise known as some miner's refuse.

Enjoy imagining the mining days and taking in the view of North Star Mountain to the southwest, which is connected by the Continental Divide to Wheeler Mountain to the west, which you probably noticed when you started your hike at Blue Lakes. When you tire of the wind, which tends to be gusty up here, head back the way you came. As you descend, look across Upper Blue Lake at North Star Mountain. You may discern signs of mines or mining scars (whatever you prefer to call them) on that mountain's flank, too.

—*Caryn, Crystal, and Robin Boddie*

47 Lonesome Lake

General description:	A day hike or overnighter to a beautiful cirque lake in the Holy Cross Wilderness. The hike offers wildflowers and wildlife, a beautiful high mountain lake with good fishing, and views of roaring East Fork Homestake Creek.
Difficulty:	Moderate.
Distance:	9 miles, round trip.
Traffic:	Moderate to heavy.
Elevation gain:	1,400 feet.
Maps:	Homestake Reservoir USGS Quad; White River National Forest Map. Trails Illustrated Holy Cross Map.
For more information:	White River National Forest, Holy Cross Ranger District, 24747 U.S. Highway 24, P.O. Box 190, Minturn, Colorado 81645, 970-827-5715.

Finding the trailhead: To reach the trail to the lake, drive south from Minturn on U.S. Highway 24 for about 10 miles or drive north from the summit of Tennessee Pass about 12 miles to the signed junction with Forest Route 703, leading to Homestake Reservoir. Turn southwest on this road and follow it for about 10 miles past the Gold Park Campground and to a signed junction. Look for the trailhead sign next to the East Fork of Homestake Creek.

Lonesome Lake

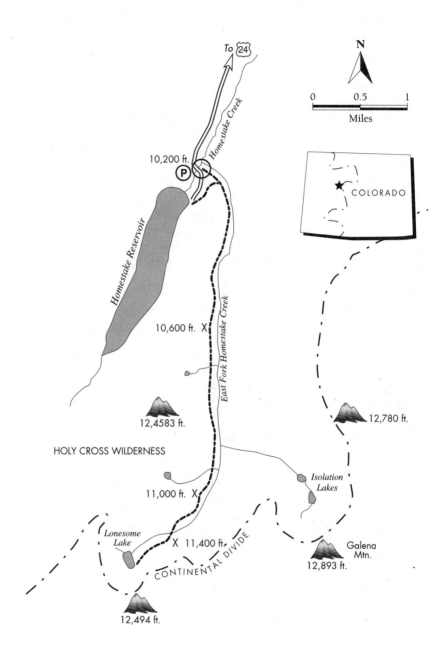

To ㉔

N

0   0.5   1
Miles

10,200 ft.
(P)

Homestake Creek

Homestake Reservoir

COLORADO

10,600 ft. X

East Fork Homestake Creek

12,4583 ft.

12,780 ft.

HOLY CROSS WILDERNESS

Isolation Lakes

11,000 ft. X

Lonesome Lake

X 11,400 ft.

Galena Mtn.
12,893 ft.

CONTINENTAL DIVIDE

12,494 ft.

The hike: This hike takes you through a long, deep glacial valley and through beautiful meadows to Lonesome Lake, one of the many alpine lakes in the Sawatch Range.

The trail climbs steeply up into the hanging valley of the East Fork. As an alternative, you can follow the steep road to the crest of the dam. From here follow the aqueduct eastward into the valley of East Fork Homestake Creek. The aqueduct ends at a small diversion pond.

This diversion, a part of the Homestake Project, is one of the many which capture water from tributaries to Homestake Creek and diverts it to Homestake Reservoir. From here the water flows beneath the Continental Divide through a tunnel to Turquoise Lake near Leadville. The Homestake Project has been the center of much controversy concerning extension of the diversion project to Cross Creek within the Holy Cross Wilderness Area. The water ultimately is used by the cities of Colorado Springs and Aurora.

The trail continues along the west (right) side of the pond. Follow the cairns, cross an open area, and then follow along the creek for about 0.5 mile through stands of evergreens. Then you will reach the first of two large meadows, this one being more than a mile in length. This beautiful spot, where wildflowers bloom profusely in the summer, might make a good destination if you are most interested in fishing.

Follow the trail around the west side of this mile-long meadow and then re-enter the woods. You will have to climb at a little steeper grade. Soon you will pass a small stream (a good spot to rest) and then come to the second of the meadows. Follow the creek to the other end of the meadow where you will find evidence of avalanches that may have roared down from the obvious avalanche chute during the previous winter. The trail then reenters the woods and begins a steady climb toward the lake. When you reach an open basin, keep to the left side for the last 0.5 mile climb to the grass-covered bench and Lonesome Lake. The trail is faint in several places. Watch for wildflowers and small mammals along your way, including marsh marigolds and marmots.

Lonesome Lake is one of many beautiful lakes to be found in this faulted anticline known as the Sawatch Range.

Fishing is said to be good for cutthroat trout in the 12 to 14-inch range. Please be sure to camp at least 200 feet away from the lake and trails to preserve the beauty of the area and be sure to watch for deer and elk on your return hike.

—Jim Haynes, Don Wagner, and Tyler Garbonza

48 Colorado Midland Railroad Trail

General description:	A unique day hike along the Colorado Midland Railroad Route, which passes through Hagerman Tunnel (now closed) underneath the Continental Divide located about 13 miles west of Leadville.
Difficulty:	Easy.
Distance:	5 miles, round trip.
Traffic:	Light to moderate.
Elevation gain:	550 feet.
Maps:	Homestake Reservoir and Mount Massive USGS quads; San Isabel National Forest Map, Trails Illustrated Holy Cross and Independence Pass.
For more information:	San Isabel National Forest, Leadville Ranger District, 2015 North Poplar, Leadville, Colorado 80461, 719-486-0749.

Finding the trailhead: From Leadville, take the Turquoise Lake Road (Forest Route 105) 0.5 mile to a three-way intersection. Go right, continuing west on FR 105 to the dam for Turquoise Lake. Continue across the dam until you reach the Hagerman Pass Road turnoff about 3 miles from the dam. Turn left onto this dirt road and drive past the Ivanhoe-Busk Tunnel outlet until you come to a Forest Service sign for the old railroad route of the Midland Railroad on the left. (Watch carefully for the sign, as it is small and set back 10 to 20 feet from the road.)

The hike: The Midland Railroad Trail offers a unique hike, taking you up through the San Isabel National Forest along the old railroad bed to the Continental Divide and the old Hagerman Tunnel.

Park and begin your hike at the Forest Service sign, starting up the historic bed of the Colorado Midland Railroad, known in its day as perhaps the most scenic railroad route in America. At the end of the first mile, you will drop into a meadow. This was the site of the famous Colorado Midland "Loop" bridge. A construction camp existed here once for the sole purpose of building a giant wooden bridge, now non-existent. Photographs of the famous bridge are abundant throughout the town of Leadville.

From the "Loop," continue on to the sign that marks a trail to Douglas City, an old railroad town now overgrown with trees. Continue on the old grade and you will come to beautiful, secluded Hagerman Lake, a great spot for camping (stay 200 feet away from the lake and off-trail) and fishing, which is fair for small cutthroat trout.

Continue on past Hagerman Lake another 0.75 mile and you will come to the large, cavernous opening in the rocks that is the long-abandoned Hagerman Tunnel. It once provided a standard gauge route through the

Colorado Midland Railroad Trail

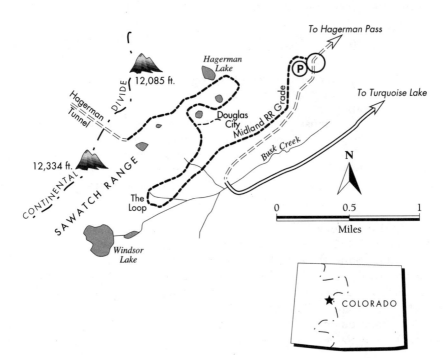

Rockies. Trains would travel through the tunnel to Lake Ivanhoe on the other side and then on to Basalt and Glenwood Springs. After having a good look, return as you came.

We are sure you will agree this is a beautiful and interesting hike, well worth your effort.

—Ruth and Sandy Mooneyham

49 Lost Man Pass and Deadman Lake

General description:	A day hike or overnighter into the high glacial basins that feed the Roaring Fork River and one of its tributaries, Lost Man Creek, or an overnighter to Deadman Lake in the Hunter–Fryingpan Wilderness, just 18.5 miles east of Aspen.
Difficulty:	Moderate.
Distance:	2.5 miles one way to Lost Man Pass; 6 miles one way to Deadman Lake; or 8.5 miles between trailheads.
Traffic:	Moderate to heavy.
Elevation gain:	1,900 feet from west to east on the trail.
Maps:	Mount Champion, Independence Pass, and New York Peak USGS quads; White River National Forest map; Trails Illustrated Independence Pass map.
For more information:	White River National Forest, Aspen Ranger District, 806 West Hallam, Aspen, Colorado 81611, 970-925-3445.

Finding the trailhead: To reach the Roaring Fork trailhead, take Colorado Highway 82 east from Aspen 18.5 miles to the point where it crosses the Roaring Fork River and begins the final climb to the summit of Independence Pass. From the parking lot on the north side of the highway there are trails ascending on either side of the river. The trail on the west (left) side leads to Linkins Lake, and the trail on the east (right) side leads to Independence Lake, Lost Man Pass, and the Lost Man Creek drainage. Those wishing to make the full 8.5-mile horseshoe trip over the pass and down the Lost Man drainage could leave an auto at the Lost Man Trailhead, 4.5 miles west on Highway 82 (14 miles east of Aspen).

The hike: The trails in the glacially formed basins that spawn the Roaring Fork River, its tributary Lost Man Creek, and the Fryingpan River make high country more than ordinarily accessible. However, because of this accessibility, the area is heavily used. Backpackers should be aware of stove-only regulations in this area and camping near the trails or any of the close-in lakes is discouraged. The trails do provide quick access to nearby country that is less heavily traveled.

The hiking alternatives in the Roaring Fork and Lost Man drainages range from the short climb of less than 1 mile to Linkins Lake to the full 8.5 mile traverse over Lost Man Pass between the Roaring Fork and Lost Man trailheads. You also have the option of hiking over South Fork Pass to Deadman Lake, a trip of 6 miles one way from the Lost Man trailhead.

Lost Man Pass and
Deadman Lake

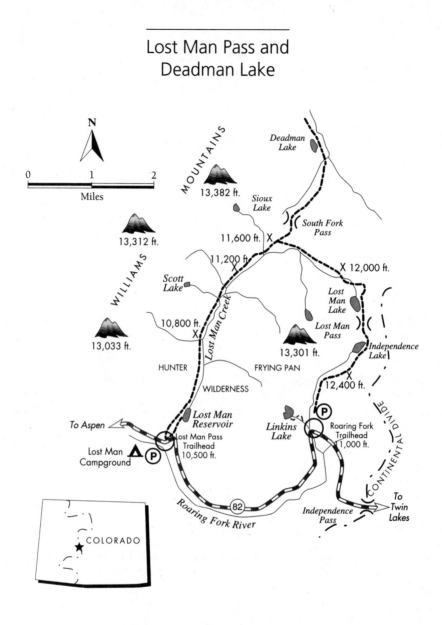

For a good picnic hike, or a short introduction to high country traveling, Linkins Lake is a good destination from the Roaring Fork trailhead. Follow the short trail on the west (left) side of the river, which soon leads away from the river, and climbs a short, intermediate ridge into tundra. The lake, which provides fair fishing for brook trout, is 0.25 mile beyond.

To reach Independence Lake or Lost Man Pass, take the trail that parallels the river on the eastern (right) bank. It follows the course of the Roaring fork through willows and over Pre-Cambrian metamorphics and granites for 1.5 miles, then bears east and is marked by cairns up the rocky slope to the lush and marshy ground surrounding Independence Lake. Fishing in Independence Lake and in the Upper Roaring Fork is fair for brook trout.

The environs of Independence Lake demonstrate the adaptability of tundra flora to the cold, high altitude, and short growing season. The area is also an excellent study in a process of succession from alpine lakes to tundra meadows: a glacial lake slowly filled by sediment, then taken over by tundra mosses and plants to become a marsh, which may in turn be drained by the erosion of the creek to form a tundra meadow. Substantial evidence of mineralization, as well as textbook examples of glacial erosion forming cirques, moraines, and glacial lakes, is also present in the area.

The impressive walls surrounding Independence Lake to the northwest are broken by the low saddle of Lost Man Pass, another 300 vertical feet above. Hikers can minimize impact through the tundra en route to the talus-covered pass by staying on the main trail. Once you encounter the talus slopes below the pass, follow the cairns to the trail's summit at 12,800 feet.

Looking back to the south, Grizzly Peak is visible in the distance, as are several bench-like moraines containing alpine lakes, including Linkins and Independence lakes. Over the pass and to the north, the trail drops in a steep descent to Lost Man Lake. Farther north, along the jagged ridge to the right, lies South Fork Pass, and beyond it the eastern slopes of the Williams Mountains, which form the headwaters of the Fryingpan River.

The descent to Lost Man Lake traverses down the right hand (northerly) slope of the basin, passes the lake and becomes somewhat obscure until it reaches the meadows surrounding Lost Man Creek. The easiest traveling and the main trail lie on the west side of the creek. The trail becomes obvious once it crosses the creek at the head of the willow-covered upper valley. The remainder of the route is a leisurely grade past serpentine falls, with wide panoramas of the Continental Divide to the south, and ends just past Lost Man Reservoir at the Lost Man trailhead on CO 82. Fishing in the reservoir is good for rainbow and brook trout. Fishing in Lost Man Creek and Lost Man Lake is fair to good for brook trout.

To make the hike to Deadman Lake, begin at the Lost Man trailhead on the north side of CO 82. It parallels the Lost Man Reservoir outlet channel about 0.25 mile to the reservoir, follows the west (left hand) shore of Lost Man Reservoir through a beautiful, mature stand of spruce and fir, and then wanders through the willows and gentle meadows to the west of Lost Man Creek, a fast, pretty stream bounding over pink and gray granites.

Within 3 to 4 miles, a comfortable walk of no more than two hours, the trail crosses one of the upper forks of Lost Man Creek. This is an ideal rest stop before the climb to the top of South Fork Pass on the switchback trail immediately to the left.

The view from the beautiful tundra of South Fork Pass is well worth the required effort. To the south lies the Continental Divide; to the north, the green slopes of the Fryingpan drainages. The trail continues northwest and descends 1.5 miles below timberline on the other side of the pass, then into a wide enchanting meadow. Across the meadow, along a faint trail marked by lonesome poles, lies Deadman Lake.

The broad expanse of the meadow and wooded hills around and below Deadman Lake are rich habitat for deer and elk, and the upper reaches of the Fryingpan offer fishing for brook trout. The area is a diverse mixture of alpine meadow, spruce-fir forest, and high country marsh. Water is readily available in the area, except on the pass, but it should be purified.

Deadman Lake itself really is dead in that it is a nonproductive fishery. This may be due to the fact that it is isolated from streams in the area, is spring fed, and is probably subject to hard freezes in winter. The lake does provide good habitat for waterfowl and a variety of mammals, and the rolling sparsely wooded hills that surround it provide numerous attractive campsites. (Be sure to camp at least 200 feet from the lakeshore and use a backpacking stove, if possible, rather than building a fire.) The surprising mixture of meadow, woods, and steep glacially scoured ridges entices one to exploratory wandering.

One obvious topographic feature in the area below: Deadman is a very large glacial moraine that forms an intricate network of ponds behind its dam of massive hardrock blocks. The river and South Fork trail continue over steep hills and through heavy timber below and beyond the moraine and upper meadows. You can return the way you came or turn east at the Lost Man Creek trail for the climb over Lost Man Pass to the Roaring Fork trailhead.

—*Chris Frye*

50 Kroenke Lake

General description:	A day hike along a roaring stream within a lush mountain forest, leading to a subalpine lake, just 8 miles west of Buena Vista.
Difficulty:	Moderate.
Distance:	8 miles, round trip.
Traffic:	Moderate to heavy.
Elevation gain:	1,500 feet.
Maps:	Mount Harvard 15-minute USGS Quad; San Isabel National Forest Map, Trails Illustrated Collegiate Mountains.
For more information:	San Isabel National Forest, Salida Ranger District, 325 West Rainbow Boulevard, Salida, Colorado 81201, 719-539-3591.

Finding the trailhead: To reach the trail to the lake, go west from Buena Vista on Crossman Avenue, which is Chaffee Country Road 350. After approximately 2 miles, turn right on Chaffee County Road 361. You cannot miss this turn, since Crossman Avenue (CR 350) deadends here. After a short while, CR 361 will veer to the left (northwest). After 1.2 miles from your original turn onto this road, take a sharp left onto North Cottonwood Creek Road (CR 365). You will be heading south again. Shortly afterward the road will turn west again. From this point it is approximately 3 miles along an extremely bumpy road to the dead-end at the trailhead.

The hike: This hike takes you into the beautiful Collegiate Mountain Range to Kroenke Lake in a subalpine setting surrounded by evergreens and vast mountain meadows.

The trail begins by crossing North Cottonwood Creek via a wide, sturdy bridge about 50 yards from the trailhead. It then continues on the south side of North Cottonwood Creek through a lush forest of spruce and fir with scattered small stands of aspen and stays close to the stream.

After approximately 1.5 miles, the trail will cross the stream over a second bridge. Shortly thereafter, it will cross a minor brook. As you continue on, you will occasionally have good views of the north face of Mount Yale, which is composed of brecciated gneisses and granite. Approximately 1 mile

Kroenke Lake

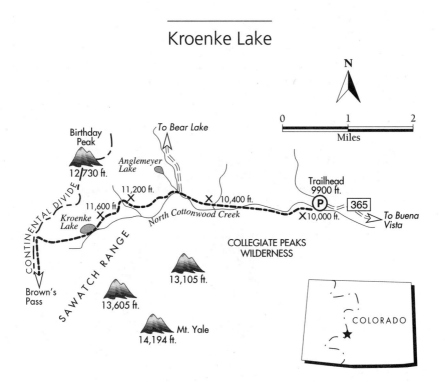

after your last steam crossing via the second bridge, the trail crosses North Horn Creek.

From this point the hiker might decide to go right to Horn Fork Basin and Bear Lake, another four miles, or stay left to Kroenke Lake. After another long mile, the trail crosses another small brook and then proceeds for less than one mile to Kroenke Lake.

All along your hike you will have seen small meadows with many wildflowers in summer. Kroenke Lake (11,530 feet) is surrounded by evergreens and is directly below the Continental Divide in a glaciated valley where there are vast alpine meadows. It is a very beautiful area and the lake promises good fishing. You may want to stay awhile and just enjoy your surroundings, or ascend to the summit of Mount Yale (14,196 feet), or go to Brown's Pass (12,010 feet) on the Continental Divide, or any of the other high peaks in the area. Then you will want to return as you came.

—*Pieter Dahmen*

THE CONTINENTAL DIVIDE THROUGH THE WEMINUCHE WILDERNESS

Probably one of the most scenic and high-alpine stops along the divide, the Weminuche Wilderness and the South San Juan Mountains share 12,000 foot airspace with hikers. The area has a well-maintained section of the CDT and receives many visitors a year. Most of these visitors, like you, will have to wait until the snow melts as most of the wilderness is above 10,000 feet and holds snow late into the summer. Check the snowpack before planning a trip in June.

51 Rincon La Vaca and Rio Grande Pyramid

General description: Moderate day hike with the option of a long day hike or overnight trip. Could include a climb of Rio Grande Pyramid, located about 30 miles southwest of Creede in the Weminuche Wilderness Area. This hike offers an excellent entry point for the vast Weminuche Wilderness; access to the Continental Divide Trail; wildflowers in spring; aspen in fall; chances to see elk, deer, black bear; relatively easy access to spectacular alpine terrain.

Difficulty:	Moderate to more difficult.
Distance:	5.5 miles one way to Rincon La Vaca (11 miles round trip); 10 miles one way to Rio Grande Pyramid (20 miles round trip).
Traffic:	Light.
Elevation gain:	4,391 to the summit; 1,200 to Weminuche Pass.
Maps:	Rio Grande National Forest Map; Weminuche Pass USGS Quad,; Trails Illustrated Weminuche Wilderness map.
For more information:	Rio Grande National Forest, Divide Ranger District, Third and Creede Avenue, P.O. Box 270, Creede, Colorado 81130, 719-658-2556.

Finding the trailhead: Drive 24 miles south from Lake City or 20 miles west from Creede on Colorado Highway 149. Turn west on Forest Road 520 and proceed 11 miles to Thirty Mile Campground where there is a trailhead.

The hike: A short distance from the signed trailhead, Squaw Creek Trail forks off. Stay on the Weminuche Creek Trail. Pass Rio Grande Reservoir dam, follow the contour of the land up above the reservoir through the aspen. Sometimes there is quite a bit of horse traffic from commercial stables on this part of the trail (mostly day trips), so you may have to step off the trail for horses. Columbine is abundant here in spring.

The trail bends left abruptly up Weminuche Creek Canyon and is moderately steep for a while. The trail is built through a rockslide, then crosses a

The San Juan Mountains.

Rincon La Vaca and
Rio Grande Pyramid

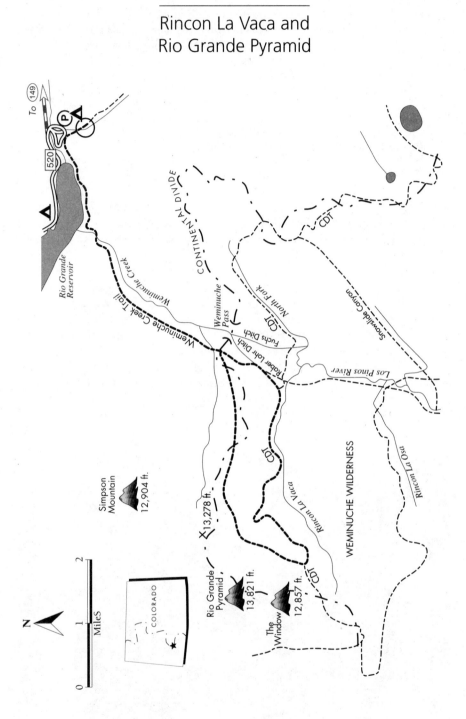

small stream, just before crossing Weminuche Creek on a bridge at about 2 miles. The creek here is an impressive torrent in the peak run-off season, increased further by the diversion into Weminuche Creek from Los Pinos River via the Raber Lohr Ditch. The trail continues up quite steeply for a bit, then the valley opens up into the broad meadows of Weminuche Pass. From this point up to Rincon La Vaca the trail is much more gentle.

The trail stays well above Weminuche Creek for about 2 miles, crossing two streams (the second is the larger) coming off Simpson Mountain. Weminuche Creek is encountered at about mile 4.5 and must be forded. There can be a lot of water in the spring, but the wading isn't difficult.

Weminuche Pass (10,622 feet) is crossed a short distance beyond the creek (a very gentle Continental Divide crossing). Pack horses are often seen grazing in the grassy meadows near the Pass.

The trail parallels the Raber Lohr Ditch for about 0.5 mile, bends right, joins with the Continental Divide Trail, then heads up the Rincon La Vaca drainage. Rincon La Vaca is a good place to stop if you are day hiking. It is a good camping spot if you are continuing.

This is good elk and deer country, but they are usually higher up after early June. Weather permitting, a good view of Rio Grande Pyramid (13,821 feet) will be visible where the forest opens up. Proceed across the bottom of an avalanche chute, then climb up the moderately steep incline to continue on toward the peak.

To climb Rio Grande Pyramid, leave the trail at a broad switchback at timberline, skirt the willows on the left and hike up to the ridge where a large, square geologic feature called the "Window" or the "Devil's Gateway" becomes visible. The trail coming directly up the ridge from Weminuche Pass is joined at about 12,300 feet and continues to the summit of the pyramid (about four miles from the lower Rincon La Vaca). The climb is rocky and steep in places, but not difficult for experienced hikers. Red Cloud, Sunshine, Uncompahgre, Wetterhorn, Mount Sneffels, Mount Wilson, Wilson Peak, the Grenadiers, and the Needles can all be seen from the summit in good weather.

52 Wolf Creek Pass–Divide Trail

General description:	An easy day hike or the starting point for an extended backpacking trip along the Continental Divide in the San Juan Mountains, located about 50 miles west of Alamosa and 60 miles east of Durango.
Difficulty:	Easy.
Distance:	As long as you want.
Traffic:	Light to moderate.
Elevation gain:	None.
Maps:	Wolf Creek Pass and Spar City 15 minute USGS quads, Trails Illustrated Weminuche Wilderness map.
For more information:	Rio Grande National Forest, Divide Ranger District, Del Norte Office, 13308 West Highway 160, P.O. Box 40, Del Norte, Colorado 81132, 719-657-3321.

Finding the trailhead: Take U.S. Highway 160 southwest from Del Norte or northeast from Pagosa Springs to the summit of Wolf Creek Pass. Just on the east side of the pass, look for a gravel road, which climbs the north

Wolf Creek Pass-Divide Trail

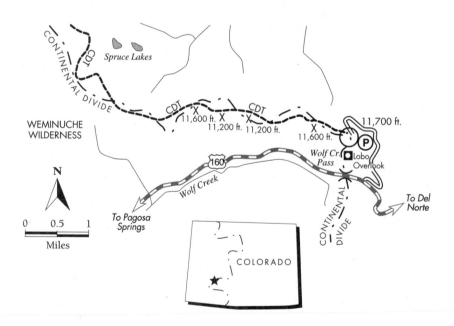

mountain to the Lobo Overlook at an elevation of about 11,700 feet and overlooks Wolf Creek Pass. The road is steep but accessible to passenger cars once the snow has been cleared in late spring or early summer. Park in the area provided at the end of the road.

The hike: This hike takes you west and northwest along a portion of the Continental Divide Trail from the top of Wolf Creek Pass. The trail is easily accessible and leads you immediately into the beautiful timberline country along the divide. You will have spectacular views of the surrounding mountain ranges as you hike into the Weminuche Wilderness Area.

Begin your hike by walking down past and to the west of the microwave tower, staying on the ridgetop through timber until you encounter the trail where it leads out across an alpine meadow. From here, the trail is easy to follow, except where it may disappear into snow drifts if you are hiking early in the summer season.

Within the first 0.5 mile, you may come across side trails which descend both north and south from the divide. These side trails are indicated differently on both the USGS and Forest Service Maps and are difficult to follow.

About 0.75 mile along, the trail drops down on the south side of the divide to avoid the steep ridgetop. The trail then traverses a beautiful bowl above Wolf Creek. At this point you may notice some timber cuts across the valley on the slopes of Treasure Mountain. They are clearcuts, but have been made in irregular shapes to approximate natural openings in the forest. These are a far cry from the square blocks so commonly associated with clearcutting in the past.

As you climb back toward the ridgetop and pass several outcroppings of rock, look for indications of the volcanic geology of this area. Extensive deposits of volcanic breccia and lava cover most of the San Juan Mountains.

After you reach the ridgetop, you will descend by way of a long meadow to a saddle along the divide. This would make a good destination for a short day hike or provide a good camping spot if you plan on going farther.

The possibilities for longer hikes are unlimited along this trail, which takes you through meadows of unsurpassed beauty full of wildflowers, and provides you with spectacular views along its length. The trail will eventually extend all the way from the New Mexico border to the Wyoming border, following both existing trails and trail sections yet to be built as it traces the Continental Divide through the state. You may continue as far as Silverton, some 60 miles away, or just to Archuleta Lake, 8 miles farther. There are side trails to be explored, too. Or you can always simply return as you came.

—Peter, Caryn, and Crystal Boddie

West Chama Trail

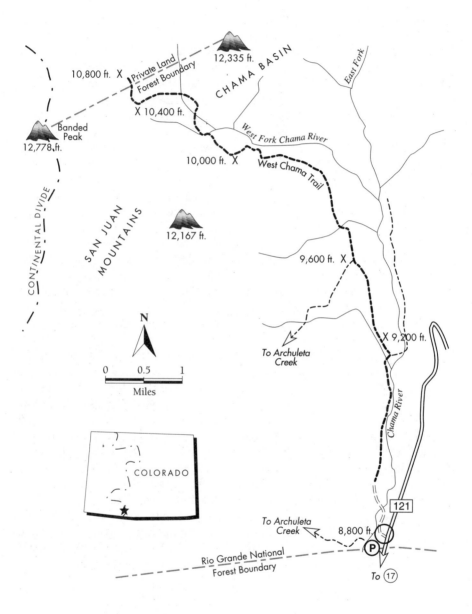

10,800 ft. X

Private Land
Forest Boundary

12,335 ft.

CHAMA BASIN

East Fork

X 10,400 ft.

West Fork Chama River

Banded Peak
12,778 ft.

10,000 ft. X

West Chama Trail

CONTINENTAL DIVIDE

SAN JUAN
MOUNTAINS

12,167 ft.

9,600 ft. X

N

X 9,200 ft.

0   0.5   1
Miles

To Archuleta
Creek

Chama River

COLORADO

121

To Archuleta
Creek

8,800 ft.

P

Rio Grande National
Forest Boundary

To 17

53 West Chama Trail

General description:	A day hike or overnighter along the Chama River into the upper Chama Basin, located approximately 7 miles north of Chama, New Mexico; about 35 miles southwest of Antonito, Colorado.
Difficulty:	Moderate.
Distance:	8 miles, one way.
Traffic:	Light.
Elevation gain:	1,600 feet.
Maps:	Chama Peak 15-minute USGS Quad, Rio Grande National Forest Map.
For more information:	Rio Grande National Forest, Conejos Peak Ranger District, 15571 County Road T-5, P.O. Box 420, La Jara, Colorado 81140, 719-274-8971.

Finding the trailhead: Take Colorado Highway 17 southwest from Antonito into New Mexico or drive 7 miles north from Chama, New Mexico, on CO 17 to the Chama River Road (Forest Road 121). The Lobo Ranch is a good landmark at the intersection. Take this road north through private property for 6 miles to the Rio Grande National Forest boundary. At the forest boundary, take the left fork of the road to the campground beside the river. The road is closed on the east bank of the river. It may reopen eventually. Ford on foot and go about 2 miles to West Chama Trail, which begins at the road closure.

The hike: The West Chama Trail leads you along the Chama River up into the beautiful Chama Basin, one of the most scenic areas in the Rio Grande National Forest and in the San Juan Mountain Range.

The trail climbs steeply away from the Chama River along a small tributary stream bordered by stands of aspen that are spectacular in the fall. As the trail leaves this tributary and follows the Chama River to the confluence of the East and West forks, it stays high above the river and passes through dry subalpine meadows and more stands of aspen and then through virgin spruce fir forests. A spectacular view of the entire valley is afforded from the trail above the confluence.

While the glacial valleys of the Conejos Plateau Area are steep and narrow, the Chama River Valley is wide and spacious. Steep cliffs of colorful, intricately eroded volcanic and sedimentary rock, surround the valley. Waterfalls cascade over the cliffs from the plateau above.

The gentle slopes that descend from the foot of the cliffs to the river below are covered by forests of aspen, interspersed with spruce and fir. Fingers of forest creep up the ravines dissecting the cliffs. Willows and cottonwoods follow the river as it meanders through the grasslands of the lower valley. At the trailhead of the West Chama Trail, the valley narrows and narrowleaf alder and willow dominate the streamside vegetation.

Massive Banded Peak, a local landmark, rises to your left as you continue the strenuous climb up the trail to the Forest Boundary and the Continental Divide. Here, at the trail's end, you have superb views of the Chama Basin and south into New Mexico.

This is not only a very scenic area, but a historic one as well. To the west is the Tierra Amarilla Land Grant and to the south is the route of the Cumbres and Toltec Railroad, a narrow gauge steam route which runs from Antonito, Colorado, to Chama, New Mexico.

Water and camping sites are abundant along the entire length of the trail, but drinking water should be treated before consumption. Fishing is good for rainbow and cutthroat trout in the Chama River. Be extremely careful in fording the river during spring runoff.

After enjoying the view from this, the headwaters of the West Fork, return as you came.

The Continental Divide in New Mexico

New Mexico is a diverse state, with almost any kind of terrain and climate imaginable. One day you can be sweltering in the desert backcountry and the next you can be shivering at an alpine pass. Although New Mexico does not have much of a CDT, the divide does pass through some of New Mexico's most scenic areas. Highlights included in this book are hikes along the divide in the San Pedro Parks Wilderness, El Malpais National Monument, the Gila Wilderness, and the Aldo Leopold Wilderness.

54 San Pedro Parks

General description:	A two- or three-day hike into the lush meadows and forests of the San Pedro Parks Wilderness, located about 90 miles northwest of Albuquerque. Best time to hike is May through October. Water is available at Rio de las Vacas and Clear Creek. The area offers large meadows, solitude, and winter cross-country ski potential.
Distance:	About 15 miles, round trip.
Difficulty:	Easy to moderate.
Traffic:	Light to moderate.
Elevation gain:	900 feet.
Maps:	San Pedro Parks Wilderness, Santa Fe National Forest, Nacimiento Peak 7.5-minute USGS Quad.
For More Information:	Cuba Ranger District, P.O. Box 130, Cuba, New Mexico 87013, 505-289-3664.

Finding the trailhead: From Cuba, drive east on New Mexico Highway 126 up into the mountains about 6 miles to the end of the pavement. About 0.25 mile from the end of the pavement, turn left onto gravel Forest Road 70 and drive 2.8 miles to the parking lot, marked with signs for Trail 51 and the San Pedro Parks Wilderness.

From Los Alamos, start at the junction of New Mexico Highways 4 and 501 a few miles southwest of town. Drive west on NM 4 into the mountains for 24.5 miles to the junction of NM 126. Turn right onto NM 126 and follow it 29.8 very scenic miles to the turnoff of FR 70 above. The first 9 miles of NM 126 is paved, the remainder is dirt. The gravel surface is

Boulders dot one of the many meadows in the San Pedro Parks Wilderness.

generally good in dry conditions, but a mile or two in the middle can be treacherous in wet weather. The dirt section of NM 126 is closed in winter.

The hike: This is one of my favorite hikes in New Mexico, in part because it is so different from most of the state's mountain areas. The 41,132-acre San Pedro Parks Wilderness is basically a big, relatively level area of forest and meadows. Crystal-clear, slow moving mountain streams meander down through broad marshy valley bottoms. Multiple large meadows give the area a manicured, park-like atmosphere. Instead of having a few high peaks, much of the entire wilderness lies at about 10,000 feet. No sheer cliffs or jagged peaks break up the terrain. Most other New Mexico mountains are very steep, with level areas few and far between.

Because the area is not very steep or mountainous, hiking is very easy, even over long distances. Additionally, plentiful water is available in the many creeks (as usual, treat it before using). This 15-mile hike gains only about 1,100 feet and can be done in a day fairly easily by someone in rea-

San Pedro Parks

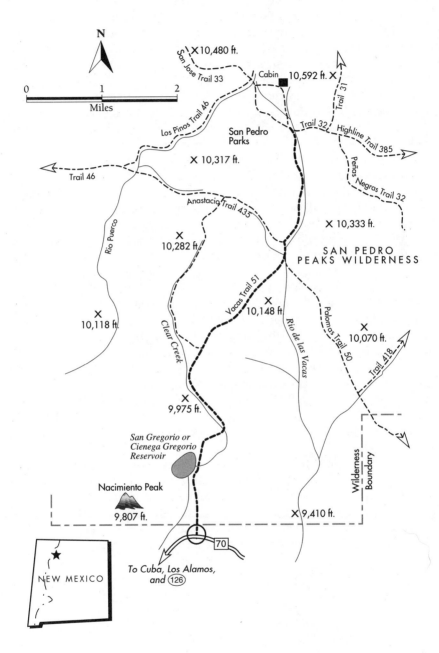

N

0   1   2
Miles

X 10,480 ft.

San Jose Trail 33

Cabin   10,592 ft. X

Los Pinos Trail 46

Trail 31

San Pedro
Parks

Trail 32   Highline Trail 385

X 10,317 ft.

Trail 46

Peñas Negras Trail 32

Anastacio Trail 435

X 10,333 ft.

Rio Puerco

X
10,282 ft.

SAN PEDRO
PEAKS WILDERNESS

Vacas Trail 51

X
10,118 ft.

X
10,148 ft.

Rio de las Vacas

Palomas Trail 50

X
10,070 ft.

Clear Creek

Trail 418

X
9,975 ft.

San Gregorio or
Cienega Gregorio
Reservoir

Wilderness Boundary

Nacimiento Peak

9,807 ft.

X 9,410 ft.

70

To Cuba, Los Alamos,
and 126

NEW MEXICO

sonable shape. Once you see it however, you will regret not spending two or three days. Potential campsites are almost innumerable.

From the parking lot, follow Trail 51, the Vacas Trail, through spruce and fir about 0.75 mile to San Gregorio Reservoir. On summer weekends, the lake and the trail leading to it can be busy. Once you leave the reservoir behind, you probably will not see many hikers. Weekdays are even better. When I did the hike on a summer weekday, I only saw one couple and one family in the entire 13 miles of hiking past the lake.

Follow the trail around the right (east) side of the small reservoir and away to the north. A little past the lake, a trail forks back to the lake on the left. Keep going north. At almost 2 miles you will hit Clear Creek, marked by a sign. The trail follows the creek for more than a mile, before climbing out a tributary into a long, flat wooded stretch. Here and there a few faint old trails fork off, but the main trail is obvious.

Occasionally the trail crosses marshy meadows and creek bottoms. It can be difficult to keep your feet dry during the crossings, especially right after the snow melts in the spring and after late summer rains. For overnight trips, you might want to carry an extra pair of tennis shoes. The trail sometimes gets faint in the marshy areas, so look carefully for the trail on the opposite side of the meadow. Wooden posts often mark the way in these confusing sections. The junctions are generally well marked, but having a copy of the San Pedro Parks Wilderness map will help immensely in avoiding any confusion in the large open meadow areas.

At about 5.25 miles, the trail reaches the Rio de las Vacas. After this point, you will mostly be hiking across meadows. Be careful of lightning in the open areas, especially in late summer. Right after crossing the stream, Palomas Trail 50 forks off to the right. Turn left up the creek, staying on Trail 51 toward San Pedro Parks. About 0.25 mile up the creek, the Anastacio Trail 435 forks off to the left. Stay right on Trail 51 toward San Pedro Park. The rest of the hike follows the broad, grassy creek bottom of the Rio de las Vacas.

At about 7.5 miles, the trail reaches the junction with the Penas Negras Trail, 32, on the right. From here, either return the same way, or continue as far as time and energy allow. By adding an easy 3 or 4 miles, a loop can be done by following Trail 51 a mile further up to Trail 46. Turn left on Trail 46, follow it for about 2.5 miles, and turn left again on the Anastacio Trail 435, to make a loop back to the 5.5-mile point on Trail 51.

55 Big Skylight Cave

General description:	A day hike to an extensive lava tube cave system, located about 35 miles southwest of Grants. This hike is best anytime of year when the roads are dry.
Distance:	1 mile, round trip to tube. No water is available.
Difficulty:	Easy.
Traffic:	Light.
Maps:	El Malpais brochure, National Park Service "Big Tubes Area" brochure, Ice Caves 7.5-minute USGS Quad.
For more information:	El Malpais National Monment, P.O. Box 939, Grants, New Mexico 87020, 505-783-4774.

Finding the trailhead: From Grants, take New Mexico Highway 53 south from Interstate 40 about 27 miles to County Road 42. Follow the dirt county road about 6.5 miles to a small dirt road heading east through a gate. A high clearance vehicle is mandatory for the next 3.8 miles to the parking area. Be sure that your tires are in good condition and you have a spare; the lava rocks are jagged. Do not attempt after a heavy rain or snow; even a four-wheel-drive vehicle will have difficulty (mine was stuck here once). Leave all gates as you find them. Several roads fork off to the right; bear left at the junctions. The parking area is marked with a "Big Lava Tubes" sign.

The hike: From the National Park Service "Big Lava Tubes" sign at the parking area, look for rock cairns heading east. Follow the cairns out onto the black lava flow. Watch carefully, so that you do not lose the cairns. You are entering a rolling sea of lava that is fairly heavily wooded with ponderosa pine, alligator juniper, and pinyon pine. It is easy to get lost if you lose the route. The trail is not worn into the lava flow; only the cairns mark the way. Be sure to take a compass and a topo map.

The marked route reaches the lava tube in about 0.5 mile. Just before you get to the tube, the cairns seem to go in two directions. Don't worry; they just go to different sections of the continuous tube.

The huge area of volcanoes and lava flows in El Malpais National Monument was formed over the past three million years in a series of many eruptions. The lava flows are new enough to be rough and jagged to hike over, but the activity here has been calm long enough for much of the area to become wooded with trees and shrubs.

Big Skylight and Four Windows Caves, at the end of the trail, are just two openings into a lava tube over 17 miles long, including collapsed sections. By following the tube, many other entrances can be found. Some of the entrances, such as Big Skylight, are deep pits requiring ropes to enter. However, you can find easy places to scramble down into the tubes at many of

Big Skylight Cave

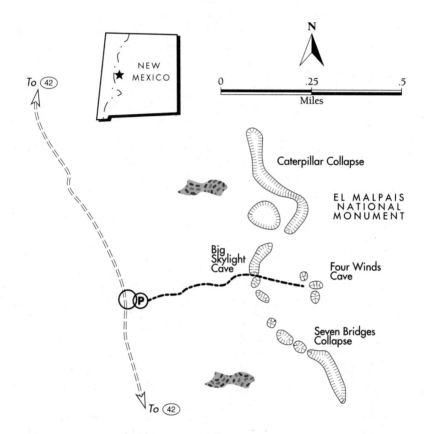

the entrances. The floors of the tubes are commonly boulder piles of loose shifting rock. Use extreme caution. To go beyond daylight in the tubes, be sure that each member of your party has a hard hat and three sources of light. A Coleman lantern has to be handled carefully while scrambling along the uneven floor, but will greatly help in lighting up the tubes. The dark colored rock and ceilings as high as forty feet easily soak up other smaller sources of light. If you exit the tube from an entrance different from the one you entered, be careful not to become lost on the surface.

THE CONTINENTAL DIVIDE THROUGH THE GILA AND ALDO LEOPOLD WILDERNESS AREAS

The Aldo Leopold Wilderness was named after one of the most famous conservationists ever. Together, the Gila and Aldo Leopold Wilderness Areas make up the largest and most intact wild area in New Mexico. The deep canyons and steep ridges thwarted development long enough for the area to remain intact for wilderness designation. The area features multiple trails and even several sections of the CDT. The area is a complicated ecosystem with regular natural fires, which sometimes hinder trail maintenance.

56 Mogollon Baldy

General description:	A two- to three-day backpacking trip to a remote mountaintop fire lookout in the heart of the Gila Wilderness, located about 85 miles northwest of Silver City. Best hiked during mid-May through October. Water is available at Bead, Hummingbird, Apache, Hobo, Little Hobo, and Blacktail Springs. Special attractions include lush high mountain forest, spectacular views, and isolation.
Distance:	About 24 miles, round trip.
Difficulty:	Moderate.
Traffic:	Moderate.
Elevation gain:	1,600 feet.
Maps:	Gila Wilderness, Gila National Forest, Grouse Mountain, and Mogollon Baldy Peak 7.5-minute USGS quads.
For more information:	Glenwood Ranger District, P.O. Box 8, Glenwood, New Mexico 88039, 505-539-2481.

Finding the trailhead: From Silver City, drive about 65 miles northwest on U.S. Highway 180 to Glenwood. From Glenwood, drive about 3.7 miles north on US 180 to the junction with paved New Mexico Highway 159. Turn right and follow the steep, winding mountain road to the old mining ghost town of Mogollon. A few escapees from civilization are bringing new life to the picturesque village. The pavement ends in Mogollon, but a good all-weather gravel surface continues to and past the trailhead. After the first snows, the road is closed beyond Mogollon until late spring. From Mogollon, the road continues to climb up into forest thickly wooded with Douglas-fir,

Mogollon Baldy

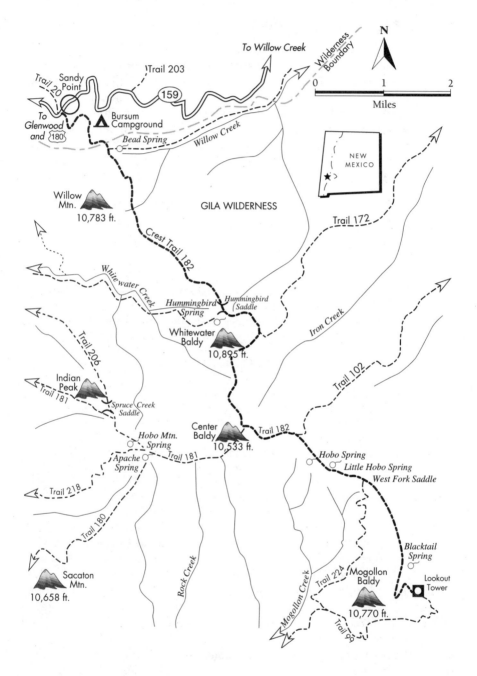

To Willow Creek

Wilderness Boundary

N

Trail 203

Trail 20

Sandy Point

159

To Glenwood and 180

Bursum Campground

Bead Spring

Willow Creek

GILA WILDERNESS

NEW MEXICO

0   1   2

Miles

Willow Mtn.
10,783 ft.

Crest Trail 182

Trail 172

Whitewater Creek

Hummingbird Spring

Hummingbird Saddle

Whitewater Baldy
10,895 ft.

Iron Creek

Trail 206

Trail 102

Indian Peak

Trail 181

Spruce Creek Saddle

Center Baldy
10,533 ft.

Trail 182

Hobo Mtn. Spring

Hobo Spring

Little Hobo Spring

West Fork Saddle

Apache Spring

Trail 181

Trail 218

Trail 180

Blacktail Spring

Sacaton Mtn.
10,658 ft.

Rock Creek

Mogollon Creek

Trail 224

Mogollon Baldy
10,770 ft.

Lookout Tower

Trail 99

ponderosa pine, and aspen. Stop at the marked Sandy Point trailhead, approximately 18.2 miles from the turnoff at US 180.

The hike: This hike follows the crest of the Mogollon Range, the highest range in not only the Gila Wilderness, but all of southern New Mexico, except Sierra Blanca many miles east. Most of the trail lies above 10,000 feet, so prepare to do a little heavy breathing. The Sandy Point trailhead is probably the most commonly used access point to the high country, but is rarely crowded.

The Gila Wilderness contains 558,065 acres, making it the largest in New Mexico. The wilderness lies in the heart of a rugged mountainous area that covers several million acres of southwestern New Mexico and stretches far into Arizona. The Gila forms the oldest wilderness area in the United States, having been set aside in 1924. Congress made the designation permanent in 1964 for the Gila Wilderness and many other areas. The headwaters of much of the Gila River start high in the Mogollon Range. The large mountain area supports healthy populations of deer, elk, bear, mountain lion, and other wildlife.

Be sure to take warm clothes and rain gear, especially in late summer when the rainy season is in full swing. Since the trail follows the crest of the range, it does not go near any creeks. Fortunately, however, the trail does pass several springs, making it unnecessary to carry large quantities of water. Before driving up the mountain from Glenwood, check at the Forest Service ranger station there about the status of the various springs along the route. I last did the hike at the end of an extended drought, and Bead, Hummingbird, and Apache Springs were still all flowing well. Hobo and Little Hobo were very low, however, with only a small quantity of somewhat stagnant water. I did not visit Blacktail Spring. Be sure to treat your water before using.

The well-marked, well-maintained Trail 182 is easy to follow. It immediately begins climbing at a moderate grade from Sandy Point, passing some of the largest Douglas-firs I have seen in the Southwest. At about 1.5 miles, the trail's grade lessens and it crosses into the wilderness.

Shortly afterwards, the marked side trail to Bead Spring goes downhill to the left. The reliable, strongly flowing spring is only about 500 feet down the trail. Be careful not to trample the lush ferns, mosses, and other delicate vegetation at the spring. Huge aspens are mixed in with the spruce at the spring. After Bead Spring, most of the rest of the hike consists of relatively small ups and downs along the crest.

The trail maintains a very easy grade for the next 1.5 miles. Then a short, moderate climb brings the trail to a high point before dropping down slightly to Hummingbird Saddle. At about 4 miles out, the forest opens up for a short distance, giving a great view of the Whitewater Creek drainage below and far out into Arizona. Hummingbird Saddle, at about 4.75 miles, is a popular camping area because of many possible level sites and nearby Hummingbird Spring. It also makes a good destination for day hikers. The spring is a few hundred yards down below the saddle to the right (west). A marked trail leads to it. The trail, 207, continues on past the spring to Redstone Park and all the way down Whitewater Creek. Whitewater Baldy, the highest point in the Mogollon Range, rises right above the south side of the saddle. A faint, unofficial trail follows the crest from the saddle up to the summit. A bare area on its south side offers great views.

At all the trail junctions, just follow the signs to Mogollon Baldy. Usually the distances shown are less than exact, but still close enough. The Forest Service trail numbers may not be on all signs, but Trail 182 is the route all the way to Mogollon Baldy.

From Hummingbird Saddle, Trail 182 drops slightly for the next mile or so. At about 5.5 miles (about 0.75 miles from the saddle), marked Trail 172 forks off to the left, to Iron Creek Lake. Stay right, towards Baldy. In another 0.75 mile or so, the trail reaches another saddle on the crest. The level area makes an ideal campsite, although there is no close water source. The trail then climbs back up some, reaching the junction with Trail 181 at about 7.25 miles. Plentiful campsites exist in the crest area around the junction. The marked right-hand trail goes to Spruce Creek Saddle and many other destinations. Apache Spring and possible campsites lie about 1.5 miles out on Trail 181. To continue on to Baldy, follow the sign onto the left-hand fork.

The trail begins to descend a short distance beyond the trail 181 junction. At a little more than 8 miles, marked Trail 102 climbs steeply off to the left to Turkeyfeather Pass. Bear right to Baldy. Hobo Spring is next to the trail on the right about 0.5 mile beyond the Turkeyfeather Pass junction. A small area has been leveled out for camping near the spring. Check with the Forest Service about the spring's status before you start your hike. Little Hobo Spring is on the left side of the trail another 0.5 mile down the way.

At about 10 miles, the trail reaches West Fork Saddle. At about 9,600 feet, it is the lowest point on the hike other than the start of the trail at Sandy Point. The saddle has several excellent, level campsites. Trail 224 to Mogollon Creek forks down to the right from the saddle. The last 2 miles (1.5 miles according to the sign) to Baldy make up the longest sustained climb of the hike, gaining over 1,100 feet. Blacktail Spring is to the left of the trail a little below the summit.

The summit commands tremendous views of not only the Gila Wilderness, but of mountains over much of southern New Mexico and Arizona. So much of the hike passes through dense woods that the views from the treeless summit are breathtaking in contrast. Such a large area surrounding the peak is undeveloped that virtually no sign of man is visible as far as the eye can see. The Forest Service, being aware of the peak's prominent summit, long ago built a fire lookout and ranger cabin on the summit. The lookout is staffed from May through August. The facilities are for Forest Service use only, but the rangers usually enjoy visiting with hikers.

Camping is allowed on the summit, but not in the immediate vicinity of the tower and cabin. Be sure to pick up water on the way up; the rangers' supply on the summit is extremely limited. Please do not disturb the Forest Service facilities if the rangers are not in residence. Believe it or not, even here vandals have struck.

Lightning is a threat along most of the crest trail, but is particularly dangerous on the bare summit of Mogollon Baldy. Thunderstorms can build within minutes in the mountains, especially in late summer afternoons. If you get wet, hypothermia is also a danger. While early summer is usually the driest time of year for hiking in the Mogollons, the mountains look their lush green best in August. Even here in southern New Mexico, patches of snow can cover the trail as late as early June in good snow years. I day-hiked up Whitewater Baldy on Memorial Day weekend one year and had to push through drifts for much of the last half of the hike. Check with the Forest Service for current conditions.

57 Mimbres River

General description:	A day hike or overnight trip along the Mimbres River in the Aldo Leopold Wilderness, located about 50 miles northeast of Silver City. Best season for hiking is April through December. Water is available Mimbres River.
Distance:	About 13 miles, round trip.
Difficulty:	Moderate.
Traffic:	Light.
Elevation gain:	700 feet.
Maps:	Gila National Forest, Aldo Leopold Wilderness, Hay Mesa 7.5-minute USGS quads.
For more information:	Mimbres Ranger District, P.O. Box 79, Mimbres, New Mexico 88049, 505-536-2250.

Finding the trailhead: From Silver City, drive about 8 miles east on U.S. Highway 180 to Central. Turn left on New Mexico Highway 152 and drive about 14.4 miles east to New Mexico Highway 35. Turn left and follow NM 35 about 15.2 miles north to NM 61, the Wall Lake turnoff. Turn right onto gravel New Mexico Highway 61. If you had any doubt that you were entering a remote area, read the sign: "Road Ahead Restricted—Four-Wheel-Drive and High Axle Vehicle." This is a state highway? Another sign says: "No Food, Lodging, or Gasoline Next 120 Miles."

Follow NM 61/Forest Road 150, a good, all-weather gravel road, for about 7.3 miles to the marked FR 150A turnoff to Cooney and the Mimbres River on the right. The road crosses North Star Mesa, where the forest has been practically clearcut by firewood cutters. The dry, slow-growing southwestern forests used for firewood cutting are not a renewable resource with the current large human population. Turn right onto FR 150A.

The first 0.7 mile is very good and the next 0.7 mile down to the river is steep, but usually passable by any vehicle. Cross the river and continue up the canyon to the end of the road at a ranch house at 2.8 miles. Park outside the fence surrounding the ranch house.

The hike: The Black Range is long, stretching almost 100 miles from north to south along a high crest. Several peaks along the crest top out at over 10,000 feet. The mountains make up a major component of the enormous 3.3-million-acre Gila National Forest. Most of the mountains are accessible only by horse or foot, with the heart protected by the 202,000-acre Aldo Leopold Wilderness. The heavily forested range is crisscrossed with several hundred miles of trails, most infrequently, if ever, used. The very long trails are ideal for multi-day backpacking trips.

The almost undiscovered mountains make a great place to lose yourself, far from civilization. This trail was chosen because it is usually accessible by any vehicle and it follows one of the range's permanent streams. It is one of the most popular entry points into the Aldo Leopold Wilderness, popular being a relative term. You probably will see but a handful of people on the trail at most.

From the parking area in front of the ranch house, hike up the rough road to the right along the fence and around the house, staying out of the private yard. Trail 77 goes upstream, skirting the ranch on the slopes above, before rejoining the river. A sign marks the trailhead in front of the house, but it was in bad shape when I last visited. It says that Mimbres Lake is 11.75 miles and Reeds Peak is 12.25 miles.

The trail is excellent, smooth, and well maintained. The hiking is easy; I gave this hike a moderate rating only because of its length. Most of the first part of the hike is in open ponderosa and cottonwood forest. The trail enters the wilderness area a bit less than a mile up canyon. Shortly afterward you hit the first of many stream crossings. The Mimbres River is really more of a stream than a river, except in flood. However, it is still large enough to be a nuisance to cross. In early spring and late summer, plan on getting your feet wet since a dry crossing point will not exist. Backpackers should take an extra pair of shoes. Many beautiful campsites lie all along the hike. Camp well away from the stream and trail.

At about 3 miles, in a park-like area of ponderosa pine in a broad part of the canyon, you will pass an old corral. Shortly afterward, you will hit lush patches of Douglas-fir and aspen mixed in with the ponderosa. At about 5 miles, another even more deteriorated corral is passed. At about 6.5 miles, at the end of this hike, the trail forks. To the left, according to the sign, Reeds Peak lies 5.75 miles away on Trail 77. To the right, Mimbres Lake lies 5.25 miles away on Trail 78. The Mimbres River also forks, with Trail 77 following the North Fork and Trail 78 following the Middle Fork.

For a tremendous three-day backpacking trip, follow Trail 78 up to Mimbres Lake (See the Mimbres Lake hike), take Crest Trail 79 north to Reeds Peak, and return via Trail 77 to the fork at the end of this hike.

Mimbres River • Mimbres Lake

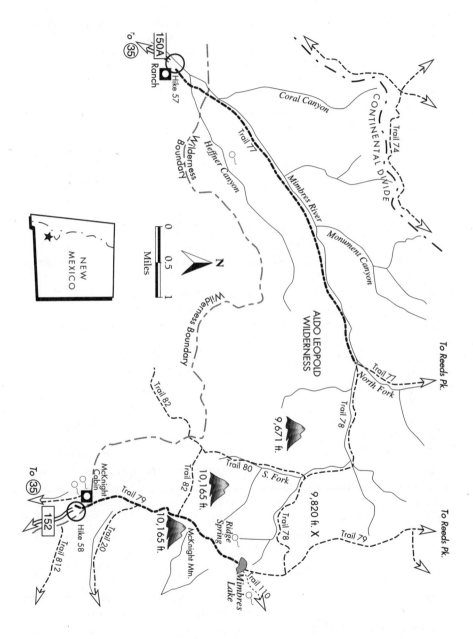

58 Mimbres Lake

See map on page 185

General description:	A day hike to a small, marshy, natural pond in the Aldo Leopold Wilderness, located about 50 miles northeast of Silver City. Best hiked May through November. Water is available at Mimbres Lake, Ridge Spring, North Seco Spring, and McKnight Cabin Spring.
Distance:	About 7 miles, round trip.
Difficulty:	Moderate.
Traffic:	Light.
Elevation:	600 feet.
Maps:	Gila National Forest, Aldo Leopold Wilderness, Victoria Park 7.5-minute USGS quads.
For more information:	Mimbres Ranger District, P.O. Box 79, Mimbres, New Mexico 88049, 505-536-2250.

Finding the trailhead: From Silver City, take U.S. Highway 180 about 8 miles east to Central. Turn left onto New Mexico Highway 152 and continue east about 14.4 miles to New Mexico Highway 35. Turn left and go north on NM 35 about 12.3 miles to McKnight Road (Forest Road 152). Follow FR 152 about 17.4 miles up onto the crest of the Black Range. Park at the Trail 79 sign. The end of the road is only 0.3 mile further at the McKnight Cabin. FR 152 is an excellent gravel road for about the first 9 miles to the junction of Forest Road 537. After this point, a high-clearance vehicle is recommended to negotiate the rocks and ruts. I made it to the top in a sedan, but I would only recommend it for short wheelbase sedans with very able drivers. Check with the Forest Service in advance.

The hike: This trail starts on the crest of the Black Range and is one of the most scenic hikes in the mountains.

Much of the heart of the range is protected by the enormous Aldo Leopold Wilderness. This trail enters the wilderness area almost immediately. Most of the mountains have never had much impact from the activities of man. Even today, the extensive mountain range is relatively undiscovered, making it unlikely that you will see many people. Most people who actually make it to this corner of New Mexico head for the better-known Gila Wilderness.

The hike can easily be done as a day hike, but begs to be done as a two or three day trip. If you are doing more than a day hike, be sure to check on the status of the springs and lake before starting. Usually water can be found in at least some of the sources, but you need to know ahead of time. Water is usually available at McKnight Cabin Spring by the corral just below the cabin at the end of the road.

The trail starts out by heading straight into an aspen grove. The sign at the trailhead, saying "Mimbres Lake 4.5" miles, is wrong; the distance is about 3.5 miles. The trail is somewhat more difficult than the elevations and length indicate because it climbs up over a couple of mountains before reaching the lake, which lies at almost the same elevation as the trailhead. The trail quickly begins climbing. At about 0.3 mile, an unmarked trail forks downhill to the left, going to the cabin. The trail then climbs steeply to the top of a flat-topped, unnamed summit.

The trail then drops down to a saddle in the crest, passing in and out of young aspen stands. The next 1.5 miles follow the narrow crest, giving great views both east and west. The young aspens and frequent views are the result of the 40,000-acre McKnight fire in the 1950s. The maps show Trail 20 as forking off to the right, but I did not see it. Many Black Range trails are disappearing from lack of use.

At about 1.5 miles, the trail begins the steep climb up McKnight Mountain, gaining about 500 feet. The top is reached at about 2 miles. A 50-yard, marked side trail on the right takes you to the rocky summit. Be sure to

Mimbres Lake is a small marshy natural lake in the Aldo Leopold Wilderness.

climb up and enjoy the 360-degree views from the highest point in the Black Range. You'll see endless miles of mountains with almost no sign of man.

Just past the summit, marked Trail 82 forks uphill to the left to Forest Road 151. Go downhill to the right toward Mimbres Lake.

The observant will notice that the rest of the trail appears to follow what was a four-wheel drive road many years ago. The trail leaves the old burned area and descends steeply for a short distance off of the peak. The trail now passes through dense fir and spruce forest on a broader, flatter portion of the crest. At about 3 miles, a drainage is passed on the left, down which lies Ridge Spring. I did not visit the spring, although a faint trail appeared to lead down the drainage toward it.

Just before reaching the lake, hikers will notice an enormous Douglas-fir on the right side of the trail. The tree is probably the largest tree of its kind that I have seen in New Mexico. It appeared to be about 7 feet in diameter at chest height and towered high up in the canopy.

The shallow, marshy Mimbres Lake lies in a beautiful, level clearing, surrounded by a dense forest of spruce, fir, and aspen. I day hiked to the lake and regretted not being able to camp. Be sure to find a site well away from the lake to avoid polluting it or scaring away wildlife. Innumerable campsites exist in the large, level, mountaintop area around the lake. The area would make a great base camp for day hikes along the Crest Trail and side trails. Marked Trail 110 forks off of Trail 79 at the lake. Although I did not visit it, the map indicates North Seco Spring as lying about 0.5 mile down Trail 110. Ridge Spring, or North Seco Spring, would probably make better water sources than the marshy lake. If all are dry, try walking down the Mimbres River on Trail 78 until the stream appears (see map).

A tremendous three-day backpacking trip could be done by following Trail 79 to Reeds Peak and looping back to the lake via Trails 77 and 78. See the map and the description of the Mimbres River hike for ideas.

59 Signal Peak

General description:	A day hike to the summit of one the highest peaks in the Pinos Altos Range, located about 15 miles north of Silver City. Best hiked in April through November. No water is available. The hike offers tremendous views of Gila Wilderness and as far as the Chiricahua and Pinaleno Mountains of Arizona; thick conifer forest.
Distance:	5 miles, round trip.
Difficulty:	Moderate.
Traffic:	Light
Elevation gain:	1,741 feet.

A fresh winter snow blankets Signal Peak.

Maps:	Gila National Forest, Twin Sisters 7.5-minute USGS Quad.
For more information:	Silver City Ranger District, 3005 East Camino del Bosque, Silver City, New Mexico 88049, 505-538-2771.

Finding the trailhead: Take New Mexico Highway 15 north from Silver City through the village of Pinos Altos. About 4 miles past Pinos Altos, the road passes the Ben Lilly Memorial and then enters Cherry Creek Canyon. The highway soon passes Cherry Creek and then McMillan Forest Campgrounds. The marked trail (742) takes off from the right side of the road about 1.5 miles past McMillan Campground. The Signal Peak road (154) turns off to the right only a couple of hundred yards farther.

Signal Peak

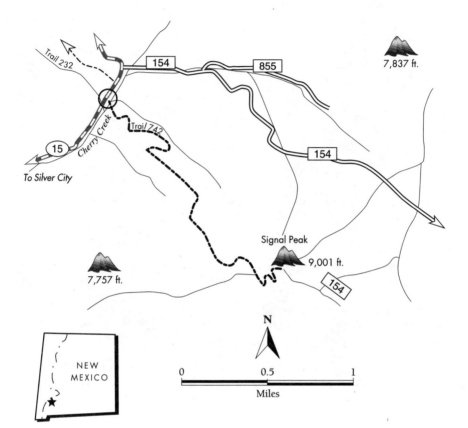

Trail 232

154   855

7,837 ft.

Trail 742

15   Cherry Creek

154

To Silver City

Signal Peak

9,001 ft.

7,757 ft.

154

N

NEW
MEXICO

0   0.5   1

Miles

The hike: The Pinos Altos Range is the southernmost mountain range of the Gila Wilderness, the largest wilderness in New Mexico. Although this hike does not enter the wilderness area, great views of the wilderness greet hikers from the trail and the summit.

From its start on Highway 15, the trail crosses a meadow before starting its climb up into the forest covering the flanks of Signal Peak. Initially, the trail passes through thick stands of Douglas-fir on the moister north slopes of the mountain. As it climbs, it curves around onto the sunnier, drier, south-facing slopes of the peak and ponderosa pine becomes more common. While most of the hike travels through dense forest, regular breaks in the trees give increasingly dramatic views, especially to the south and southwest.

From the summit, with its fire lookout tower, you can see 360 degrees. To the east, north, and west lie the endless mountain ranges of the 3.3 million-acre Gila National Forest.

To the south and southwest, desert basin and range country stretch far into Arizona and Mexico. Sleepy Pinos Altos lies below, the site of a gold mining boom begun in 1859. Little mining continues today in Pinos Altos, but other large mines near Silver City and Santa Rita still produce enormous amounts of copper and other metals every year.

The Gila National Forest covers a large unpopulated area of high country consisting of many interconnected mountain ranges. The Continental Divide meanders though the national forest for 170 miles and crosses the Pinos Altos Range only about a mile southeast of the summit of Signal Peak. The Continental Divide Trail is being developed in New Mexico as part a route planned from Canada to Mexico. Much of it will traverse the Gila National Forest.

You can return to the trailhead via the lookout tower road, but at 7 miles, it is considerably longer than the trail.

60 Tadpole Ridge

General description: A day hike (with shuttle) or overnight trip (without) along the crest of the Pinos Altos Range.
General location: About 15 miles north of Silver City (to east trailhead).
Length: About 16.5 miles round trip (8.25 miles with shuttle).
Difficulty: Moderate with shuttle, strenuous without.
Traffic: Light.
Elevation gain: 7,150 to 8610 feet.
Maps: Gila National Forest, Twin Sisters and Reading.
For more information: Silver City Ranger District, 3005 East Camino del Bosque, Silver City, New Mexico 88049, 505-538-2771.

Finding the trailhead: Take paved New Mexico Highway 15 north from Silver City about 6.6 miles to the mountain village of Pinos Altos. Continue along NM 15 almost an additional 8 miles to the marked eastern trailhead for Tadpole Ridge Trail 232 on the left. It lies just across the road from the Signal Peak trailhead and a couple of hundred yards before the obvious junction with the Signal Peak Road, Forest Road 154. To get to the western trailhead, continue along NM 15 another 3.1 miles to the Sheep Corral Canyon Road, Forest Road 282, on the left. Follow the narrow, but good gravel road for 6.8 miles to the marked trailhead in the bottom of a canyon by a corral and water tank. There are several road junctions along FR 282; stay on the better, main road (which is FR 282) to get to the trailhead.

Tadpole Ridge

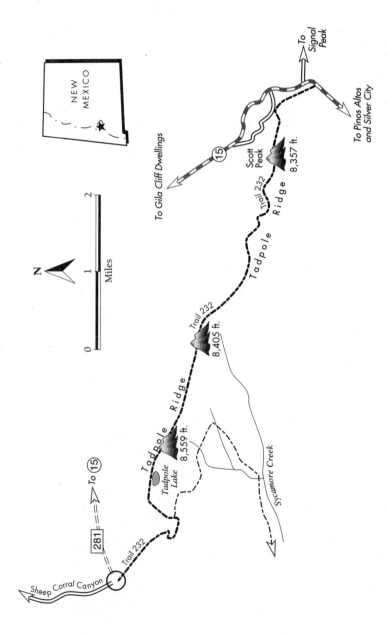

NEW MEXICO

N

0   1   2
Miles

To Gila Cliff Dwellings

15

Scott Peak

8,357 ft.

To Signal Peak

To Pinos Altos and Silver City

Trail 232

Tadpole Ridge

Trail 232

8,405 ft.

Tadpole Ridge

8,559 ft.

Tadpole Lake

Sycamore Creek

281

To 15

Trail 232

Sheep Corral Canyon

The hike: Tadpole Ridge is a long, narrow ridge that runs roughly northwest to southeast and forms the crest of part of the Pinos Altos Range. The mountains are one of many ranges that lie within the massive Gila National Forest. Part of the Pinos Altos Range is in the Gila Wilderness, but not the section traversed by this trail.

This hike is an easy escape into the cool pines from nearby Silver City. Although parts of Tadpole Ridge burned during dry years in the mid-1990s, most of the hike is still shaded by pines and firs. Because most of the maintained trail follows the crest of the ridge, views are excellent. Water is usually available at Tadpole Lake; however, check with the Forest Service about its status ahead of time. It is really just a large stock tank with murky water, so unless you are backpacking, plan to carry enough.

The hike is most easily done as a one-way hike with a shuttle. Drop one vehicle at the eastern trailhead and start your hike at the western trailhead. This description describes the hike by starting on the west side.

Marked Trail 232 starts at the road by a corral and water tank. From the road, start up the hill past the rusty water tank. Look carefully for a big cairn and follow the trail past it up a narrow canyon bottom. Ponderosa pines and Douglas-firs shade the trail here and along much of the route. The first part of the trail was once an old road.

You will soon pass burned forest areas, but here and along much of the route the fire generally cleared underbrush and did only minor harm to the larger trees. After a little less than a mile, the trail steepens abruptly and switchbacks out of the canyon. Views of the Mogollon Range to the northwest open up. The path reaches a saddle and marked trail junction at about 1.25 miles. The faint, lightly traveled Sycamore Canyon Trail 234 turns off to the right and drops down off the other side of the saddle.

The trail sign at the junction indicates a distance of 7 miles to the eastern trailhead on NM 15, giving a total hike length of 8.25 miles as written above. However, another source shows a total distance of 9.5 miles. Take your pick; I used the shorter distance here.

From the saddle, continue hiking up Tadpole Ridge on Trail 232. The trail climbs through a short, but heavily burned section, and then levels off some on the ridge top in 0.5 mile or so. It soon passes Tadpole Lake in the middle of a level area that would be good for camping. After Tadpole Lake, the trail follows the ridge top for most of the rest of the hike. Fortunately, at times it contours along the north slope of the ridge, rather than climb over every small summit along the crest. Even so, it does cross numerous saddles. Although no single saddle requires a lot of elevation loss and gain, the many saddles add quite a bit of climbing in addition to the initial climb up onto the ridge top. Generally, the western half of the trail has more ups and downs and is rockier that the eastern half.

Views stretch in every direction from many points along the trail. To the northwest lie the Mogollon and Diablo Ranges in the heart of the Gila Wilderness. To the east lies the Black Range, high north-south trending mountains. On clear days, the Chiricahua and Pinaleno mountains of Arizona can be seen far to the southwest. Notice that the south side of Tadpole Ridge is much less lush than the north side because of greater sun exposure. On early or late season hikes, you may have to walk through patches of snow where the trail crosses shady north slopes.

After roughly the mid-point of the hike, the trail becomes smoother and follows a long stretch of mostly level ground through thick, relatively un-burned ponderosa pine forest. From here on, the trail is relatively level or downhill trending. It really begins to descend when it reaches a heavily burned area. Here the trees are quite dead and hazardous to be under in strong winds. Signal Peak is visible across Cherry Creek Canyon to the south-east. Soon after leaving the heavily burned area, the trail drops down the north side and off of the ridge top for good. After a couple of switchbacks, the trail becomes a rough, unofficial woodcutter's road. Turn right (east) and follow the road a short distance downhill until it turns back into a trail. Continue downhill along the trail. Soon paved New Mexico Highway 15 is visible below to the left. Stay on the trail another 0.25 mile or so to the trailhead—it is shorter than following the highway.

61 Fort Bayard Champion Tree

General description:	A day hike to an enormous alligator juniper, a New Mexico record-sized tree, located about 12 miles northeast of Silver City. No water available.
Distance:	About 5.5 miles, round trip.
Difficulty:	Easy.
Traffic:	Moderate.
Elevation gain:	450 feet.
Maps:	Gila National Forest, Fort Bayard 7.5-minute USGS quad.
For more information:	Silver City Ranger District, 3005 East Camino del Bosque, Silver City, New Mexico 88049, 505-538-2771.

Finding the trailhead: Start at the well-marked Fort Bayard turnoff on U.S. Highway 180 in the village of Central, about 7 miles east of Silver City. Drive north from US 180 to the fort, now a hospital. Follow signs for the Gila National Forest and Forest Road 536 through the grounds. After passing the fort, the paved road turns to a good gravel surface and becomes FR 536. It enters the national forest about 1.6 miles from US 180. Ignore Forest Road 775 splitting off to the right; stay on FR 536. The road reaches a forest service work camp at 4.5 miles. Go left at the entrance to the camp and follow the sign for the National Recreation Trails. Stop at the large, marked parking area on the right in less than a 0.25 mile.

Fort Bayard Champion Tree

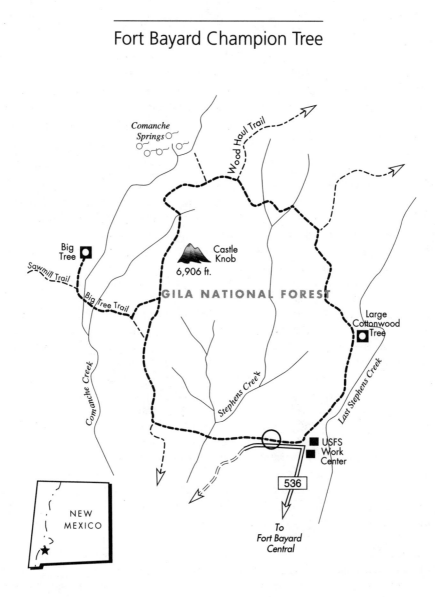

The hike: Alligator junipers thrive in the lower elevations of the mountains around Silver City. They usually grow in mixed stands with pinyon pines and oaks. They are easily recognized because their deeply checkered bark resembles alligator skin. Older junipers usually have a thick, gnarled trunk, but rarely get more than 30 or 40 feet tall. This hike leads to a mammoth, thick-trunked tree that towers more than 60 feet into the sky. It also makes an easy loop through the foothills of the Pinos Altos Range.

The trail is good any time of year. In summer it can be hot, so plan to start early. In winter snow usually melts off within a few days. Water is sometimes available in Cameron Creek behind the massive alligator juniper, called the Big Tree, but not dependably. It can also sometimes be found by taking a side trip to Comanche Springs about halfway around the loop. However, with this short a hike, it is better just to carry enough water.

The national forest map is somewhat confusing for this hike. The topo map or the map with this guidebook is better.

The parking area is the starting point for three trails. A color-coded sign at the trailhead shows red for the Big Tree Trail, green for the Sawmill Trail, and pale blue for the Wood Haul Trail. All three trails share the same route initially. The trail cuts through the fence and then follows it west, crossing a small canyon in about a quarter mile. A short distance after climbing out of the canyon, the trail goes through a gate and then hits an old unused road. As directed by the trail sign, turn right and follow the road uphill to the north.

After about 0.7 mile you will come to a marked junction with another old road. (You may notice a small, unmarked trail turning off to the left a bit before the junction. This is just a small shortcut to the Big Tree Trail.) Turn left onto the Big Tree/Sawmill Trail at the marked junction. You will return here after visiting the tree.

The trail soon drops into a broad, grassy valley bottom dotted here and there with cottonwoods. The trail crosses the valley to the junction with the Sawmill Trail. The Sawmill Trail can be followed using a topo map to Pinos Altos, a good day hike if a shuttle or pick-up is arranged ahead of time. Stay right at the junction and go only another 0.13 mile or so to the Big Tree. The tree is so massive that it is hard to believe that it really is a juniper. A short distance behind the tree, along sometimes flowing Cameron Creek, is a very large cottonwood.

From the Big Tree, retrace your route back to the junction of the two old roads. Go left on the Wood Haul Trail and climb north further into the foothills. The trail was once a wagon road used by historic Fort Bayard for gathering firewood and harvesting construction timber. It climbs at a moderate grade through a few ponderosa pines onto a low mesa, and then levels off. The old road forks in front of a gate. The left fork goes downhill to Cameron Creek and Comanche Springs. Take the right fork and go through the gate. In less than 0.25 mile, the marked Wood Haul Trail forks to the left and ascends a ridge. It makes an excellent side trip off of the main loop of this hike. It climbs up and over the main ridge of the Pinos Altos Range and goes to the Mimbres Valley, the Signal Peak Road, and other destinations. Along the way, it passes deep ruts cut into the rock by wagon wheels. However, for this hike stay right and continue hiking along the old road on a relatively level bench.

In about 0.5 mile, a little-used, unmarked trail goes left to the upper part of Stephens Creek. Stay straight on the main route. The trail soon begins to descend, offering good views to the south. The massive open pit copper mine at Santa Rita is partly visible. The descent is the only really rocky part of the entire hike; the rest of the trail is quite smooth. The trail drops into another broad, grassy valley with a huge, solitary cottonwood. Be sure to walk over to this impressive tree.

From the cottonwood, the old road continues south down the valley to the Forest Service work camp. Go through three gates in quick succession and turn right on the road that leads to the starting trailhead visible only a short distance away.

62 Hillsboro Peak

General description:	A day hike to a lookout tower on one of the high peaks of the Black Range, located about 40 miles east of Silver City. Water is available at Hillsboro Spring. Best hiked from May through November.
Distance:	About 10 miles, round trip.
Difficulty:	Moderate.
Traffic:	Light.
Elevation gain:	1,845 feet.
Maps:	Gila National Forest, Aldo Lecpold Wilderness, Hillsboro Peak, 7.5-minute USGS Quad.
For more information:	Black Ranger District, 1804 Date Street, P.O. Box 431, Truth or Consequences, New Mexico 87901, 505-894-6677.

Finding the trailhead: From Silver City, drive about 8 miles east on U.S. Highway 180 to Central. Turn left onto New Mexico 152 and continue east about 32 miles to the trailhead at the top of Emory Pass. From I-25 to the east, drive west on NM 152 past Hillsboro and Kingston to Emory Pass at the top of the Black Range.

The hike: The Black Range stretches almost 100 miles from north to south, west of the Rio Grande Valley. The Continental Divide follows the crest along the north end of the range. The rugged mountains have fewer people in them now than at the turn of the century. Mining towns in the foothills boomed in the 1880s, including Kingston, Hillsboro, and Lake Valley on the southeast side below Hillsboro Peak, and Winston and Chloride on the northeast. Lake Valley had one of the most famous mining discoveries in the West. A single underground room, the "Bridal Chamber," contained over three million dollars of pure silver. The metal was so easy to mine it was loaded directly onto railroad cars without any smelting. Today, the mines have closed and the saloons have disappeared, leaving the communities to slumber peacefully in the New Mexico sun. The mountains towering over the towns now contain one of New Mexico's largest wildernesses and are almost forgotten.

When you do this hike, be sure to spend a little time in Kingston and Hillsboro, just down NM 152 from the trailhead. The sleepy little villages, with their old buildings and apple orchards, invite exploration. Paved NM 152 winds over the crest of the southern end of the mountains and provides the easiest access to Black Range trails. The trails leading from the pass are probably the most popular in the mountains, but are still relatively lightly used. You will probably only see people on summer weekends. Several nice campgrounds lie along NM 152, just down the west side of the pass.

Park at Emory Pass Vista, located just off the highway at the pass. Well-marked Trail 79 starts about 200 feet up the short paved side road that leads to the vista parking lot. The well-maintained trail immediately begins climbing to the north from the road. Just up the way, you hit a dirt road. The short road just leads from the highway to some Forest Service facilities. Turn right and follow it uphill a short distance, passing a building, heliport, and radio tower. Go through a gate and follow an old, unused road which is now the trail. About 200 yards past the gate, the old road is blocked off. The trail

A fire lookout tower caps the flat summit of Hillsboro Peak.

drops below and parallel to the abandoned road before rejoining it in about 0.25 mile.

The trail passes through Douglas-fir and ponderosa pine, alternating with patches of oak scrub that have grown up after an old fire. Open areas provide great views as you follow the crest north. At about 2 miles, you hit the Aldo Leopold Wilderness boundary, marked by a small sign. The rest of the trail roughly follows the edge of the wilderness. At a little over 3 miles, the trail hits a well-marked, four-way intersection. A large sign formally announces the wilderness. To the right, little-used Trail 127 descends 6 miles to Kingston, a nice hike with a car shuttle. To the left goes the more popular

Hillsboro Peak

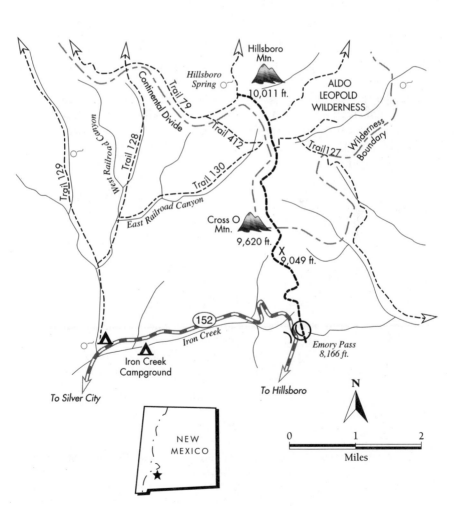

Hillsboro Peak Bypass Trail 412. Trail 412 makes a good cutoff for early season hikers wanting to continue north along the crest. Trail 79, up on the north side of the peak, retains snow until later in the spring.

Continue straight ahead, uphill, on Trail 79 to the summit. An unmarked trail forks off to the right, descending into Mineral Creek, about 0.5 mile up Trail 79 from the intersection. Like many Black Range trails, it is faint and so unused you may not even notice it. Another unmarked, but much more obvious, intersection is reached just short of the summit. The right fork is Trail 117. Stay left and climb the last 50 yards or so onto the large, flat summit at just less than 5 miles. A tall lookout tower and some Forest Service buildings are clustered at one side of the summit. The tower is occupied in the fire season of late spring and early summer. Please do not disturb any of the facilities. The views from the summit, and especially the tower, are tremendous. On a clear day, the view stretches from Sierra Blanca in southeastern New Mexico to mountains in southeastern Arizona.

Since much of the trail and the summit in particular are exposed to lightning, start your hike early in the day. Good campsites can be found on several saddles along the way and on the summit (but not too close to the buildings). Hillsboro Spring lies below the summit to the northwest off of Trail 117. Ask the Forest Service ahead of time about its status and exact location. For a long one-day or good two-day hike with a car shuttle, continue north on Trail 79 to Trail 128. Turn left on Trail 128 and follow it down Railroad Canyon to Trail 129 in Gallinas Canyon. Continue down Trail 129 to NM 152. The hike can be enlarged by continuing further along Trail 79 to Trail 129 and following it all the way down Gallinas Canyon to NM 152. The Black Range has miles and miles of empty trails to explore. Use this hike as an introduction. If some of these trails do not get more use, the Forest Service will probably abandon them.

63 Sawyers Peak

General description:	A day hike to a southern peak of the Black Range, located about 40 miles east of Silver City. Best hiked from May through November. No water available. The hike features mountain views, lush forest, and solitude.
Distance:	About 8 miles, round trip.
Difficulty:	Moderate.
Traffic:	Light.
Elevation gain:	1,500 feet.
Maps:	Gila National Forest, Hillsboro Peak and Maverick Mountain 7.5-minute USGS quads.
For more information:	Black Ranger District, 1804 Date Street, P.O. Box 431, Truth or Consequences, New Mexico 87901, 505-894-6677.

Sawyers Peak

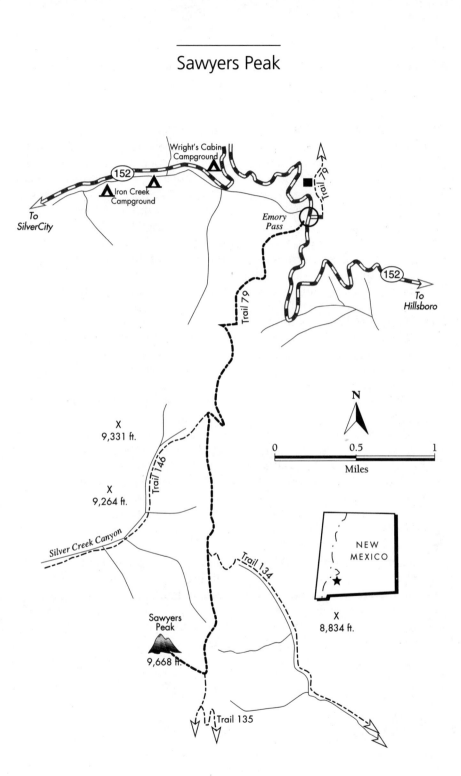

Finding the trailhead: Follow the same directions as those for the Hillsboro Peak hike. Park in the gravel lot right on the highway at the pass, rather than in the Emory Pass Vista parking area.

The hike: Like the Hillsboro Peak hike, the Sawyers Peak trail is easily accessible from New Mexico Highway 152 at Emory Pass. The trail is one of the more popular trails in the Black Range, but "popular" is relative. Some trails near Santa Fe and Albuquerque probably get more visitors on a summer weekend than Sawyers Peak gets all year. This trail follows the crest of the Black Range south from NM 152. The bulk of the mountains lie to the north of the highway, but the smaller southern section is very scenic and little-visited. The southern end does not lie in a formal wilderness like much of the central and northern parts, but it still has all the trappings of one.

Trail 79 climbs southwest from the gravel parking lot. A trail sign marks the start. The well-maintained trail climbs at a moderate grade on or near the crest for most of the hike. Unlike Hillsboro or McKnight peaks, the area around Sawyers Peak has not had any forest fires for many years. Because of the lack of fires and the trail's location on shady north-facing slopes for much of the way, lush forest lines almost the entire route. Broad views open up occasionally, but for the most part the trail winds through dense fir, spruce, aspen, and pine.

At a little over 2 miles, little-used Silver Creek Trail 146 forks off to the right. Stay left on Trail 79 and continue climbing. At about 3 miles, even less-used Trail 134 forks left down Trujillo Canyon. Continue to the right on Trail 79 to Sawyers Peak. Finally, about 0.75 mile further on, you reach the base of the peak on the southeast side. At this point, Trail 79 begins to descend to the south, following the lowering crest of the mountains. Views start to open up to the south. The summit is reached by climbing back to the northwest on a short side trail up the crest through the trees. The rounded peak is heavily wooded, allowing few clear views. Better views lie just to the south of the peak along Trail 79.

The best campsites probably lie on the summit or along Trail 79 near the base of the summit. To leave any remaining people behind, just continue south along the Crest Trail. Very few people go beyond Sawyers Peak. Be sure to take topographic maps, since the trail gets faint in places. If a car shuttle can be arranged, an excellent hike would follow Trail 79 all the way to Forest Road 886.

Afterword:
A Good Idea

It has been whispered here and there, usually by "locals," that books like this are a bad idea.

The theory goes something like this: Guidebooks bring more people into the wilderness, more people cause more environmental damage, and the wildness we all seek gradually evaporates.

I used to think like that. Here is why I changed my mind.

When I wrote and published my first guidebook, *Hiking Montana* (Falcon 1979), some of my hiking buddies disapproved. Since then, I've published over fifty hiking guides, and I'm proud of it. I hope these books have increased wilderness use.

Experienced hikers tend to have lofty attitude toward the inexperienced masses. They think anybody who wants to backpack can buy a topographic map and compass and find their own way through the wilderness. But the fact is, many people want a guide. Sometimes inexperienced hikers prefer a live person to show them the way and help them build confidence, but most of the time they can get by with a trail guide like this one.

All guidebooks published by Falcon (and most published by other publishers) invite wilderness users to respect and support the protection of wild country. Sometimes, this is direct editorializing. Sometimes, this invitation takes the more subtle form of simply helping people experience wilderness. And it is the rare person who leaves the wilderness without a firmly planted passion for wild country, thus waiting for a chance to vote for more of it.

While teaching backpacking classes for the Yellowstone Institute, I had taken hundreds of people into the wilderness. Many of them had on a backpack for the first time. Many of them were not convinced that we need more wilderness, but they were all convinced by the time they arrived back at the trailhead. Many, many times, I've seen it happen without saying a single word about wilderness.

It doesn't take preaching. Instead, we just need to get people out into the wilderness where the essence of wildness sort of sneaks up on them and takes root, and before you know it, the ranks of those who support wilderness has grown. But what about overcrowding? Yes, it is a problem in many places and probably will become one along the Continental Divide. The answer to overcrowded, overused wilderness is not limiting use of wilderness and restrictive regulations. The answer is more wilderness. How can we convince people to support more wilderness when they never experience wilderness?

That is why we need guidebooks. And that is why I changed my mind. I believe guidebooks have done as much to build support for wilderness as pro-wilderness organizations have ever done through political and public relations efforts.

And if that's not enough, here is another reason. All FalconGuides (and most guidebooks from other publishers) contain sections on leave-no-trace camping and wilderness safety. Guidebooks provide the ideal medium for communicating this vital information.

In thirty years of backpacking, I have seen dramatic changes in how backpackers care for wilderness. I've seen it go from appalling to exceptional. Today, almost everybody walks softly in the wilderness. And I believe the information contained in guidebooks has been partly responsible for this change.

Having said all that, I hope many thousands of people use this book to enjoy a fun-filled vacation hiking along the Continental Divide—and then of course, vote for wilderness protection and support national trails like the CDT.

Bill Schneider, President

The Continental Divide National Scenic Trail

Congress officially designated the Continental Divide National Scenic Trail (CDT) in 1978. When completed it will travel 3,100 miles from Canada to Mexico, and rival the Pacific Crest Trail and the Appalachian Trail. Lack of funding and disagreement about the need or importance of the project has kept it stalled in some areas, but in others, it is near completion. According to the Continental Divide Trail Alliance, the trail is 70% completed, but large hurdles remain.

The section through Idaho and Montana is on 795 miles of trails, logging roads, and cross-country routes. The most complete section occurs in southern Montana, where in the Anaconda–Pintler Wilderness the trail is well marked and very traveled. Other areas of southern Montana, like the section crossing Nicholia and Deadman Creeks (Hike 23) past Lemhi Pass are getting more attention and are among the more followable sections of the CDT. However, much of the non-wilderness Montana/Idaho Section is open to motorized recreation, something less than desired for hikers. Refer to *The Hiker's Guide to Montana's Continental Divide Trail* (Falcon, 1990) for specific route information.

The 760-mile Colorado Section is arguably complete, a testament to the work started by James R. Wolf's Continental Divide Trail Society and continued by the Continental Divide Trail Alliance. The section follows the well-developed Colorado Trail for a large section and has sections open to mountain bikers. The section through the Weminuche Wilderness is particularly spectacular and high alpine. See Hike 52 (Wolf Creek Pass–Divide Trail) for an introduction. Also, look for *Hiking Colorado's Wemminuche Wilderness* coming soon from Falcon. For detailed information on the Colorado Section of the Continental Divide see *Colorado's Continental Divide Trail: The Official Guide* (Westcliffe, 1997).

Unfortunately, throughout Wyoming, the CDT is incomplete. Although you can hike many sections of it, a trail or designated trail does not exist. Sections through the Wind River Range are closest to completion. Other areas have shown little progress. For example, near the Ferris Mountains in Wyoming, the trail negotiates large tracks of private land and patches of Bureau of Land Management Land along dirt roads without trail signs or designated routes. I hope that with public support this area will improve for through-hikers soon. Until then, see Hike 40 for instructions on exploring this remote wild area. The only documentation of the route that I found was in James Wolf's *Guide to the Continental Divide Trail, Volume 3: Wyoming* and his 1993 Wyoming Supplement.

In New Mexico, the CDT is even less complete. Here, the divide passes through the Jicarilla Indian Reservation. The tribe refused to allow access for the proposed trail. In addition, many of the lands in Northern New Mexico are disputed Hispanic Land Claims. Finally, many sections in New Mexico cross private land and CDT designation has been met with resistance. For example, *Backpacker* magazine quoted one county commissioner in New Mexico as saying, "The last thing we need is bunch of backpackers and tree huggers tramping through our yards." These issues make the New Mexico section the most difficult. One very bright spot in New Mexico is where the divide crosses through the Gila and Aldo Leopold Wilderness, a fitting area for the southern trip. See Hikes 56 through 63 for routes to explore in the southern end of the Continental Divide before it continues into Mexico. There is not currently any route guide to the CDT in New Mexico. The Continental Divide Trail Society states in their web site that, "A preliminary guidebook to Northern New Mexico will be published when sufficient information is available to provide detailed recommendations." Perhaps cooperation is the first step for gaining more public support for the CDT in New Mexico.

Because of the these difficulties, it is unclear when a completed route will exist, but with this guide you can still visit the best areas along the divide and skip the conflict prone and unpleasant areas. We also think that limiting your exploration of the divide to the United States misses some of the best alpine areas, including Banff and Jasper in Alberta. For those reasons, this book does not focus on doing a point to point Continental Divide hike, but we would like to draw attention to the notable efforts of those trying to make the trail route a reality.

In order to guarantee that the remaining 1,000 miles of unconstucted or unprotected trail receive the proper funds and protection, we encourage you to support the Continental Divide Trail Alliance. Falcon donated $3,000 worth of books on the Montana Section of the CDT to the Alliance and we hope that getting you to explore the areas around the CDT will whet your appetite for exploring and supporting preservation along the Continental Divide. For more information on supporting the development of the scenic trail route contact:

> Continental Divide Trail Alliance
> P.O. Box 628
> Pine, CO 80470

Or:

> The Continental Divide Trail Society
> 3704 North Charles Street #601
> Baltimore, MD 21218-2300
> cdtsociety@aol.com

Lastly, if you wish to try the trip from Mexico to Canada, James Wolf has scouted the CDT since 1973 and put together a series of route guides. These are the most comprehensive guides to attempting the border to border trip (See Appendix A: Sources of Information).

Appendix A:
Sources of Information

Boddie, Caryn and Peter. *Hiking Colorado*. Helena: Falcon Publishing, 1991.

Brooks, Tad and Sherry Jones. *The Hiker's Guide to Montana's Continental Divide Trail*. Helena: Falcon Publishing, 1990.

Harmon, Will. *Hiking Alberta*. Helena: Falcon Publishing, 1992.

Hunger, Bill. *Hiking Wyoming*. Helena: Falcon Publishing, 1998.

Jones, Tom and John Fielder. *Colorado's Continental Divide Trail: The Official Guide*. Englewood: Westcliffe Publishers, 1997.

Molvar, Erik. *Hiking Glacier and Waterton Lakes National Parks*. Helena: Falcon Publishing, 1994.

———.*The Trail Guide to Bob Marshall Country* Helena: Falcon Publishing, 1994.

Parent, Laurence. *Hiking New Mexico*. Helena: Falcon Publishing, 1998.

Schneider, Bill. *Hiking Montana*. Helena: Falcon Publishing, 1994.

———.*Hiking Yellowstone National Park*. Helena: Falcon Publishing, 1997.

Wolf, James R. *Guide to the Continental Divide Trail, Volume 1: Northern Montana*. Bethesda: Continental Divide Trail Society, 1991.

———.*Guide to the Continental Divide Trail, Volume 2: Southern Montana and Idaho*. Bethesda: Continental Divide Trail Society, 1979.

———.*Guide to the Continental Divide Trail, Volume 2: Southern Montana and Idaho, 1995 Supplement*. Bethesda: Continental Divide Trail Society, 1995.

———.*Guide to the Continental Divide Trail, Volume 3: Wyoming*. Bethesda: Continental Divide Trail Society, 1980.

———.*Guide to the Continental Divide Trail, Volume 3: Wyoming, 1993 Supplement: Wyoming*. Bethesda: Continental Divide Trail Society, 1993.

Wolf, James R. *Guide to the Continental Divide Trail, Volume 4: Northern Colorado*. Bethesda: Continental Divide Trail Society, 1982.

———.*Guide to the Continental Divide Trail, Volume 5: Southern Colorado*. Bethesda: Continental Divide Trail Society, 1986.

Appendix B: Hiker's Checklist

Not every item on this checklist will be needed for every trip, so customize the list based on your needs and comforts, the duration of the outing, weather, and the unexpected. Use this list as an organizing tool for planning, packing, and minimizing oversights. Feel free to pencil in items that you find critical to a successful trip.

Ten Essentials

- [ ] extra food
- [ ] extra clothing
- [ ] sunglasses
- [ ] knife
- [ ] firestarter
- [ ] matches in waterproof container
- [ ] first-aid kit and manual
- [ ] flashlight
- [ ] map(s) for the trail
- [ ] compass

Clothing

- [ ] lightweight underwear
- [ ] longjohns
- [ ] under socks
- [ ] wool boot socks
- [ ] long pants
- [ ] shorts
- [ ] long-sleeved shirt
- [ ] T-shirts
- [ ] wool sweater or shirt
- [ ] wool hat and gloves
- [ ] visor or cap
- [ ] raingear
- [ ] warm coat or parka
- [ ] belt
- [ ] bandanna
- [ ] swimsuit or trunks
- [ ] hiking boots
- [ ] sneakers or camp shoes

Personal Items

- [ ] contacts or eyeglasses
- [ ] comb
- [ ] toothpaste and brush
- [ ] biodegradable soap/towelettes
- [ ] towel
- [ ] nail clipper and tweezers
- [ ] facial tissue or handkerchief
- [ ] toilet paper and trowel
- [ ] sunscreen and lip balm
- [ ] insect repellent
- [ ] wallet and keys
- [ ] emergency medical information
- [ ] watch

Gear

- [ ] water bottles
- [ ] pack(s)
- [ ] tent, with required poles and pegs
- [ ] ground cloth
- [ ] sleeping bag and foam pad
- [ ] stove and fuel
- [ ] pots and eating utensils
- [ ] can opener
- [ ] rope
- [ ] stuff bags
- [ ] large trash bags for emergency shelter for self or gear
- [ ] plastic bags for trash
- [ ] zip-locked bags for foodstuffs
- [ ] aluminum foil

Food

- [ ] 3 meals, plus snacks for each day
- [ ] extra food for delays
- [ ] salt/pepper
- [ ] vegetable oil
- [ ] drink mixes

Health & Safety Items

- [ ] medications
- [ ] emergency blanket
- [ ] water pump or purification tablets
- [ ] whistle
- [ ] pencil and paper
- [ ] picture wire for emergency repairs

Miscellaneous

- [ ] mosquito netting
- [ ] binoculars
- [ ] camera and film
- [ ] guidebooks
- [ ] identification books
- [ ] fishing gear and valid license

get FALCON GUIDED

FALCON GUIDES ® are available for where-to-go hiking, mountain biking, rock climbing, walking, scenic driving, fishing, rockhounding, paddling, birding, wildlife viewing, and camping. We also have FalconGuides on essential outdoor skills and subjects and field identification. The following titles are currently available, but this list grows every year. For a free catalog with a complete list of titles, call FALCON toll-free at 1-800-582-2665.

HIKING GUIDES

Hiking Alaska
Hiking Alberta
Hiking Arizona
Hiking Arizona's Cactus Country
Hiking the Beartooths
Hiking Big Bend National Park
Hiking Bob Marshall Country
Hiking California
Hiking California's Desert Parks
Hiking Carlsbad Caverns
     and Guadalupe Mtns. National Parks
Hiking Colorado
Hiking the Columbia River Gorge
Hiking Florida
Hiking Georgia
Hiking Glacier & Waterton Lakes National Parks
Hiking Grand Canyon National Park
Hiking Grand Staircase-Escalante/Glen Canyon
Hiking Great Basin National Park
Hiking Hot Springs in the Pacific Northwest
Hiking Idaho
Hiking Maine
Hiking Michigan
Hiking Minnesota
Hiking Montana
Hiker's Guide to Nevada
Hiking New Hampshire
Hiking New Mexico

Hiking New York
Hiking North Cascades
Hiking Northern Arizona
Hiking Olympic National Park
Hiking Oregon
Hiking Oregon's Eagle Cap Wilderness
Hiking Oregon's Mount Hood/Eagle Cap
Hiking Oregon's Three Sisters Country
Hiking Pennsylvania
Hiking Shenandoah National Park
Hiking South Carolina
Hiking South Dakota's Black Hills Country
Hiking Southern New England
Hiking Tennessee
Hiking Texas
Hiking Utah
Hiking Utah's Summits
Hiking Vermont
Hiking Virginia
Hiking Washington
Hiking Wisconsin
Hiking Wyoming
Hiking Wyoming's Wind River Range
Hiking Yellowstone National Park
Hiking Zion & Bryce Canyon National Parks
The Trail Guide to Bob Marshall Country
Wild Montana
Wild Utah

■ *To order any of these books, check with your local bookseller*
*or call FALCON® at **1-800-582-2665**.*
Visit us on the world wide web at:
www.falconguide.com

FALCON®

get
FALCON GUIDED

BEST EASY DAY HIKES SERIES

Beartooths
Canyonlands & Arches
Best Hikes on the Continental Divide
Glacier & Wateron Lakes
Grand Staircase-Escalante and the Glen Canyon
  Region
Grand Canyon
North Cascades
Olympics
Shenandoah
Yellowstone

12 SHORT HIKES SERIES

Colorado
Aspen
Boulder
Denver Foothills Central
Denver Foothills North
Denver Foothills South
Rocky Mountain National Park-Estes Park
Rocky Mountain National Park-Grand Lake
Steamboat Springs
Summit County
Vail

California
San Diego Coast
San Diego Mountains
San Francisco Bay Area-Coastal
San Francisco Bay Area-East Bay
San Francisco Bay Area-North Bay
San Francisco Bay Area-South Bay

Washington
Mount Rainier National Park-Paradise
Mount Rainier National Park-Sunrise

■ *To order any of these books, check with your local bookseller
or call FALCON® at **1-800-582-2665**.*

Visit us on the world wide web at:
www.falconguide.com

FALCON®

get FALCON GUIDED

BIRDING GUIDES

Birding Minnesota
Birding Montana
Birding Texas
Birding Utah

FIELD GUIDES

Bitterroot: Montana State Flower
Canyon Country Wildflowers
Great Lakes Berry Book
New England Berry Book
Pacific Northwest Berry Book
Plants of Arizona
Rare Plants of Colorado
Rocky Mountain Berry Book
Scats & Tracks of the Rocky Mtns.
Tallgrass Prairie Wildflowers
Western Trees
Wildflowers of Southwestern Utah
Willow Bark and Rosehips

FISHING GUIDES

Fishing Alaska
Fishing the Beartooths
Fishing Florida
Fishing Glacier National Park
Fishing Maine
Fishing Montana
Fishing Wyoming

PADDLING GUIDES

Floater's Guide to Colorado
Paddling Montana
Paddling Okeefenokee
Paddling Oregon
Paddling Yellowstone & Grand
   Teton National Parks

ROCKHOUNDING GUIDES

Rockhounding Arizona
Rockhound's Guide to California
Rockhound's Guide to Colorado
Rockhounding Montana
Rockhounding Nevada
Rockhound's Guide to New Mexico
Rockhounding Texas
Rockhounding Utah
Rockhounding Wyoming

WALKING

Walking Colorado Springs
Walking Denver
Walking Portland
Walking St. Louis

HOW-TO GUIDES

Avalanche Aware
Backpacking Tips
Bear Aware
Leave No Trace
Mountain Lion Alert
Reading Weather
Wilderness First Aid
Wilderness Survival

MORE GUIDEBOOKS

Backcountry Horseman's
   Guide to Washington
Camping California's
   National Forests
Exploring Canyonlands &
   Arches National Parks
Exploring Hawaii's Parklands
Exploring Mount Helena
Recreation Guide to WA
   National Forests
Touring California & Nevada
   Hot Springs
Trail Riding Western
   Montana
Wild Country Companion
Wild Montana

FALCON®

■ *To order any of these books, check with your local bookseller*
   or call FALCON® at **1-800-582-2665** .

Visit us on the world wide web at:
   www.falconguide.com

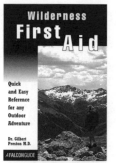

WILDERNESS FIRST AID

By Dr. Gilbert Preston M.D.

Enjoy the outdoors and face the inherent risks with confidence. By reading this easy-to-follow first-aid text, all outdoor enthusiasts can pack a little extra peace of mind on their next adventure. *Wilderness First Aid* offers expert medical advice for dealing with outdoor emergencies beyond the reach of 911. It easily fits in most backcountry first-aid kits.

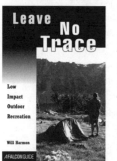

LEAVE NO TRACE

By Will Harmon

The concept of "leave no trace" seems simple, but it actually gets fairly complicated. This handy quick-reference guidebook includes all the newest information on this growing and all-important subject. This book is written to help the outdoor enthusiast make the hundreds of decisions necessary to protect the natural landscape and still have an enjoyable wilderness experience. Part of the proceeds from the sale of this book go to continue leave-no-trace education efforts. The Official Manual of American Hiking Society.

BEAR AWARE

By Bill Schneider

Hiking in bear country can be very safe if hikers follow the guidelines summarized in this small, "packable" book. Extensively reviewed by bear experts, the book contains the latest information on the intriguing science of bear-human interactions. *Bear Aware* can not only make your hike safer, but it can help you avoid the fear of bears that can take the edge off your trip.

MOUNTAIN LION ALERT

By Steve Torres

Recent mountain lion attacks have received national attention. Although infrequent, lion attacks raise concern for public safety. *Mountain Lion Alert* contains helpful advice for mountain bikers, trail runners, horse riders, pet owners, and suburban landowners on how to reduce the chances of mountain lion-human conflicts.

Also Available

• *Wilderness Survival* • *Reading Weather* • *Backpacking Tips*
• *Climbing Safely* • *Avalanche Aware*

To order check with your local bookseller or

call FALCON® at **1-800-582-2665.**

www.falconguide.com